To my parents
Norman and Catherine Zurick

HAWAII, NATURALLY

*An Environmentally Oriented Guide
to the Wonders
and Pleasures of the Islands*

David Zurick

Wilderness Press
BERKELEY

First Edition July 1990
Second printing August 1991

Copyright © 1990 by David Zurick
Design by Thomas Winnett
Maps by Tim Krasnansky
Cover photo by the author
Cover design by Larry Van Dyke
Photos by the author except as noted
Library of Congress Card Catalog Number 90-12558
International Standard Book Number 0-89997-108-3
Manufactured in the United States of America
Published by Wilderness Press
          2440 Bancroft Way
          Berkeley, CA 94704
          Write for free catalog or phone (414) 843-8080

Library of Congress Cataloging-in-Publication Data

Zurick, David.
   Hawaii, naturally : an environmentally oriented guide to the
wonders and pleasures of the islands / David Zurick. -- 1st ed.
      p.   cm.
   Includes bibliographical references (p.) and index.
   ISBN 0-89997-108-3
   1. Hawaii--Description and travel--1981- --Guide-books.
   2. Natural history--Hawaii.   I. Title.
   DU622.Z87 1990
   919.6904'4--dc20   90-12558
                                         CIP

Acknowledgements

Thank you: Kilali Alailima for your companionship and graceful assistance; Sam and Linda Pearsall for the office in your home; the folks at the Bishop House; Bobby Camara for your island insights and for showing me the stones; Annette Kaohelaulii at the Sierra Club; Jennie Peterson at the Hawaii Nature Center; The Nature Conservancy of Hawaii; Marjorie Zieglar and other staff members at the Sierra Club Legal Defense Fund; Scott Exo, Margie Robinson, and son Galen for companionship, ideas, and the use of the bicycle; Charlie Johnston for sharing waves, reefs, and walks; Tim Krasnansky for the maps; Peggy Lehman for assistance with the photographic prints.

Contents

Notes

Hawaiian word spellings are used in this book for place names and a few commonly used terms, such as *kamaaina*—meaning "local resident". Persons interested in acquiring a casual command of the Hawaiian language can consult the *Hawaiian Dictionary* by Mary K. Pukui and Samuel H. Elbert or the condensed version *The Pocket Hawaiian Dictionary* by M. K. Pukui, S. H. Elbert, and Esther T. Mookini. Another book of interest is *Place Names of Hawaii* by M. K. Pukui, S. H. Elbert, and E. T. Mookini.

Two Hawaiian terms that are used frequently in this book are *makai* ("toward the ocean") and *mauka* ("toward the mountains"). These words are common geographic reference terms in Hawaii; they are generally more useful for indicating directions in Hawaii than the cardinal compass points.

"Hawaii" is distinguished from "Hawai'i"; the latter is the Hawaiian name for the largest island in the archipelago, while the former refers to the state of Hawaii. Throughout the book, the island of Hawaii is referred to as the Island of Hawaii (capital "I").

Geostats

Hawaii's environment is frequently described in superlatives, to the point that the Islands seem to be a cliche. But in fact, most of the descriptions are apt and true. Hawaii is a place of unsurpassed beauty. It has an almost perfect tropical climate, and its qualities of light and color are exquisite and rare. The terrain is extremely varied, and it contains about every conceivable feature—from coastal formations to high alpine deserts. In the context of such a land, it is interesting to observe some statistics of geography.

• The Great Circle distance between the state's two most distant points is 1523 miles; the closest continental point to Hawaii is 2315 miles distant.

• The largest natural lake in Hawaii is located on the smallest main island (182-acre Halulu Lake on Niihau).

• The Northwest Hawaiian Islands group stretches for 1084 miles, but includes only 3.2 square miles of land.

• Tidal changes in Hawaii daily cover and uncover 302 miles of shoreline.

• The maximum ocean depth between any two adjacent Hawaiian Islands is 9950 feet (between Kauai and Oahu).

• Hawaii's highest waterfall is located on Molokai (Kahiwa at 1750 feet); the greatest number of named waterfalls is on Kauai (8), the largest river (measured by discharge) is on the Island of Hawaii (Wailuku River—185 million gal./day), and the longest stream is on Oahu (Kaukonahua Stream—33 miles).

• Fifty percent of the state's land area lies at an elevation greater than 2000 feet.

• Hawaii has 33 miles of sea cliffs over 1000 feet high.

• The largest volcanic crater in both area and depth is Haleakala on Maui (12,575 acres and 3,028 feet deep).

• Hawaii's narowest dam impounds the state's largest reservoir (Wahiawa Dam—460 feet long; 7671 acre feet reservoir).

• Oahu's highways in 1988 averaged 6.8 abandoned vehicles per 1,000 miles of driving, down from 23.6 in 1981.

• In 1988 an average of 892 visible litter items occurred along each mile of Oahu's highways, down from 2,135 items in 1978.

- Waikiki has the highest noise levels on Oahu (55.3 decibels exceeded 90% of the time).

- The lowest extreme temperature of record was at the Mauna Kea summit on the Island of Hawaii (11 degrees F.); the highest recorded temperature was at Kihei on Maui (98 degrees F.).

- Trade winds in Hawaii blow 65 percent of the time.

- The average water temperature at Waikiki on summer afternoons is 82° F.; on winter afternoons it is 77°.

- One hundred plants, 88 invertebrates, and 24 birds are now extinct in Hawaii; 19 plants, 41 vertebrates, 29 birds, 2 reptiles, 8 marine mammals, and 1 land mammal are endangered.

- In 1987, 121,000 trees were located along Honolulu's streets and highways.

- For detailed statistical information about Hawaii, consult the *The State of Hawaii Data Book* or the *Atlas of Hawaii.*

Introduction

Given a resident population of approximately one million, and an additional six million annual visitors, all competing for space on 6425 square miles of land, it is a wonder and a delight that any natural areas remain in Hawaii at all. At the same time, it is painfully apparent that we are loving this acclaimed paradise to death.

In the midst of incessant demands on the land by newcomers, old-timers, speculators, hoteliers, and others, preserving areas in wilderness, in native habitat, or in naturally occuring plant and animal communities is tenuous. The 1988 State of Hawaii Data Book reports that 47% of Hawaii's land area is in conservation land use of one type or another, but much of this land has been intensively used, first by Polynesians and later by Europeans, so that most of it now lacks any resemblance to native ecosystems. The intact native ecosystems are fast disappearing.

The existing natural areas in Hawaii are places of extraordinary but fragile beauty. To visit, use, and understand these natural places, one needs a special image of the Islands. On the one hand, Hawaii is everything the travel brochures claim. Bronze-skinned girls really do wear flowers in their hair as they frolic on idyllic beaches, silhouetted against flaming sunsets. Beach bars really do concoct the tropical drinks with splashy names, served by sunny blondes sporting perpetual tans. Hotels do offer jet skis, parasails, water bikes, and the chance to swim with captive dolphins. This is what several million annual visitors to Hawaii demand, and it is what the Waikiki-based tourism industry serves up.

So—has Hawaii really become Waikiki? As tourists, aided by perhaps the world's largest and most effective travel industry, multiply and spread beyond Oahu's south shore, the more distant island regions become tainted with the glitz and glamour of the tropical cliche. In this rush to the last paradise, has paradise been lost?

No. It is both ironic and poetic that the built resorts pale against the power of their natural backdrop. While lovers frolic in the artificial waterfall of a hotel resort, cascades plummet more than 3500 feet down nearby cliffs to crash in a fury of surf and rock. The counterpoint to the fern bars and the muzak of Waikiki are the mist-shrouded mountains where rare forest birds sing a twilight song. Lavish luaus offer tourist food under tiki lights, but they still fall short of a quiet picnic on a secluded beach at sunset.

To encounter natural Hawaii, it is not necessary to journey to its most remote recesses. Even within the urban space of Honolulu there are many opportunities to explore and to learn about Hawaii's natural environment. Indeed the island of Oahu, often disdained by wildlands advocates as overdeveloped—an urban wasteland—contains some absolute gems of nature. But they must be sought out. To visit the natural places with understanding, it is important to become familiar with Hawaii's tropical environment. For many visitors and residents alike, it will be a radically new and unfamiliar experience.

An excellent entry point into natural Hawaii for newcomers is the botanical parks, natural history museums, and other interpretive centers that exist in the Islands. These can brief you on the local natural world. A second means of entry is to link up with someone who is knowledgeable about the wild places, to briefly travel with

---

On the one hand, Hawaii is everything the travel brochures claim. Bronze-skinned girls really do wear flowers in their hair as they frolic on idyllic beaches, silhouetted against flaming sunsets.

---

them, and to learn from them. The natural areas that remain in Hawaii benefit from the advocates of natural Hawaii who play a fundamental role of stewardship. Many of these same persons and organizations lead people into the wild areas and provide opportunities for environmental education. A third means of entry is background reading that will prepare one to explore the environment alone in intelligent and sensitive ways. There exist many important writings on Hawaii's nature, and the reader is encouraged to explore the books and other readings named in this book. And a final means is to gain a familiarity with the specific information necessary to visit a place, including travel directions and restrictions. These means of entry into natural Hawaii will be emphasized throughout the book; indeed they make up the book. Thus, it differs from the genre of travel guides by emphasizing natural experiences, and it differs from most outdoor guides by being less a trail guide and more a contextual guide for visiting the natural areas.

Book Organization

The state of Hawaii contains discrete land areas: the six frequently visited islands of Hawaii, Kauai, Lanai, Maui, Molokai, and Oahu; a number of other prominent islands (including Kahoolawe, which is used as a bombing range by the U.S. Navy, and as a spiritual retreat by native Hawaiians, and Niihau, a privately owned island); and a series of atolls that extend 1367 miles northwest of Honolulu. This book covers the 6 main islands. With the exception of the Maui group, each island constitutes a separate section of the book. Lanai, Maui, and Molokai share a chapter.

To introduce the reader to Hawaii's tropical island environment, the book begins with a brief overview of the natural history and the cultural history of the islands. Here, we look at the geological evolution of the islands, the development of plant and animal communities, and the appearance of human and societal demands on the land. Journeys into natural Hawaii provide travelers with the opportunity to see how these histories have produced the Hawaiian landscapes.

The second chapter of the book, "The Hawaiian Islands," presents state-wide information about environmental opportunities pertinent to all 6 main islands. Thereafter, each chapter covers a separate island (in the case of the Maui group, several islands). The informational headings for each island chapter remain the same throughout the book—with some exceptions where one island offers unique opportunities not found on the others.

Each island chapter details opportunities specific to that island. How to get to places, where and how to stay, what to do and what to expect. Quite obviously, the information potential is overwhelming—witness the multitude of Hawaii guidebooks currently available. Also overwhelming is a zeal to take it all in, the downfall of many a traveler. In this book, conventional visitor services (restaurants, hotels, commercial amusements) are not covered. Instead, the book highlights the less advertised, more subtle, and ultimately more "Hawaiian" attractions on the islands. These provide a quality of experience that differs sharply from the experiences of commercial destinations contrived by the hospitality industry.

The book encourages a slow and steady exploration of the islands. It identifies places and opportunities that require considerable time to visit, and therefore not all the places can be discovered in a single visit or even multiple visits to Hawaii. While the book is intended to be a window on natural Hawaii, it also is a doorway through which the reader steps, with occasions to pause along the path.

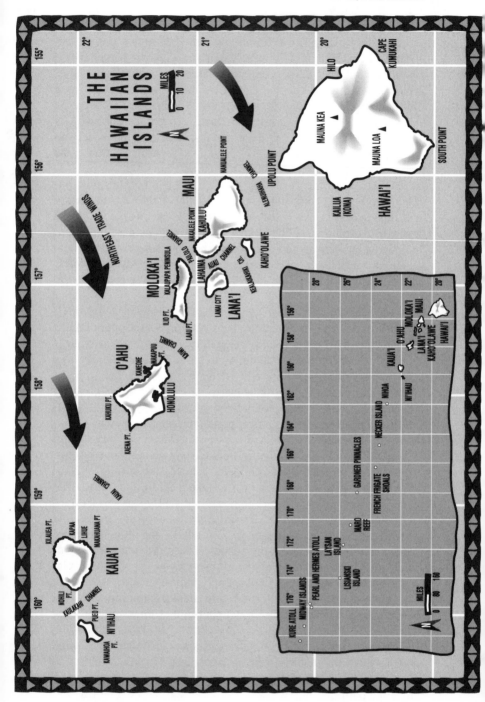

Chapter One

The Nature of the Place

For millions of years the Hawaiian Archipelago remained uninhabited. From their fiery origins over a mid-Pacific volcanic "hot spot," the islands are drifting northwestward as a 1600-mile arc of atolls, shoals, and volcanic peaks. The distance from Hawaii to the North American continent is over 2300 miles; from Hawaii to the Asian mainland is almost 5,000 miles. In this splendid isolation, Hawaii evolved as a geological and biological rarity.

Sometime about 1500 years ago, Polynesian sailors from the Marquesas Islands arrived in Hawaii. They reached the islands after navigating by the stars and the ocean currents. From their home islands, some 2500 miles to the southeast, they brought to Hawaii their domestic plants and animals, their technologies, and a vast knowledge of the tropical environment. They settled in dispersed rural communities called *ohanas*. They fished in the offshore waters, cleared land, built their dwellings from local materials, hunted and collected in the forests, captured birds for plumage, re-routed waterways for agriculture, and cultivated the land. Archaeologists have reconstructed early Hawaiian life and have found a society that was initially fitted into the island environment, extracting little that they did not replace. Over time and with increasing human numbers, the ecological balance between nature and man became less even. The eventual changes in the landscape that the Polynesian colonizers made over half a score of centuries were pronounced and extensive.

In 1795, seventeen years after the explorer Captain James Cook "discovered" Hawaii, Polynesian society on all the islands except Kauai consolidated into a single Hawaiian Kingdom under Kamehameha the Great. It was not to last for long. The development of the Hawaiian monarchy coincided with the European settlement of the islands. Among the first Westerners to visit and then to stay were the traders and the whalers; then came missionaries, businessmen, farmers, and drifters—all seeking to extract some wealth from the natural riches of the tropical land and seas. During the early decades of the 1800s, the U.S. and various European countries jockeyed for position in the lucrative Hawaiian merchant trade. Every bit as eager as the entrepreneurs were the early missionaries, although their quarry was souls, not profit. The two forces, economic and religious, commingled during the 19th century, and exercised tremendous claims on the land of Hawaii and the spirit of her people. The influence of the U.S. persisted throughout this period. In 1900, after a short-lived provisional government that terminated the reign of Hawaii's last queen, Liliuokalani, the islands were organized as the Territory of Hawaii under the U.S. government.

Every bit as eager as the entrepreneurs were the early missionaries, although their quarry was souls, not profit.

When Hawaii became a territory, it was put under the jurisdiction of the U.S. Coast and Geodetic Survey. An island-wide survey was conducted that determined the basis for future land subdivisions, boundary drawing, and zoning. It was as if, once the lines had been drawn, all further development was justified. The 20th century has witnessed a widespread transformation of the islands' landscapes. Now, as it enters the Pacific Age, Hawaii sustains its tripartite economy of cash crops, the military, and tourism.

The results of human occupation have been dismal for Hawaii's natural world. Hundreds of species of native plants have become extinct or are now endangered. Over 75% of the native birds are now gone or threatened with extinction. Hawaii has the dubious distinction of harboring 30% of the total number of endangered species in the U.S. This vivid but sad record of environmental change in Hawaii is eloquently presented in the book *Islands in a Far Sea*, by John L. Culliney.

In the paragraphs that follow, I provide a brief introduction to Hawaii's natural history, the role of culture in transforming Hawaii's landscape, and the conservation issues that today are critical. Much of what appears here has been informed by Culliney's book and by a host of others. *Hawaii: A Natural History* by Sherwin Carlquist is the definitive book on terrestrial ecology in the Hawaiian Islands. Persons interested in Hawaii's geology should look at *Volcanoes in the Sea* by Gordon Macdonald, Agatin Abbot, and Frank Peterson. Several field guides to Hawaii's flora and fauna are available, mentioned in the chapters where they apply. Material on cultural history appears in a number of books that were written for the nonspecialist. All these items, along with other references, are in the bibliography at the end of the book.

Islands of Fire

Puna is shaking in the Wind,
Shaking is the hala grove of Keauu
Tumbling are Haena and Hopoe
Moving is the land—Moving to the Sea.

—Hawaiian chant

A century ago, Mark Twain visited Hawaii and called it "the loveliest fleet of islands anchored in any ocean in the world." Twain was more correct than he knew. The islands indeed are anchored to the earth's suboceanic crust, and they are slowing moving with it, as a fleet, northwestward.

In Hawaiian myth, the islands were formed when the demigod Maui snagged a piece of the ocean floor and hauled it to the surface, where it shattered into the Hawaiian Archipelago. According to modern geological theory, tectonic forces are driving a huge section of the Pacific crustal plate across a fissure, a "hot spot" below the crust. From this hot fissure a continuous plume of upwelling magma slowly formed the seamounts, which eventually breached the ocean surface amid shattering eruptions, roiling gases, and boiling water to become an island. This is how each of the Hawaiian Islands came into being. Then the island grew for a while longer as it slowly drifted northwest astride the oceanic plate, moving from its undersea volcanic source at an estimated 1.2 inches per year.

This process accounted for every island of the Hawaiian chain. Hence, each island to the northwest is much older than its southeastern neighbors. Erosion of the volcanic surfaces by wind and water has given each island its unique appearance, such as the low lagoon atolls of Kure, the fluted sea cliffs of Kauai, and the rolling, gentle slopes of the Island of Hawaii.

The creation of new land continues today most vividly on the Island of Hawaii. Here one can witness at close quarters the violent yet fascinating power of the volcano fires. Thousands of visitors each year watch in Hawaii Volcanoes National Park as gaseous, molten rock flows from vents across the land to the sea. In the flames and the red glow of the lava is the face of Pele, the volcano goddess; no less visible today than in earlier times when the poet Tennyson was moved to write,

Dance in a fountain of flame with her devils or
Shake with her thunders and
Shatter her island.

When magma pours onto the earth's surface it is called lava. The volcanic landscapes of Hawaii are built of layer upon layer of lava, some hundreds of feet thick, others only inches deep. As you stride across the lava surfaces of the islands, you note two distinct forms: the smooth, billowy, ropy type is called *pahoehoe;* the rough, clinkery surface is called *aa.*

Everywhere in Hawaii is evidence of the volcanic origins of the islands, most immediately on the Island of Hawaii, where eruptions still occur with great frequency. This island is the youngest of the main islands, composed of five volcanoes: Kohala, Mauna Kea, Hualalai, Mauna Loa, and Kilauea—in chronological order from oldest to youngest. On this island, observe how the volcanoes differ in appearance. The oldest, Kohala, has been severely weathered.

Lava flow enters ocean on Island of Hawaii

Along its windward slopes, where rainfall is heavy and wave action intense, the slopes have been carved into a rough pattern of deep valleys and towering sea cliffs. From the Waipio Valley overlook one can see the first of a series of coastal valleys and headland cliffs that score the windward Kohala coast. Unlike weathered and severely eroded Kohala, the southern mountains of Mauna Kea and Mauna Loa still retain their gentle slopes. Hawaii's most active volcano is the southern mountain of Kilauea, the showpiece of Hawaii Volcanoes National Park.

Traveling north along the Hawaiian Archipelago, from Hawaii to Maui, and then on to Molokai, Oahu, and Kauai, one clearly can observe the effects on the terrain of long exposure to erosion. The northern islands are smaller and not as tall. They lack the round domelike slopes of the Island of Hawaii, showing instead the steep cliffs and deep valleys where waves and streams have cut through the lava rock. Many visitors to Hawaii find the sharp relief of the northern islands most appealing. Through the power of the media, especially motion pictures and television, we have developed our image of a tropical Pacific island as one with the jagged contours seen in the northern Hawaiian islands. Actually in Hawaii are found all of the many faces of volcanic islands—from the young slopelands of Hawaii Island to the ancient pinnacles, shoals and lagoons of the Northwest islands.

Islands of Life

If the Hawaiian Islands were no more than bare volcanic surfaces, they would certainly not have been the quest of early Polynesian migrants, nor would they have become the latter-day paradise for modern tourists. But in fact, the islands are home to an extraordinary assemblage of natural and introduced plant and animal communities. They are virtual gardens of tropical life. The subtitle given to this section, "Islands of Life", is taken from a campaign recently initiated by The Nature Conservancy of Hawaii to preserve outstanding features of Hawaii's unique but endangered habitats and wildlife. In support of this campaign, The Hawaii Nature Conservancy recently published a lavish book, *Hawaii: The Islands of Life* by Gavin Daws. It portrays both the beauty and the fragility of Hawaii's natural environments. In the paragraphs that follow, I discuss some of the natural heritage of Hawaii that organizations like The Nature Conservancy are working to preserve.

The great distances between Hawaii and the nearest continents made it extremely difficult for plants and animals to reach the newly

formed islands, but some managed the journey. The feet and the
feathers of migrating birds carried hitch-hiking burrs and other plant
seeds. Ocean currents and surface winds carried shallow-water
marine life across great expanses of deep ocean. Crabs, barnacles,
and other drifters clung to flotsam or drifting mats of rotting vegetation to make the passage. Small, airborne insects drifted with the
wind. A few of the many migrating plants and animals survived after
reaching the islands. The colonization of the land by the plants was
slow; scientists estimate that only one new plant species arrived in
Hawaii every 100,000 years.

The great distances between Hawaii and the nearest continents made it extremely difficult for plants and animals to
reach the newly formed islands, but some managed the
journey.

As plant populations established themselves, they contributed
shade and nutrients, they moderated moisture, and they created new
habitats for new species. The great range of environmental conditions in Hawaii offered opportunities for the early founder species to
expand into a variety of habitats. With evolution, new species filled
new ecological niches, giving rise to the many species that are
unique to Hawaii. Ecologists and biogeographers call the process by
which species colonize new habitats, adapt, and evolve into wholly
new species "adaptive radiation", and it accounts for a great deal of
the native biotic diversity in Hawaii. Over 90% of the island's plants
and birds are endemic (occurring naturally here and nowhere else),
making the islands one of the most unusual natural laboratories on
earth. Not even the famous Galapagos Islands can claim such a per-
centage of endemic species.

Ecologists have identified almost 200 types of habitats in the
Hawaiian Islands, ranging from alpine tundra on the summits of
Mauna Loa and Mauna Kea to the lush lowland rainforests found
along the coasts. Biologist Sherwin Carlquist simplifies this pattern
considerably in his book *Hawaii: A Natural History*. He describes
six main terrestrial biological regions: Coast, Dry Forest, Wet
Forest, Epiphytic Vegetation, Bogs, and Alpine Zone. These regions
differ primarily in climate, altitude, and vegetation. Even casual
visitors to the island can observe the biological differences between
one broad region and another.

The coastal sections of the main islands are inhabited by native
shrubs and grasses that tolerate drought and salt. Characteristic of

these areas are the shrubby beach naupaka (*Scaevola taccada*) and the trailing vines such as the nehe (*Lipochaeta integrifolia*). But from earliest times of human settlement, the coasts have been greatly modified, many introduced species having overtaken the native communities. Today, about 75% of the native Hawaiian coastal plants are considered to be rare.

On the lower dry slopes, particularly on old lava flows, native trees such as the lama (*Diospyros*) and the naio (*Myoporum sandwicense*) are common. At higher elevations on the dry slopes, the koa (*Acacia koa*) becomes conspicuous. The understories of the dry forests contain numerous shrubs and vines, including the fragrant maile (*Alyxia*). The dry plant communities are fast disappearing, though, since these areas are preferred for agriculture and for seaside resorts.

The wet mountain forests occur mainly where moist winds, rising over ridges, precipitate along the windward slope. Plant diversity is great in these locations, and some trees, such as the ohia lehua (*Metrosideros polymorpha*), attain majestic stature. The understory of the wet forests contains extraordinary foliage, including the huge hapuu tree ferns (*Cibotium splendens*), without which the rain-

Tree ferns

forest would lose much of its primordial appearance. In these moist regimes, a variety of plants, called epiphytes, grow on the trunks and limbs of the rainforest trees. The most familiar of the epiphytes are the bromeliads (of which the pineapple is a member), and the orchids. Lush with towering canopy trees, ferns, and flowering plants, the rainforests are the delight of many journeys into Hawaii's wilderness.

Annual rainfall exceeds 200 inches in some places on the islands. In these areas, some streams drain into large depressions to form bogs. In Hawaii, these areas represent a distinct biological region, though small and fragmentary. The Hawaiian bogs are tussocked pools of mud and standing water. Most occur at high elevations (for example, near the summits of Mt. Waialeale on Kauai, Mt. Kaala on Oahu, and Puu Kukui on Maui). They are cool places, draped in clouds most of the time. Some of the Hawaiian bog plants are the most curious of Hawaiian flora, evolutionary oddities that are adapted to a difficult environment. These are some of the most fragile lands in the world. Fortunately, many of the bogs in Hawaii are now official natural areas managed for the preservation of the native species.

The last biological region is found at the highest elevations (above 6000 feet). These alpine locations are restricted to Mt. Haleakala on Maui, and Mauna Loa, Mauna Kea and Hualalai on the Island of Hawaii. The high mountain landscape is predominantly bare volcanic surfaces. Frost, subfreezing temperatures, low precipitation, and dry cindery soils characterize the summit. Snow blizzards are common in these stony high deserts, and it is surprising that any life exists here at all. Yet some of Hawaii's most striking plants thrive in alpine locations. Many are low-lying herbs and shrubs, including the naenae (*Dubautia menziesii*) and the ohelo (*Vaccinium*). The most spectacular of the alpine plants is the Haleakala silversword (*Argyroxiphium sandwicense*), a member of the daisy family found in the Haleakala crater. Because they are so limited in geographic extent and biotic diversity, all the alpine species in Hawaii are considered rare.

These diverse environments and the plant communities that they support can be found throughout the islands, in accessible as well as remote places. Natural area reserves, the Nature Conservancy

---

Snow blizzards are common in these stony high deserts, and it is surprising that any life exists here at all.

preserves, national wildlife refuges, and national and state parks contain areas of native habitat. These parklands and preserves, and the outstanding opportunities that they present for natural wanderings, are identified in the subsequent chapters of this book.

The habitats described above are important not only because of the plants they contain, but also because they provide ecological niches for Hawaii's unique wildlife. Of all the fauna forms, the native Hawaiian forest birds have most compellingly captured the attention of conservationists and the general public. Perhaps it is because of their colorful plumage and whimsical songs. Perhaps it is because over one third of the endemic birds that lived in Hawaii before human contact are now extinct. Of those that remain, over two thirds are classified as endangered species. The plight of Hawaiian forest birds signals an island-wide crisis—the loss of crucial habitat and the competition for space from introduced flora and fauna.

Cultural Encounters

The remote Hawaiian archipelago was first visited by seafaring oceanic peoples sometime between the years 200 and 500 A.D. The

Hawaiian goose (nene)

earliest settlers probably arrived by chance, since it is unlikely that navigational routes were established between the far-flung islands of the eastern Pacific. These early forebearers of the people we now call Polynesians very likely drifted to the islands, made successful landfalls, and stayed. Waves of accidental migrants probably arrived in this way, after veering off course while on deliberate long voyages. It is unclear to archaeologists when two-way travel to Hawaii became established, certainly not for a long time after the islands were first populated. At some point, though, return navigation did occur, and thereafter a steady flow of people reached Hawaii from islands far to the southeast.

Hawaiian culture developed as a component of the Polynesian cultural realm. Traveling in large, seaworthy canoes and navigating by stars, the early inhabitants of Hawaii roamed the ocean, maintaining contact with the people of the other east Pacific islands with whom they shared appearance, language, and culture. Hawaii is at the north apex of a huge cultural triangle that extends to New Zealand in the southwest and Easter Island in the southeast. This oceanic triangle contains numerous island groups ("Polynesia" means "many islands"), including Tonga, Samoa, Cook, Marquesas, Easter, and Hawaii.

Traveling in large, seaworthy canoes and navigating by stars, the early inhabitants of Hawaii roamed the ocean, maintaining contact with the people of the other east Pacific islands with whom they shared appearance, language, and culture.

The Polynesians who settled in Hawaii were resourceful farmers and fishermen. They used coastal land intensively for growing taro, the staple tuber of the Polynesian diet. They fished in the lagoons and in the offshore waters. To regulate their subsistence activities, the early Hawaiians organized themselves into groups, initially kinship-based and egalitarian, but later according to hereditary rank. An aristocratic society of chiefs and kings developed in Hawaii, accompanied by complex codes of behavior and personal relationship (the *kapu* system). A feudal system of land allocation developed, whereby kings granted to chiefs (called *alii*) large parcels of land. They in turn allocated to commoners small plots of farmland. This land-tenure system divided Hawaii's land into wedgelike shapes that extended from the mountains to the ocean. The products of the land—taro, sugar cane, coconuts, and fruits—

Taro fields on Kauai

were taxed heavily by the alii. The descendents of pigs, fowl, and other domestic animals brought to Hawaii by the Polynesians provided meat primarily for the *alii's* diets. As the island's population grew, and as the conspicuous consumption of the alii increased, the land was pressured to produce more food.

The environmental impacts of the early Hawaiians were considerable. From their homelands they transported to Hawaii medicinal and food plants, cultivation techniques, domesticated animals, and settlement forms. Land-clearing for agriculture, especially in the large lowland valleys, contributed to deforestation. Magnificent waterworks were developed in places such as Hanalei on Kauai, Waipio Valley on the Island of Hawaii, and Honolulu on Oahu. These water systems allowed the redistribution of rainfall from natural catchments to the taro fields. Archaeological evidence suggests that the period 1100 to 1500 A.D. marked an era of significant land transformations, initiated by the Hawaiians as they cleared and burned vast forests for agriculture.

The loss of habitat and over-hunting pressures led to the demise of many bird species during the Polynesian days before Western contact. Hawaiians introduced numerous plants, including the coconut (*Cosos nucifera*), kukui (*Aleurites moluccana*), hau (*Hibiscus tiliaceus*), and breadfruit (*Moraceae*) trees. Some of these spread from cultivated areas to the wildlands, changing the makeup of native forests. While these prehistoric land transformations certainly domesticated the landscape, making it more usable for settlement by the Hawaiians, they pale beside the changes instituted by later migrants from the West whose technologies and ambitions, and consequent impacts, were far greater than those of the Hawaiians.

After Captain Cook's arrival in 1778, the western world recognized the vast bounty of Hawaii's land. Early American and European traders were supplied on their ocean journeys of exploration with food and articles provided by the Hawaiians. These provisions fostered a growing island trade in agriculture and lumber. Sandalwood became the first valuable export article of trade. Whaling and ranching followed, and the Hawaiian economy slowly became oriented to that of the *haoles* (white foreigners). Cattle, pigs, goats, sheep, and horses were introduced to Hawaii by Westerners, together with cats and rats (and later mongooses, to combat the rat problem in the sugar fields). Rice, coffee, and other commercial crops were planted. The domesticated landscape of the early Hawaiians underwent further transformations.

In 1848, 70 years after Captain Cook made his discovery, the indigenous land-tenure system that had protected land as the property of the king was abolished in the Great Mahele (land division). Land was redistributed among the king, the chiefs, the fledgling government of Hawaii, and the native tenants. The latter group gained control of only a tiny fraction of the available land (less than 1%). In 1850, land sales to foreigners were authorized, and thus began a period of land transference from the Hawaiians to the Western plantation owners and land speculators. In the mid-1800s, sugar became the king of Hawaii's economy. Ranchlands were converted to sugar lands wholesale with the expansion of irrigation into dry, leeward locations. Later joined by pineapple, the sugar plantation economy carried Hawaiian agriculture into the mechanized 20th century. Influxes of Asians to work on the plantations began in 1852 with Chinese contract laborers; soon thereafter came Filipinos and Japanese, adding to the ethnic mix of the islands.

Due to its location in the mid-Pacific, Hawaii made an attractive base for the U.S. military, which has been important in Hawaii since its annexation as a U.S. territory in 1900. The armed forces now control about 6% of the land in the islands (26% of Oahu). In additional to installations on most of the large islands, the military maintains the entire island of Kahoolawe as a bombing site, and Makua Valley on leeward Oahu as a live-firing area.

With statehood in 1959, commercial development and urbanization further intensified. The old port towns of Lahaina on Maui and

Pineapple field on Oahu

Hilo on the Island of Hawaii expanded into the surrounding rural areas. But the main urban development took place on Oahu, centered in Honolulu. In a matter of decades Honolulu lost much of its old world charm and took on the appearances of a modern high-rise city. Urban sprawl on Oahu has led to a gradual "suburbanization" of much of the island. On the outer islands, the viability of rural life is threatened in places by extensive resorts: Kaanapali, Wailea, and Kihei on Maui; the "gold" Kona Coast on the Island of Hawaii; and Poipu on Kauai. The most dramatic landscape changes in Hawaii are the result of post-contact agricultural expansion, militarization, tourism, and metropolitan growth. These have degraded the quality of the Hawaiian environment on a scale more massive than the changes introduced by the Polynesians, but the threatened condition of Hawaii's natural areas is actually an outcome of many centuries of habitation, beginning with the first Polynesian settlers and extending through the various subsequent waves of Western development.

On the outer islands, the viability of rural life is threatened in places by extensive resorts.

Conservation Concerns

Hawaii's record of investment in the Islands' natural heritage is a poor one. Historical land abuses have degraded many natural areas, resulting in the wholesale elimination of many plant and animal species. The main threats to natural communities are continued habitat destruction and the disruptive effects of introduced plants and animals. To avert continued land degradation in Hawaii, conservationists think it necessary to develop a high level of environmental awareness among both residents and visitors, and to create a strong advocacy and political action base in Hawaii. It is heartening to note that new environmental groups are taking on responsible roles in Island conservation (these groups are described in the chapters of this book).

Visitors to Hawaii's unique environment not only can observe and enjoy its tropical wonders, but can actively participate in their preservation by becoming informed of current conservation issues. The foremost environmental crisis in Hawaii is the crisis of extinction. It exists in all of Hawaii's biological regions. It can be observed in the montane cloud forests of Mauna Kea on the Island of Hawaii, where five endangered bird species and numerous endemic plants find habitat. It is the basis for new feral pig control programs in Haleakala National Park; fencing off extensive forest areas allows natural regeneration of endangered plants on land degraded by the browsing animals. Kawainui Marsh, near Kailua on Oahu, is the state's largest wetlands ecosystem, but unfortunately it is under pressure from local residents and the City and County of Honolulu, who want a flood-control program at the expense of the marsh's unique wildlife.

It is heartening to note that new environmental groups are taking on responsible roles in Island conservation.

Statewide, the number of threatened natural areas is large. Visitors to these areas should realize the sensitivity of their destinations. Marjorie Ziegler, a resource analyst for the Sierra Club Legal Defense Fund in Honolulu, prepared a list of key endangered areas that residents and visitors frequent. Virtually all wetlands are threatened. Motorized ocean recreation in many areas disrupts breeding habitat for humpback whales and sea turtles. Helicopters in the National Parks disturb the serenity and peace, and possibly disrupt native birds. Coast resort development encroaches upon sea strand natural communities, ancient fishponds, and reef habitats.

On an island-by-island basis the following conservation "hot-spots" are identified with tourism: On Kauai, backpackers on the Na Pali Coast can observe the serious problem of feral goats, and at the Kauai Westin Resort non-native species were introduced as visitor attractions. On Oahu, off-road vehicles disturb the dune ecology at Kaena Point, and the Campbell Industrial Park in Honolulu destroys unique sinkholes that have archaeological and paleontological (prehistoric bird bones) significance. On Molokai, The Hawaii Nature Conservancy Preserves at Moomomi and Pelekunu protect rare coastal and upland rainforest ecosystems. On Maui, the Crater and the Kipahulu regions of Haleakala National Park contain native habitat threatened by pigs and hunters. On Lanai, native upland dryland forests at Kanepuu have recently come under the stewardship of The Hawaii Nature Conservancy, but resort development at Manele-Hulupoe Bay threatens marine ecosystems and curtails public shoreline access. On Hawaii, the proposed resort at Punaluu will endanger hawksbill turtle nesting sites and anchialine ponds; the current resort complex at Waikoloa involves a host of issues including captive dolphins, breeding endangered goose and duck, and the destruction of coastal ecosystems; and the proposed "Hawaiian Riviera" at South Point would disturb important archaeological sites.

The issues described are only a few in the range of problems that confront Hawaii's unique natural environment. The state's own actions in supporting the conservation effort in Hawaii fall short of meeting the need. The monies devoted to parks and preserves is less than one fifth of the amount viewed as necessary by the Natural Resources Defense Council. It is unrealistic to assume that the state's 1.1 million residents can shoulder the entire burden, when almost five times that many visitors annually travel among the Islands. For the sake of Hawaii's environment, it is crucial that both visitors and residents come to see this paradise as more than a visual feast—it is a paradise of life. If we come away from the islands with a greater sense of their beauty and with a commitment to preserve natural Hawaii, we have been responsible visitors.

Chapter Two

The Hawaiian Islands

Background

Hawaii consists of 132 islands and shoals. Eight of these are main islands, which combined make up over 99% of Hawaii's land area. Most of the minor islands are included in the Northwest Hawaiian Island group, and they are rarely visited. The eight main islands are Niihau (off-limits to non-Hawaiians), Kauai, Oahu, Molokai, Lanai, Maui, Kahoolawe (restricted access), and Hawaii. Of these 8 islands, the major visitor destinations are on Kauai, Oahu, Maui, and Hawaii; Molokai and Lanai receive far fewer tourists.

In 1987 the resident population on all islands was 1,083,000. Most of these were on Oahu, which had a population of 830,600, and they lived primarily in the city of Honolulu. The remaining 252,000 persons live on the other main islands: Hawaii (114,400), Maui (81,100), Lanai (2,200), Molokai (6,700), Kauai (47,400), and Niihau (202). In addition to the residents of the state, on any average day about 133,000 visitors are in Hawaii. In 1986 approximately 5,600,000 visitors arrived in Hawaii, most coming from the U.S. but considerable numbers from Japan, Canada, and western Europe. To accommodate the tourists, in 1986 there were 510 hotels in Hawaii, almost half of which were on Oahu.

Behind these statistics lies the fact that for such a small place, Hawaii has captured the imagination of millions of people throughout the world. Many come for the equable temperatures (the coldest temperature on record at Honolulu International Airport is 53 degrees, the warmest 94), the persistent trade breezes, or the dependable sunshine. Others visit to enjoy the cultural amenities of the islands, the mix of ethnic groups, and the lavish displays of tourist recreation. A growing number of people come to explore and enjoy the unique tropical environment of the islands. They also share with many island residents a keen desire to preserve the natural areas.

This chapter provides information on island-wide environmental opportunities for both visitors and residents—mostly on the main islands. The activities, the natural areas, and the environmental organizations included in this chapter span the Hawaiian Islands, and they provide a context for exploring individual islands, covered in the separate chapters. Detailed information on island natural areas, alternative lodging, hiking, camping, parks, environmental tours, outfitters, and equipment sources are in the individual island chapters.

Alternative Energy

Hawaii's almost exclusive dependence upon imported petroleum (over 90% of the state's energy use), primarily crude oil from Alaska, puts the state in a precarious energy position. Conservation measures and alternative energy generation are therefore important to the islands' future. While Hawaii lacks a fossil-fuel base due to its volcanic origins, it has abundant sources of potentially renewable low-polluting energy—biomass, geothermal, hydropower, wind, solar, and ocean thermal. These natural energy sources are the focus of considerable commercial development statewide, as well as low-tech projects locally. As a result, several ongoing energy projects are located on the various islands, mainly on Oahu and the island of Hawaii, which can be visited and which serve as energy education centers. They demonstrate how the natural features for which Hawaii is noted—abundant sunshine, strong and steady trade winds, volcanoes, luxurious vegetation, and ocean waters—can provide usable energy.

The Hawaii Natural Energy Institute (HNEI) undertakes and coordinates a great deal of research on renewable energy in the state, and it has an excellent resource materials collection. It is located on the campus of the University of Hawaii, 2540 Dole St., Honolulu, HI 96822. 808/948-8788.

They demonstrate how the natural features for which Hawaii is noted—abundant sunshine, strong and steady trade winds, volcanoes, luxurious vegetation, and ocean waters—can provide usable energy.

The Tropical Research House demonstrates numerous residential energy-conservation systems. Set up your visit well in advance. The house is located adjacent to the University of Hawaii campus: Tropical Research House, University of Hawaii, College of Tropical Agriculture and Human Resources, 2515 Campus Road, Miller Hall 10, Honolulu, HI 96822. 808/948-8105.

General state level energy information can be obtained by contacting: Department of Business and Economic Development, Energy Division, 335 Merchant St., Room 110, Honolulu, HI 96813. 808/548-2334.

Neighbor island inquiries can be made at the following field extension offices:

Island of Hawaii: Hawaii Energy Extension Service, Hilo Lagoon Center Annex Building, Room 214, 101 Aupuni St., Hilo, HI 96720. 808/961-7558.

Maui: Office of Economic Development, 200 S. High St., Wailuku, Maui, HI 96793. 808/244-7783.

Kauai: Office of Economic Development, 4396 Rice St., Lihue, Kauai, HI 96766. 808/245-7305.

The current alternative energy programs in Hawaii include biomass, geothermal, hydropower, wind, solar, and ocean thermal energy conversion.

BIOMASS

Tree plantations and crop residues are currently the main sources of biomass energy production in Hawaii, supplying 9 percent of the state's energy needs and being the most flexible renewable energy resource. The sugar industry now is the main contributer, burning bagasse (the fibrous residue of sugar cane stalks and leaves) to produce steam and electricity. 605 million kWh of biomass energy was produced during the year 1987–88. Hawaii's 200,000 acres of commercial forestland constitute a potential supply of woodchips, another promising biomass source. Logging for energy poses its own problems, however, as already has been noted on Molokai, where clear-cutting for energy chips is contributing to erosion in some places on the porous volcanic slopes.

Biomass energy projects and research facilities are found on Hawaii (4 sites), Maui (2 sites), Oahu (2 sites), and Kauai (1 site). Not all are open to the public, but many conduct tours and all will provide additional information upon request.

Island of Hawaii

BioEnergy Development Corporation: They conduct research and development on biomass energy production from 714 acres of eucalyptus trees planted in the South Hilo district north of Hilo. Tours last 3–4 hours and must be set up in advance. Office hours are Mon.–Fri. 8–3. Contact: 888 Kalanianaole Ave., Hilo, HI 96720. 808/961-0411.

Mauna Loa Macadamia Nut Company: Nut shells and husks are processed for thermal energy at this factory located near Keaau. A visitor center located near the factory allows viewing the procedure. Open 7 days a week, 9–5. Located 6 miles south of Hilo airport on Highway 11. Contact: S.R. Box 3, Hilo, HI 96720. 808/966-9301.

Hamakua Sugar Company, Inc.: No tours are conducted, but educational materials are available upon request. The company supplies the bulk of alternative energy on the Island of Hawaii (40% of all electric power). Contact: P.O. Box 250, Pauilo, HI 96776. 808/776-1511.

Hilo Coast Processing Company: The main power base is bagasse from cane remnants. The company is the single largest alternative energy producer in the state. Education materials are available on request. No regular tours.

Maui

Hawaiian Commercial and Sugar Company: Their Puunene factory on Maui is located near Kahului; a second factory is located at Paia. Both are in the isthmus valley of Maui, where the company owns 37,000 acres. Contact: P.O. Box 3440, Honolulu, HI 96801. 808/525-6645 (Honolulu office); 808/877-5523 (Maui office).

Happy Hula Hog Farm: Vegetation is turned to swine waste and then to energy on this farm. Excess power from the biogas plant is sold to the Maui Electric Company. No group tours can be accommodated on the farm, but information is available upon request. Contact: RR1, Box 612, Kula, Maui, HI 96790. 808/878-1582.

Kauai

The Lihue Plantation Co.: A cogeneration facility is located in Lihue where bagasse is converted to steam and electricity. The plant provides about 30% of Kauai electric energy sales. Technical information is available upon request. Contact: P.O. Box 751, Lihue, Kauai, HI 96766. 808/245-7325.

GEOTHERMAL

Natural heat from the earth's interior is unusually close to the surface in Hawaii, particularly on the Island of Hawaii. One of the world's most active volcanoes, Kilauea, is located on Hawaii. It pumps superheated magma onto the land surface, where it, along with residual heat from other magma bodies, provides an enormous potential geothermal energy resource. The Kilauea East Rift Zone, where much of the most recent volcanic activity has occurred, is estimated to be able to provide 600 megawatts of electricity for the next century if properly harnessed. The main project development, in

Puna on the Island of Hawaii, is a source of controversy for local residents, however. Many people are upset over the damage the plant has wrought on the local environment; others are opposed to geothermal energy on higher grounds—believing it to be a drain on the energy powers of Pele, the goddess of Hawaii's volcanoes. The community controversies are strong, and the potential of geothermal must be considered in light of them.

Advocates of geothermal energy point to its relatively clean operation, its ability to meet large-scale energy needs in the near future, and the many potential spin-off benefits (nursery greenhouse warming, geothermal kilns for drying wood, aquaculture applications of warm residue water,). The commitment to geothermal energy research is strong, evidenced by the more than 30 research projects undertaken by the Hawaii Natural Energy Institute. The main project site is located in Puna on the Island of Hawaii. The HGP-A geothermal plant in Puna produced 14.8 kWh of electricity in the year 1987–1988, and associated research projects are being conducted on the role of heat byproducts for drying fruit, seasoning wood, dyeing cloth, heating greenhouses and making glass.

Island of Hawaii
Natural Energy Laboratory of Hawaii, Puna Geothermal Facility: The NELH-Puna Geothermal Facility is located near Kapoho in the Puna District, about 21 miles from Hilo. It consists of the HGP-A power plant and the Noii O Puna (Puna Research Center). The 3.0 MW HGP-A plant has been in production since 1982. Group tours must be arranged two weeks in advance. Individuals can visit any day. The visitor center is open daily 7:30–5:30. To reach the facility, take the Hawaii Belt Road (Hwy 11) to Keeau, turn left and proceed 11 miles on Hwy 130 to Pahoa. Pass through Pahoa, turning onto Hwy 132 toward Lava Trees State Monument. At the Kapoho-Pohoiki junction, stay right and go another mile to the geothermal facility. Contact: P.O. Box 2172, Pahoa, HI 96778. 808/965-9699.

HYDROPOWER
Hawaii's volcanic soils are so porous that few substantial rivers can form, but the mountain areas receive heavy rains and the vertical drops of many streams are very large, giving some potential for hydropower generation. There are currently 20 plants in operation, and an additional 8 are proposed. Of those currently operating, 9 are located on the Island of Hawaii, 4 are on Maui, and 7 are on Kauai. They are owned and operated by various corporations, and they differ in size and capacity. Most are located in remote places.

Contact: Department of Business and Economic Development, Energy Division, 335 Merchant St., Honolulu, HI 96813. 808/548-2334.

WIND POWER

The northeasterly trade breezes that stir the palms and cool the air prevail almost 70% of the time in Hawaii, averaging speeds of 15–25 miles per hour—well exceeding the 12–14 mph winds needed to make use of this resource as an energy source. Wind-power harnessing goes back at least as far as 1837 in Hawaii, and today there are over 400 wind energy conversion systems (WECS) in the state, with combined generating potential of about 16 MW. Land use and aesthetics pose a serious problem for the large scale development of wind energy, but in some favored locations WECS are proving successful without major environmental impacts. Seven locations are on the Island of Hawaii, 3 on Maui, 1 on Molokai, 4 on Oahu and 1 on Kauai. The windfarms vary in size and in number of turbines. The largest are the Kahuku windfarms on Oahu and the Lalamilo and Kamaoa windfarms on the Island of Hawaii. It is possible to visit the larger farms, and it is quite an exhilarating experience: Don Quixotian landscapes peppered with massive white-and-red rotating turbines, each sounding a steady whoosh! with the turn of their giant blades.

Wind-power harnessing goes back at least as far as 1837 in Hawaii, and today there are over 400 wind energy conversion systems in the state.

Oahu

Kahuku Windfarms: The world's largest wind turbine, the MOD-5B, capable of generating 3 megawatts, is located here, together with 15 smaller turbines. The MOD-5B's blade is longer than the wingspan of a jumbo jet, and its red and white colors stand out among the green north coast hills. Tours can be arranged through Hawaiian Electric Renewable Systems, Inc. The farm is easily accessible from Kamehameha Highway (Hwy 83) between Kuilima and Kahuku. Arrangements must be made in advance to visit the farm. Contact: P.O. Box 730, Honolulu, HI 96808. 808/293-9255.

Island of Hawaii

Lalamilo Ventures: Two windfarms are operated by Lalamilo Ventures, one at Kahua Ranch, on the upper slopes of North Kohala, and a second in Waikoloa, near the sea. The Kahua Ranch windfarm has 197 turbines, while the Waikoloa farm consists of 59 wind machines. Lalamilo is located along Waikoloa Road (Hwy 20), mauka of the coastal village of Puako. Tours need to be arranged at least 3 weeks in advance. Contact: P.O. Box 2195, Kamuela, HI 96743. 808/882-7315.

Kamaoa Windfarm: Located in the extreme southern part of the Island of Hawaii is this 37-turbine, 90-acre windfarm. The farm is on South Point Road, about 60 miles south of Hilo off Mamalahoa Highway (Hwy 11).

Solar Energy

Every 15 minutes the earth's surface receives enough sunlight to theoretically meet humankind's annual energy needs. Hawaii's location in the energy-surplus tropical latitudes and its clear skies make it a prime candidate for efforts to harness some of the insolation for use as energy. Solar thermal power, primarily in water heating systems, is the third largest energy source in Hawaii, after imported petroleum and domestic biomass. A number of small photovoltaic (PV) systems that convert sunlight directly into electricity have been installed in Hawaii, and plans have been initiated for the construction of a large PV power system in Hawaii to be run by the Maui Electric Company. Currently, two operating solar-energy systems can be visited on the Island of Hawaii.

Rainbow Harvest Hawaiian Solar Dried Fruit: Solar dryers process tropical fruit at this location in coastal Puna, near Cape Kumukahi. Contact: P.O. Box 1592, Pahoa, HI 96778. 808/965-9262.

Mana o Kala Solar Energy Farm Complex: Vegetables and about 2000 fruit trees have been planted on this organic farm operated by solar energy (both photovoltaic and solar thermal). Solar-powered automobiles, tractors, power tools and the Mana La world class solar-powered racing car are located here. Arrangements to visit the farm must be made well in advance. Contact: P.O. Box 379, Pauuilo, HI 96776. 808/776-1039.

OCEAN THERMAL ENERGY CONVERSION (OTEC)

Deep, cold ocean waters lie very close offshore around the Hawaiian Islands, and they pose a sharp contrast to the warm surface waters. The temperature difference between these ocean layers "fuels" a form of solar energy captured by a heat exchanger that drives a turbine to generate electricity. This process is known as ocean thermal energy conversion. Nutrient-rich, pathogen-free cold water is a by-product that is being used in aquaculture research at the Hawaiian Abalone Farms and the Royal Hawaiian Sea Farms and Aquaculture Enterprises. The research on OTEC is based at the

Natural Energy Laboratory of Hawaii (NELH) Kona Seacoast Test Facility.

Natural Energy Laboratory of Hawaii: The NELH's OTEC facility comprises 322 acres along the ocean at Keahole Point, near Keahole Airport. Proceed on Route 19 for one mile south of the airport entrance. Arrange a visit at least 2 weeks in advance. Contact: P.O. Box 1749, Kailua-Kona, HI 97620. 808/329-0648.

Alternative Lodging

In 1988 there were about 70,000 hotel and rental condominium units in Hawaii (33,661 in Waikiki alone). These capture most of island visitors, but alternatives exist. They include cabins, rustic lodges, small inns, and bed-and-breakfast establishments. The alternative lodgings are mentioned throughout this book under the island chapters. Most of them are located near natural areas, and they specifically appeal to more active visitors. The single largest category of alternative lodgings is the bed-and-breakfasts. Individual B&Bs are mentioned in the various island chapters. I avoid making recommendations, but I attempt to provide enough descriptions of settings and relative locations for you to make informed choices. On a statewide basis, two agencies provide extensive B&B directories:

Hawaiian Visitors Bureau

Lush tropical plant life surrounds a lovely waterfall near Hana on Maui

✓ ~ific-Hawaii Bed and Breakfast: 19 Kai Nani Place, Kailua, HI 96734. 808/262-6026.

✓ Bed and Breakfast Hawaii: P.O. Box 449, Kapaa, HI 96746. 808/822-7771.

Aquaculture

Fishponds have long been a part of Hawaii's landscape. The early Hawaiians created extensive intertidal channels by sealing off coastal water from the surrounding ocean. Lava rock walls were laboriously placed to enclose ponds where fish were kept and fed with agricultural scraps. The fish provided the local people with a steady protein source. Along some protected coastlines, such as at the Kaneohe Bay area on Oahu and the southern shore of Molokai, extensive series of fishponds make up elaborate prehistoric aquaculture systems. In Captain Cook's time it is estimated that there were some 350 ponds scattered among the islands. Most of the traditional fishponds have long been abandoned.

Modern aquaculture in Hawaii began fairly recently with oyster and mullet farming. Fifty aquafarms now are located in the state, where prawns, shrimp, seaweeds, trout, tilapia, abalone, catfish, oysters, koi, and microalgae are raised. General information about aquaculture in Hawaii can be obtained from the office of the Aquaculture Development Program in Honolulu: 335 Merchant St., Rm. 359, Honolulu, HI 96813. 808/548-5495.

Attributed to Hawaii's legendary elves, the Menehune, this fishpond is on Kauai

Hawaiian Visitors Bureau

Several aquaculture consulting projects have sprung up in Honolulu:

Aquatic Farms: in Honolulu, HI. 808/531-8061.

Mariculture Research and Training Center of the Hawaii Institute of Marine Biology: 49-139 Kam Hwy, Kaneohe, HI 96744. 808/237-8615. Arrange tours through this office.

Prawn Aquaculture Program: in Honolulu, HI. 808/847-6015.

It is possible to visit some of the aquafarms by advance arrangement. Prawn, shrimp, tilapia, seaweed, and bullfrogs are raised on Oahu's north shore fish farms. "Hawaii Aquaculture" at The Natural Energy Laboratory of Hawaii's Puna operations on the Island of Hawaii is experimenting with raising fish in the controlled water effluent of the geothermal plant located there. Trout and salmon are raised in cold water ponds at the OTEC program in Kailua-Kona, also located on the Island of Hawaii.

Oahu

Amorient Aquafarm: Located in Kahuku, on the north shore of Oahu, they raise prawns on 23 acres of ponds. They sell some of the catch in a roadside stand along Hwy 83 between Kahuku and Kuilima. The bulk of their production is sold at Tamashiro Market in Honolulu—a premier seafood store and a colorful place of local fame. Contact: 808/293-8531.

Hanohano Enterprises: This prawn farm is located on Kamehameha Highway, between Kahana Bay and Hauula along Oahu's windward coast. Contact: 808/293-8209.

Island of Hawaii

The Natural Energy Laboratory of Hawaii at Keahole Point in Kailua-Kona is also an experimental aquaculture site. Cold-water aquaculture is researched by the Hawaiian Abalone Farms and the Royal Hawaiian Sea Farms and Aquaculture Enterprises: Natural Energy Laboratory of Hawaii, P.O. Box 1749, Kailua-Kona, HI 97620. 808/329-0648.

Hawaii Aquaculture is conducting projects in association with the Puna Geothermal Facility: P.O. Box 2172 Pahoa, HI 96778. 808/965-9699.

Environmental Education

Several organizations in Hawaii promote environmental education by various means. They share the philosophy that learning can best be achieved by direct interaction with nature, so the programs generally entail an outdoors approach. But the structure of the programs varies widely, as do the target population. Some programs are restricted to certain age groups; others are open to all ages. The programs described below span the range of nonformal environmental education in Hawaii.

Hawaii Nature Center: Located in the Makiki forest only minutes from Honolulu is one of the state's premier environmental education centers. In 1986 it was chosen as one of the top 3 environmental education organizations in the nation. The main interpretive building now has a red, white and blue banner across the entrance advertising the fact that it won the national "Take Pride in America" award in 1987 for its work with nature stewardship and childrens' environmental education. This is a high quality organization. The center's hands-on approach to learning puts the *keikis* (little ones) in direct contact with the natural world, where they explore the flora and fauna, the natural life cycles, and the conservation issues of the surrounding forest. Incorporated in 1981, the Hawaii Nature Center serves 23,000 people a year.

If you or your children want to take advantage of the center, there are many programs to choose from. They offer school year and summer classes of varying lengths. A regular schedule of hikes and interpretive programs is offered each month for both children and adults: walks in the nearby Makiki Forest Reserve; longer hikes to natural areas on Oahu with docents (naturalist guides) who are local authorities on geology, flora, fauna, and island geography; nature photo classes; and many others. The center publishes a regular newsletter as well as interpretive brochures for the Makiki Forest Reserve trail systems ("Manoa Cliffs Trail: Plant Identification Guide"; "The Natural History of the Makiki Valley Loop Trail"). For information on events and services, contact: Hawaii Natural Center, 2131 Makiki Heights Drive, Honolulu, HI 96822. 808/973-0100. To reach the center, head mauka from Honolulu up Makiki Street, turn left onto Makiki Heights Drive, and after one-half mile turn right at the Nature Center signboard.

Wilderness Hawaii: Wilderness Hawaii conducts small group backpacking expeditions into Hawaii's wildlands. Their purpose is to combine education and adventure with wilderness-skills development, and with teamwork, leadership, and self-esteem training. A 20-day course for teenagers offered in the summer explores, on physical, emotional, and spiritual levels, the wildness of Hawaii Volcanoes National Park. This is the peak "Wilderness Hawaii" experience best summed up in the simple words of one of the teens who completed the course, "I feel more peaceful inside." Shorter, 4-

day courses are offered for teens, women, and coed adults. The courses allow participants a chance to learn what can't be taught. As one person put it, "I remembered how to relax and play . . . I opened my eyes underwater for the first time—yea-a-a!".

For details on their programs, including itineraries, costs, and logistics, contact: Wilderness Hawaii, P.O. Box 61692, Honolulu, HI 96839. 808/737-4697.

Sea Life Park: One of Hawaii's most popular tourist attractions doubles as an environmental learning center, with a focus on marine education. This alternative role that Sea Life Park plays is less visible to the general public than the commercial amusements, but it is authentic, unique and highly respected. Each year nearly 30,000 people come from the community, from the U.S. mainland, and from abroad to participate in the marine education program at Sea Life Park. Tidepool treks, marine photography, seabirds, dolphin research and marine crafts are part of the scheduled educational programs that are offered to all levels, from preschoolers through adults. Contact: Sea Life Park, Education Department, Makapuu Point, Waimanalo, HI 96795. 808/259-7933. The park is on Kalanianaole Highway (Hwy 72) near Makapu Point, on Oahu.

The School for Field Studies: This nontraditional field school offers college and high-school students outdoor study opportunities in Hawaii. The focus is on the natural history of the islands. They have both summer and winter programs, which can be taken for college credit (most students are co-enrolled at their own university). For details, contact: The School for Field Studies, 16 Broadway, Beverly, MA 01915. 508/927-7777.

This is the peak "Wilderness Hawaii" experience best summed up in the simple words of one of the teens who completed the course, "I feel more peaceful inside."

Wildlands Research: This is a field studies program that offers college credit through San Francisco State University. Semester-long courses are held each year in the wildlands of Hawaii. A summer session runs from June 28 to August 9, and a winter session runs from January 11 to February 22. The programs focus on the changing relationships between island culture, wilderness areas, and tourism. The field study is conducted on the islands of Kauai, Molokai, Maui, and Hawaii. For information, contact: Wildlands Research, 3 Mosswood Circle, Cazadero, CA 95421. 707/632-5665.

University of Hawaii Outdoor Recreation Program: The main campus of the University of Hawaii, at Manoa in Honolulu, has a long-standing program of outdoor education during the summer months. Courses are offered in a variety of subjects: sailing, kayaking, nature studies, wilderness skills. Many of the programs involve trips to outer islands. The price is always reasonable. Contact: University of Hawaii, CCB Outdoor Recreation Program, Hemenway Hall 101, 2445 Campus Rd., Honolulu, HI 96822. 808/956-6001.

Ohia Project, Bishop Museum: This organization does not lead trips into the wild places, but it does develop and provide materials that will ensure that those who go there have a higher-quality experience. They produce environmental education materials for K-8 grades on topics including geology, geography, plants and animals, humans and the environment, natural-resource management, and global environmental interaction. Pretty heady stuff for the young ones, but necessary. Their focus is on tropical ecology and the Hawaiian setting. If you're a student, teacher, or otherwise interested, contact: Ohia Project, Bishop Museum, 1525 Bernice Street, P.O. Box 19000-A, Honolulu, HI 96817. 808/848-4108.

Interpretive Hikes and Nature Walks

Any walk into the woods is a learning experience. But if you are new to the Hawaiian Islands, or you have not studied island flora, fauna, ecology, or geology, you may want to take advantage of the excellent resource people who regularly lead hikes to natural places on the islands. Many of these people link up with environmental organizations, including the Sierra Club, The Nature Conservancy, Hawaii Nature Center, Trail and Mountain Club, the various botanical gardens, Waikiki Aquarium, and other civic groups. The information provided below will guide you to organizations that regularly schedule interpretive hikes. This certainly doesn't mean that you can't hike into natural Hawaii without a guide, but if you go with one a few times, you will better understand the place when next you go alone. And you will undoubtedly meet kindred spirits among your fellow hikers.

Sierra Club: The Hawaii Chapter of the Sierra Club, a national environmental organization, is one of the most active local chapters of the club that I have encountered. In addition to resource materials for Hawaiian wilderness, they offer outing leaders training programs, conduct service trips for federal and state environmental and recreation organizations, organize the high school hikers program, and lead interpretive outings for the community. The community

Hawaiian Visitors Bureau

Shoreline black lava glistens in the sunlight

outings are offered each Sunday of the month, and occasionally on other days. The different islands have local affliate groups: the Honolulu Group on Oahu, the Maui Group on Maui, the Moku Loa Group on the Island of Hawaii, and the Kauai Group. Contact the affiliate groups to find out about upcoming outings on particular islands. Many of the Sierra Club hikes take you into restricted areas, such as The Nature Conservancy preserves, the national wildlife refuges, and forest reserves. The leaders are knowledgeable, well-trained, and sympathetic to a range of abilities among hikers. There is a $1 fee for persons over 14 years, and hikers must provide their own food, water, and gear.
Contact:

> Honolulu Group, P.O. Box 2577, Honolulu, HI 96803
> Kauai Group, P.O. Box 3412, Lihue, HI 96766
> Maui Group, P.O. Box 2000, Kahului, HI 96732
> Moku Loa Group, P.O. Box 1137, Hilo, HI 96721

Lyon Arboretum: The exquisite gardens of the Lyon Arboretum (see Oahu Botanical Parks) are only one aspect of this organization. They also serve as an educational association by presenting opportunities for the community to learn about Hawaiian native plants, ethnobotany, and tropical horticulture. They schedule regular hikes on Oahu that feature bird-watching or forest flowers, and they occasionally organize nature trips to the outer islands. There is no regular outings schedule, but you can find out about upcoming activities by contacting: Lyon Arboretum Association, 3860 Manoa Road, Honolulu, HI 96822. 808/988-3177.

Waikiki Aquarium: Located at the eastern edge of Waikiki's glitter, the aquarium offers a soothing respite from its hectic surroundings. It also regularly offers fascinating educational classes and outings on Oahu. Some outing program titles are: "In Search of Wild Limu" (a reef-walk hunt for seaweed); "Reading the Beach" (beach sand erosion study); "Fish Watchers Workshop" (designed for 8 to 12 year olds); and "Partners for Survival: Symbiosis on the Reef". These marine education adventures, conducted by scientists, provide excellent hands-on experience with the ocean world. One of their most popular outings is the nighttime reef walk. The aquarium also conducts seasonal 3-hour ocean cruises aboard a naturalist vessel for students and community groups. Weekly lectures on Hawaiian and Pacific natural history are featured throughout the year at the Aquarium. Contact: Waikiki Aquarium, 2777 Kalakaua Avenue, Honolulu, HI 96815. 808/923-9741.

Nature Productions

The creativity of Hawaii's environmentalists shines brightly over the islands, and it provides the public with some truly imaginative ways of exploring nature, even while staying indoors.

Kaio Productions: Producers of educational videotapes on Hawaii. Some recent titles: "Eruptive Phenomena of Kilauea's East Rift Zone," "Eruption at the Sea." Contact: Kaio Productions, P.O. Box 909, Volcano, HI 96785. 808/967-7166.

Puppets on the Path: Three talented women from the Island of Hawaii have joined strengths to create a puppet stage show that is unlike all others—not the Biggest Show in Town, but maybe the Best. Since 1982 they have been entertaining audiences in Hawaii and on the U.S. mainland (including the Smithsonian Institution and the Kennedy Center for the Performing Arts) with their whimsical, musical romps through the world of nature: "Forest Friends," "Dancing in the Deep," and "Nature Notes from Land and Sea" are the titles of their puppet stage acts. They sing, they dance, and they play with a purpose. In 1990 their newest production, "A World of Difference," will begin touring. It focuses on tropical biological diversity and the problem of ocean litter.

> I'm Flotsam and Jetsam, Trash of the Sea,
> When folks throw out plastic, they make more of me.
> I'm baaaaad!
>   © 1989 Puppets on the Path

For a schedule of shows, workshops, and other activities (or to book an event) contact: Puppets on the Path, P.O. Box 810, Volcano, HI 96785. 808/885-4607.

Heiaus

The early colonizers from the Marquesas Islands brought to the Hawaiian Islands the Polynesian concept of sacred places. They believed that man and gods are linked to the earth's spirit, and that certain natural places have a strong spiritual power, which they called "mana". In Hawaii, temples for worship and sacrifice were built at many of these sites. The Hawaiians referred to their temples as "heiaus."

The location of a heiau was determined because of the physical attributes of the area, or because culturally significant events had occurred there. For example, coastal headlands and mountaintops were often used for temple sites, and some heiaus were located where a chief or a king had been born. The function of a heiau often was linked to its natural setting. Agricultural heiaus were devoted to Kane, the god of farming, and were located near fertile growing areas. Planting and harvest celebrations took place at these heiaus. Fishing heiaus, called *koa,* were established at coastal locations near productive waters for the worship of Kuula, the god of fishing. Other heiaus served as prayer and ceremonial centers for purposes of war, sports, or navigation. At all the heiaus, religious ceremonies were held to appease the gods and to solicit their blessings.

Heiaus differed in their religious and social importance. Places of refuge, called *puuhonua* heiaus, and places of human sacrifice, called *luakini* heiaus, were the two most important types of heiaus. The former were sanctuaries for persons who violated the code of sacred laws, called *kapu.* The latter were used in the ritual killing of people. In some instances, the two types were combined at the same location, resulting in a heiau of great power. Ritual activity at all the heiaus was the responsibility of a resident priest, called a *kahuna,* overseen by a local chief or a member of the higher-ranking Hawaiian royalty, the *alii.*

While Hawaiian culture flourished and evolved over the centuries prior to Western contact, heiaus occupied an important position in island life. They helped to bind islanders together in a religious system that emphasized the productivity and the overall sacredness of the land. Because the activities at the temple sites were controlled by the *kahunas* and the *alii,* the heiaus also helped to legitimize the central power structure that ruled the islanders' lives.

Western contact changed the Hawaiian system. Missionaries arrived in 1820, bringing to Hawaii a new religion, and traders eventually introduced to the islands Western forms of economy and politics. Soon the significance of the heiaus in Hawaiian culture declined, for several reasons. Land lost its spiritual meaning and became an economic good. The new religion was based on Western deities, rather than on any immediate qualities of the land. *Kahunas* and chiefs lost their power to the Western clergy and Western business-men. No longer faithfully maintained, heiaus fell into physical decay. Given warm temperatures and high humidity, the lush tropical vegetation quickly eroded and overgrew the rock-and-earthen structures built by the Hawaiians. The remnants of heiaus found today—crumbling foundations of lava rock, plants clinging to terrace walls, dislodged paving materials—hint at early designs that blended indigenous knowledge of geography, architecture and religion.

Heiaus today are important archaeological sites, a part of the prehistoric record of the Hawaiian Islands. The noted Pacific archaeologist T. G. Thrum and his successors have surveyed over 750 heiaus scattered across the archipelago. This probably is only a fraction of the total number, since new heiaus continually are being discovered. Only a small number are accessible, and fewer still are in good shape. The best-preserved heiaus retain all or part of the original constructions: priests' quarters, altars, sacrificial stones, paved courtyards where the *kahunas* and the *alii* met, terraced earthen platforms where the commoners gathered, and rock walls that partitioned the heiau from the surrounding terrain are common features. Some of the larger and more important heiaus have been

Kahuna's hut, Mookini Heiau, Island of Hawaii

restored by archaeologists, and many of the important ones now are
public parks or historical monuments. The heiaus mentioned in this
book are the most accessible and most nearly intact ones, and they
can be readily explored. Calling attention to such places poses the

While Hawaiian culture flourished and evolved over the centuries prior to Western contact, heiaus occupied an important position in island life.

obvious risk of disturbing them, so please visit with sensitivity. Many
native Hawaiians still practice the old religion, and they revere the
heiaus as their temples. Realize that you approach not only an
important archaeological site but also a spiritual place that remains
vital to Hawaiian culture and to many island residents.

Hiking and Camping

The Hawaii State Department of Land and Natural Resources
estimates that about 2% of island residents and 2% of annual
visitors use the state's 1112 miles of established hiking trails. It also
estimates that about 3% of residents and 1% of visitors stay at one
of the state's campgrounds (the total number of tent sites at all established campgrounds in the state is about 2065). Numerous hiking
guidebooks describe the trail systems on many of the islands. The
Forest Division of the Department of Land and Natural Resources
publishes trail maps and descriptions of many of its forest reserve
areas. Various community groups have developed interpretive guides
to specific natural areas. This book directs you to the camping and
hiking areas, and to the existing guidebooks that describe the areas in
detail. Hawaii's national parks constitute the largest and most
frequently visited type of natural area on the Islands (5,225,631 persons visited the national parks in 1987). But there are many others.
The camping and hiking areas mentioned in the book are organized
by island and by type of environment (for example, mountain versus
coastal locations).

Visitors unfamiliar with Hawaii's natural environment should
realize that the wilderness areas are fragile and threatened places.
Campers and hikers should stick to the designated sites and trails.
Avoid vegetation, loose and crumbly rock, and private land. If you
need a fire, use a backpacking stove. Clean boots and camping gear
thoroughly after each hike. These can harbor seeds and backpackers are often inadvertent carriers of noxious pest weeds. The
spread of alien plants is a major environmental problem in Hawaii.
Utilize the wisdom and sensibility that should be applied in all

natural areas, and realize that Hawaii's are especially rare. The Hawaii Sierra Club publishes the small booklet *Hiking Softly in Hawaii,* which outlines necessary courtesies of the Hawaiian outdoorsperson. It can be obtained from the Sierra Club in Honolulu. Another book, *Exploring Nature Safely* by Ed Arrigoni, is an excellent safety primer for those unfamiliar with backcountry travel in Hawaii.

Where hiking and camping areas fall within established parklands, detailed maps and site descriptions are often available free of charge by contacting the appropriate administering agency (these are noted throughout the book). In remote areas not under parklands jurisdiction, topographic maps are necessary. Sources of these maps and other related reference materials are given in the various island chapters. It is wise to consult these detailed maps when planning a journey to a remote area. Island topography is varied, with remarkable changes in elevation, shifts in vegetation, and abrupt changes in trail difficulty, so become familiar with these factors before you set out.

Nature Tours and Outdoor Excursions

Several adventure travel agencies operate nature tours on the main islands of Hawaii. They share the goal of providing environmentally focussed tours and outdoor activities.

Eye of the Whale Marine/Wilderness Adventures: They offer adventure travel programs that combine hiking, snorkeling and sailing. Three tours to choose from: Whale Tales (5–8 days); Earth, Fire & Sea (7 days); and Gateway to Paradise (10–14 days). Their journeys go to Lanai, Molokai and the Island of Hawaii. The excursions, limited to small groups (less than 10), emphasize participation in and appreciation of Hawaii's environment. Prices range from $700 to $1500, depending on itinerary. Contact: Eye of the Whale, P.O. Box 1269, Kapaau, HI 96755. 808/889-0227.

Hawaiian Outdoor Adventures: They offer one-week dayhike trips, extended backpacking trips, and bicycle tours. Itineraries include Maui, Kauai, and the Island of Hawaii. Trips are led by Robert Smith, author of several hiking guidebooks for Hawaii. Prices range from $375 to $895, depending on itinerary. Contact: Hawaiian Outdoor Adventures, P.O. Box 869, Huntington Beach, CA 92648. 213-438-4520.

Pacific Quest: They combine sailing and hiking in their Hawaiian outdoor adventure tours. A 14-day Adventure Quest goes to Kauai, Molokai, Maui, and the Island of Hawaii ($1295). The 6-day Sailing Adventure goes to Lanai, Maui, and Molokai ($936). Contact:

Jim Rizzuto

Camping at a state beach

Pacific Quest, Inc., P.O. Box 205, Haleiwa, HI 96712. 808/638-8338.

OCEAN TOURS

Hawaii contains about 750 miles of coastline, and no place in the islands is more than 30 miles distant from the nearest shore. The ocean, in addition to influencing Hawaii's climate, terrain, and vegetation, represents an obvious recreational resource for the state. The siren call for most tourists is the call to the beach. On any typical day, 171,000 persons are at the beach, 22,000 are riding waves, 25,000 are fishing, 3,000 are paddling canoes, and 20,000 are diving. And Hawaii has no dearth of tour operators to service the ocean recreation industry.

This book has a terrestrial focus. Hence, only those ocean tour agencies that combine land-sea options, or that include ocean conservation education in their itineraries are included in the book chapters. For information on fishing and marine conservation, contact the Division of Aquatic Resources, Department of Land and Natural Resources, 1151 Punchbowl St., Room, 330, Honolulu, HI 96813. Two coastal activities included in this book are snorkeling and surfing, both popular outdoor sports. References are made to the best spots for both on the various islands. If you plan to snorkel in island waters, pick up a copy of *Hawaiian Reefs and Tidepools* by Ann Fielding.

Parklands

Hawaii has approximately 250 established parklands in the state's natural areas (when we include urban parks, the total rises to about 700). They include national parks and historical sites, state parks, county beach parks, private preserves, botanical gardens, national wildlife refuges, city and county parks, state wildlife sanctuaries, and marine recreation areas. A lavish new book, *Hawaii Parklands* by Marnie Hagmann, provides capsule descriptions and outstanding photographs of many of the parks in Hawaii. The parklands that provide natural experiences for the public are included in this book under the various chapters. In addition to the established parks, about 1.2 million acres of land are held in 68 forest reserves, managed for watershed maintenance and multiple use.

Information about particular parklands is provided in the island chapters. The main park-administering agencies are listed in the appendix. They are sources for park information and user permits.

Preserve Lands

Federal, state, and private organizations have set aside land in Hawaii for the preservation of rare plant and animal life. These lands cover about one-half million acres, and they contain the full range of Hawaiian natural communities. The island chapters of this book cover the preserve parks that provide opportunities for camping, hiking, and nature study. The overview below places the particular island opportunities in the context of statewide natural areas. Federal lands provide the largest acreage of preserve land in Hawaii (national parks and national wildlife refuges—270,750 acres). State lands provide an additional 200,000 acres (natural area reserves, wilderness preserves, and state wildlife sanctuaries). Private preserve lands are held by The Nature Conservancy of Hawaii. Over 17,000 acres are directly managed by The Nature Conservancy on five islands, plus joint projects with the U.S. Fish and Wildlife Service and the National Park Service on an additional 17,000 acres. Because these lands are devoted to wilderness protection, their access and use are restricted. Before visiting one of these areas, check with the administering agency.

NATIONAL PARKS

Hawaii has two national parks—Haleakala National Park on Maui, and Hawaii Volcanoes National Park on the Island of Hawaii—and an additional three national historical parks—Kolako Honokohau National Historical Park and Puuhonua o Honaunau on the Island of Hawaii, and Kalaupapa National Historical Park on Molokai. The parks' combined area totals about 250,000 acres. The historical parks have resource management programs, but their primary mandate is to provide preservation and interpretation programs on cultural history.

The two national parks are premier areas for outdoor exploration and study. Haleakala National Park (27,350 acres) is covered in the chapter on Maui, Molokai, and Lanai. Hawaii Volcanoes National Park (217,297 acres) appears in the Island of Hawaii chapter.

STATE NATURAL AREA RESERVES

In 1970 the state of Hawaii established the State Natural Area Reserve System (NARS). Its charge is to preserve unique ecosystems, including bogs, grasslands, reefs, lava flows, forests, and tundra. The NARS includes 18 reserves on the islands of Hawaii, Kauai, Maui, Molokai, and Oahu, occupying 108,000 acres of land.

Many of the areas are remote and inaccessible. Others are commonly enjoyed by hikers and naturalists, although the preservation goals of the NARS restrict activities in the reserves. Reserves that provide opportunities for natural explorations are described in the island chapters. For statewide visitor information, contact: Natural Areas Reserve System, Department of Land and Natural Resources, 1151 Punchbowl Street, Honolulu, HI 96813. 808/548-7417.

The habitat diversity contained in the natural area reserves provides unparalled opportunities both for preserving and for exploring Hawaii's unique natural heritage. The NARS includes almost one half of the total number of distinct natural communities in the islands. Thus legal protection is extended to many rare wildlife habitats. To be effective, the NARS needs an aggressive management program. In some of the reserves, unfortunately, the enforcement of access and use restrictions is lax. Travelers who visit the reserves should be aware that the primary purpose of such places is preservation. Because they are of outstanding value as natural places, the reserves also provide great experiences for nature exploration.

THE NATURE CONSERVANCY OF HAWAII PRESERVES

The Hawaii Nature Conservancy maintains nature preserves on five islands. Only two areas are currently open to public visitation— Waikamoi Preserve on Maui (5230 acres) and Kamakou Preserve on Molokai (2774 acres). The other preserves strictly regulate access and use (Kaluahonu Preserve on Kauai; Ihi ihilauakea Preserve on Oahu; Pelekunu Preserve and Moomomi Dunes on Molokai; Kipahulu Valley Preserve on Maui; and Hakalau National Wildlife Refuge on the Island of Hawaii). Visits to the restricted areas are possible only by joining a Sierra Club service trip or by participating in one of The Nature Conservancy outings. The possibilities are described elsewhere in the book under Nature Tours and Outdoor Excursions, Environmental Education, or Environmental Groups. For statewide information on opportunities with The Nature Conservancy, contact: The Nature Conservancy of Hawaii, 1116 Smith St., Suite 201, Honolulu, HI 96817. 808/537-4508.

Waikamoi Preserve: This preserve is located on the island of Maui, adjacent to Haleakala National Park. It is a windswept tract of montane forest that is a delight for birders because it provides intact habitat for many endangered Hawaiian forest birds. Sometimes seen here is the crested honey-creeper (*Palmeria dolei*); more common are the scarlet iiwi (*Vestiaria coccinea*), the crimson-breasted apapane (*Himatione sanguinea*), the yellowish-green amakihi (*Hemignathus virens*), and the dark-rumped petrel, or uau (*Pterodroma phaeopygia sandwichensis*).

The preserve is open to the public on a restricted basis. Public hikes are arranged through Haleakala National Park on Monday, Thursday, and Friday of each week (make arrangements at Park headquarters). Hikes also are led by Preserve naturalists specifically for conservancy members one Sunday a month. Direct inquiries to the preserve manager, Waikamoi Preserve, P.O. Box 1716, Makawao, HI 96768. 808/572-7849.

Kamakou Preserve: The preserve is located on the island of Molokai, near the summit of Kamakou (Molokai's highest point at 4970 feet). It contains a magnificent montane rainforest that support 250 kinds of Hawaiian plants. Two extremely rare forest birds found only on Molokai live here: the Molokai thrush, or olomao (*Myadestes lanaiensis*), and the Molokai creeper, or kakawahie (*Paroreomyza flammea*). The Preserve is open to the public, but it is accessible only by 4-wheel-drive vehicle along a road that is often impassable. Visitors should first inquire of the Preserve Manager, Kamakou Preserve, P.O. Box 40, Kualapuu, Molokai, HI 96757. 808/567-6680.

The Nature Conservancy of Hawaii regularly conducts field trips to the preserves for island residents and for visitors from the mainland who are Conservancy members. The itineraries of the trips vary, but they all feature outings and hikes to the various island preserves. For information, contact the Honolulu Office of The Nature Conservancy of Hawaii.

NATIONAL WILDLIFE REFUGES

The U.S. Fish and Wildlife Service maintains a number of national wildlife refuges in the Hawaiian Islands, managed for the preservation of endangered species that are found nowhere else in the world. The oldest and most extensive refuge in Hawaii is the Hawaiian Islands National Wildlife Refuge (NWR), comprising over 250,000 acres of high islands (Nihoa and Necker islands), low islands (Laysan and Lisianski islands), sea stacks (Gardner Pinnacles) and atolls (French Frigate Shoals, Pearl and Hermes Reef, and Maro Reef). These compose the Northwest Hawaiian Island group, which stretches like a beaded pendant for 800 miles northwest from the main Hawaiian Islands. These remnants of larger islands are located far from any continental landmass, and they provide a unique window into Pacific natural history. Some endemic faunal species, including the Hawaiian monk seal, Laysan finch and

Hawaiian Visitors Bureau

Boobies on Kauai

Nihoa millerbird, are found nowhere else in the world. The endangered Hawaiian green sea turtle breeds here, as do 18 species of seabirds numbering in the tens of millions.

Of the 70 species of endemic birds (referring to those found nowhere else) in Hawaii prior to man's arrival, 24 are now gone and another 30 are threatened with extinction. Many of the imperiled birds are wetland creatures that inhabit the coastal lowlands. Five of the seven wildlife refuges on the main islands are wetlands ecosystems, the remaining two refuges occupy higher, drier sites. Like the national wildlife refuges of the Northwestern Hawaiian Islands, they exist to provide habitat for endangered species and to increase our understanding of the environment. Year-round island residents like the Hawaiian coot, Hawaiian duck, and Hawaiian gallinule are joined by migratory birds from North America and Asia to make up a diverse population that depends on the marshlands and ponds for food, shelter and breeding grounds. Four endangered waterbirds are found in the wetland refuges: Hawaiian duck, or koloa maoli (*Anas wyvilliana*), Hawaiian gallinule, or alae ula (*Gallinula chloropus sandvicensis*), Hawaiian coot, or alae keokeo (*Fulica american alai*), and Hawaiian stilt, or aeo (*Himantopus mexicanus knudseni*). Housing and resort development have altered much of Hawaii's coastal marshlands, threatening the habitat of these species. The refuges exist now to serve the habitat needs of the seabirds, as well as the educational needs of the people who visit them.

It is possible to enter the refuges with a special use permit. These are provided for purposes of nature study, research, photography, journalism, or art. Contact: Refuge Manager, Hawaiian and Pacific Islands National Wildlife Refuge, U.S. Fish and Wildlife Service, 300 Ala Moana Blvd, R. 5302, P.O. Box 50167, Honolulu, HI 96850. 808/541-1220.

Oahu

James Campbell NWR: Thirty-five species of birds, including stilts, coots, and ducks, inhabit this 155-acre marshland located in Kahuku on Oahu's north shore. The spring-fed Punamano Pond and the adjacent Kii pond unit have been restored and enhanced through water impoundments and channels to provide nesting and feeding areas. The refuge is open to the public on certain weekends and by special permit. It includes an interpretive display and a nature trail. Plans for additional wetland wildlife interpretation facilities are in the making.

Pearl Harbor NWR: Bounded by sugar cane fields that quickly give way to urban buildup, this refuge is located adjacent to Pearl Harbor, near the Honolulu International Airport. The seemingly incongruous site provides 40 acres of marshland habitat for shorebirds. It was established in 1977 as a wildlife refuge in compensation for losses of seabird feeding habitat that occurred when the reef runway was annexed to the airport. The refuge is primarily for the Hawaiian stilt, but includes 28 other species of birds.

The refuges exist now to serve the habitat needs of the seabirds, as well as the educational needs of the people who visit them.

Island of Hawaii

Hakalau Forest NWR: Lying at elevations between 4500 and 6800 feet along the windward slope of Mauna Kea, this 13,105-acre native rainforest preserve harbors several endangered bird species and an unknown number of threatened plants. It is a new refuge, jointly administered by The Hawaii Nature Conservancy and the U.S. Fish and Wildlife Service. The refuge is located about 2 hours from Hilo by 4-wheel-drive vehicle. Altitudinal zonation of habitat provides a diverse range of ecosytems: dense fern, ohia and koa forest downslope; parklands of scattered koa and ohia at midslope; and upland grasslands. The purpose of the refuge is to preserve the rainforest ecosystem in entirety. Public use is by permit only, and is generally limited to bird-watching groups.

Opaeula NWR: Located in the Makalawena District north of Keahole Airport along the Kona Coast, this refuge includes a brackish pond, a lava flow, and a kiawe thicket. It provides sanctuary for the Hawaiian coot and the Hawaiian stilt, as well as 14 additional native bird species. Bird observation and photography are possible from the perimeter.

Kauai

Hanalei NWR: The lush Hanelei Valley on the north shore of Kauai is the setting for this 917-acre refuge supporting 49 kinds of birds, including a number of endangered species. The valley has been irrigated for wetland taro farming for over 1200 years, and taro is still commercially farmed by 12 permitees. They combine cropping practices with habitat preservation in a unique arrangement with the U.S. Fish and Wildlife Service. An interpretive overlook on Hwy 56 (Kuhio Highway) north of the refuge provides an outstanding view of the entire area.

Huleia NWR: Established in 1973 on 238 acres of wooded slopes and grassy bottomlands along the Huleia River south of Lihue, this refuge includes converted rice and taro land. It hosts 31 species of birds, 13 of which are native to the islands. The refuge lies adjacent to the Menehune (Alakoko) Fishpond; the refuge can be observed from the Menehune Overlook off Hwy 58.

Kilauea Point NWR: On a rocky promontory overlooking the Pacific along Kauai's north coast lies this spectacular refuge.

Mouth of Waioli River at Hanalei on Kauai

Kilauea Point is located at the end of a paved access road about 1 mile north of the village of Kilauea off Kuhio Highway (Hwy 56). The Kilauea Point Natural History Association operates a visitors facility at the base of the Kilauea Lighthouse. Wedge-tailed shearwaters, red-footed boobies, the Laysan albatross, frigatebirds and the red-tailed tropicbird can be seen here. The refuge is open Mon–Fri. 10–4. A $2 entrance fee is charged to those not holding a national wildife refuge passport.

Molokai

Kakahaia NWR: Five miles east of Kaunakakai along Hwy 460 is the 42-acre Kakahaia refuge. It provides nesting habitat for 12 species of sea and coastal birds on a 15-acre freshwater pond amid surrounding kiawe thickets. Maui County maintains a small roadside park on the refuge where visitors can picnic and observe the birdlife.

Recycling

The need for the recycling of waste materials is great in water-locked Hawaii, particularly on Oahu, where the City and County of Honolulu has initiated a pilot program that requires residents of certain areas to recycle their refuse under threat of prosecution. Local and state governments also are supporting commercial recycling ventures, so that now a number of recycling companies exist on the islands. Oahu has 16 enterprises, and a smaller number of recycling centers is found on the outer islands.

Oahu

For a list of recycling centers around the island, contact: The Recycling Association of Hawaii, 2025 Lilika Street, Honolulu, HI 96817; 808/732-9253.

Island of Hawaii

Recycle Hawaii: 808/329-2886; a nonprofit community group that organizes pick-ups in Kona on the leeward coast. Call them for dates and locations.

Urban Forest Institute: P.O. Box 415, Honaunau, HI 96726; 808/328-8043; an advocacy group that promotes recycling of tree trimmings and other organic refuse for biomass energy and compost. They provide resources, consulting lectures, and surveys. Call them for information.

Kauai

C. M. Salvage: 4530 Kehua Street, Kapaa, HI 96746; 808/822-6076; accepts all types of ferrous and nonferrous metals.

Reynolds Aluminum Recycling: Nawiliwili Harbor, Lihue, HI 96766; 808/245-7233; takes only aluminum.

Maui

Maui Scrap Metal Company: 1791 Wainua, Wailuku, HI 96793; 808/244-0317; accepts brass, copper, lead, aluminum, radiators, batteries and scrap iron.

Reynolds Aluminum Recycling Center: 851 Loku Place, Wailuku, HI 96793; 808/244-4146; takes only aluminum.

Snorkeling and Surfing

During the winter months, the northern shores of the Hawaiian Islands get pounded by heavy surf. The swells generate from winter storms that track across the north Pacific, thousands of miles from the Hawaiian shores. The fury of the storms' energy is evident in the huge waves that strike the Hawaiian coasts from December to March. At these times, the southern shores experience calm.

During the summer months, south Pacific storms occasionally generate enough energy to drive large swells north onto the islands' south shores. When this occurs, Kona conditions are said to prevail, and the south shores become the center of surf activity.

This grand seasonal cycle of north versus south shore water conditions determines the quality of coastal areas for either surfing or snorkeling. For example, Oahu's north shore in the winter is a place of awesome power, where only master surfers venture into the water to ride the waves that can tower over 25 feet high. In the summer, though, these same waters are calm and clear, and make for excellent snorkeling in places. Add to this seasonal rhythm the unique character of individual beaches, lagoons, reefs, rocky shoals, and protected bays, and Hawaii's coasts take on a varied character for snorkeling and surfing.

The chapters in this book contain information on surfing and snorkeling. This information is meant to initially guide you to loca-

---

Oahu's north shore in the winter is a place of awesome power, where only master surfers venture into the water to ride the waves that can tower over 25 feet high.

---

tions, but not all locations are covered, nor can daily conditions be predicted, so ask around. Snorkeling equipment and surfboards can be rented or purchased at most resort locations on the islands, or bring your own. Unless you are already a practiced surfer, you will likely need some lessons. These, too, are available at many tourist beaches, especially Waikiki on Oahu. Surfing was the ritual sport of the ancient Hawaiian kings, but the hot-dogging that currently takes place in Hawaiian surfing waters is entirely new. There is a good deal of competition among surfers, and where crowded conditions prevail, beginners will find it difficult to learn the skills. Waikiki is probably still the best place to learn to surf, as it has been for a century or more. Practiced surfers will want to check the more remote surf breaks.

Snorkeling, on the other hand, is one of the more passive water sports in Hawaii, and for competent swimmers who are advised of local water conditions, it poses little difficulty. The snorkeling spots mentioned in this book do not cover the whole range of locations, many of which only locals know about. Check with local tour agencies and dive shops on the islands you visit for detailed information.

Body surfing at Sandy Beach, Oahu

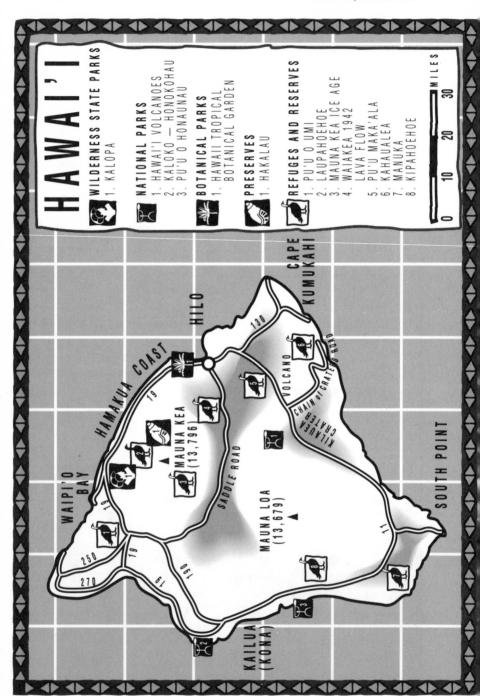

Chapter Three
Island of Hawaii

Background

The Island of Hawaii is the largest of the Hawaiian Islands, comprising 4038 square miles—an area greater than the combined territory of the other islands. This single fact of geography is quickly grasped when one begins a tour of the island. The distances between places on Hawaii are great. To travel from Upolu Point to South Point, traversing the island from north to south, requires a full day, and to make significant inroads across the island's motorable terrain requires several days. But this superficial reckoning of the island's geography fails to embrace the range of environments that prevail on Hawaii, most of which are not accessible by vehicle. The island's diversity makes it a varied and challenging place to explore.

The two main mountains—Mauna Kea (13,796 feet) and Mauna Loa (13,677)—dominate the island's topography. Together they account for over 70% of the land area. Only Haleakala on Maui towers above the surrounding terrain like these two mountains do on Hawaii. The altitudinal differences encountered on the Island of Hawaii ensure a wide range of environments, and the contrasts between windward and leeward coastal locations augment the altitudinal factor. Combine these with the youth of the island, the presence of vast wilderness tracts, and the unique evolutionary history of the island's land and life forms, and it becomes possible to imagine the extraordinary diversity of this place. More subtle than these reckonings, but ultimately more unsettling or riveting, is the presence on Hawaii of an unspoken but felt, and immensely powerful, sense of origins—geological, biological, and cultural.

As one journeys through the natural and cultural landscapes of the Island of Hawaii, it becomes readily apparent that this island holds for the visitor something different than the others. Tropical scenes duplicated on all the Hawaiian Islands are present here:

waterfalls, sunsets, swaying palm trees, clear skies, clear water, lush rainforests. But then note: Beaches contain black, not white, sand. Stinking, steaming vents of gases spew from the earth's bowels through cracks in the barren rock. The distant, gentle curves of the high mountain summits are covered by snow much of the year, when only a few miles away as the shorebird flies the coastal beaches simmer in the tropical heat. At the coastline near the former Hawaii Volcanoes National Park entrance at Wahaula one can watch as great viscous flows of lava enter the ocean. Where lava and water meet, the lava solidifies into rock and then bursts into sand-grain-size particles—the compression of geological time into milliseconds! Many visitors find the island disconcerting, and they never return. Others return again and again, until they come to stay. There is no vacillation in a person's image of the Island of Hawaii: Some find it ugly, barren and boring; others find it one of the most powerful places on earth.

For many visitors, Hawaii Volcanoes National Park dominates their image of the island. Perhaps properly so, for contained in the Park is a wide range of island habitats. It will take time to explore the inner and the outer reaches of the Park, but it will be worth it. Save time for other places, though. The coastlines of the island lack the sandy beaches of Kauai and Oahu, but they exhibit the rugged and desolate character of true wildlands. As your journey takes you along these coasts, stop to explore more intimately the places where petroglyphs and heiaus indicate ancient Hawaiian settlements.

Steam seeps up through the earth near Kilauea

Hawaiian Visitors Bureau

Spend time on the barren coasts of the Kau and Kona districts—the splendid isolation encountered in these places is uncommon.

When traveling along the barren stretches of highway traversing the lava flows on the south and west coasts, watch for kipukas—the islands of life that were formed when a lava flow split, preserving in its path some ancient land where forests now grow. These evolutionary anomalies contain some of Hawaii's most luxurious natural plant communities. Few visitors explore the kipukas, but in Hawaii Volcanoes National Park, at Kipuka Puaulu, you have an opportunity to stroll through one of these fragments of natural history.

The absence of perennial streams in the vast stretch of land along the leeward coast derives from the low rainfall and from the porous rock formed by the Kilauea, Mauna Loa, Hualali, and Kohala lava flows. Contrast this dry, barren, gently sloping landscape with the wet, heavily eroded, forested slopes of the windward Hamakua coast. Along the western slopes of Kohala, visible from the Waipio Valley overlook, heavy rainfall and rivers have carved 2000-foot deep canyons. The drive from Honokaa to Kawaihai along Highway 19 takes you from one, very wet world, into another, very dry world. Everywhere on Hawaii are reminders of the recent geological past: symmetrical volcanic peaks, cinder and spatter cones, bare lava fields, rifts and dikes forming canyons and ridges. With only about 100,000 residents, the Island of Hawaii contains vast areas of uninhabited (and uninhabitable) land. Chart some of these remote places during your visit.

Alternative Lodging

There is no problem finding a hotel on the Island of Hawaii, but locating an affordable one that is close to hiking and to natural areas may be difficult. The island hosts some of the world's fanciest resorts (the Waikaloa Hyatt, for example, where fantasies and room rates run wild). It also has some of the sleaziest hotels in Hawaii, where cockroaches are the only things that run wild. The lodgings listed below are of several types: rustic cabins, youth hostels, pleasant and cozy bed and breakfast inns, budget hotels (funky, but clean and with character), and retreats and conference centers. These places are oriented toward the active traveler exploring the island's out-of-the-way places.

CABINS
Hawaii Volcanoes National Park
Hawaii Volcanoes National Park maintains several cabins in the park for visitors. The most accessible of these are the Namakani

Paio Cabins operated by Volcano House. The cabins are located about 1 mile west of Park Headquarters on Mamalahoa Highway (Hwy 11). Each cabin accommodates 4 persons maximum. They rent for $24 per night (includes linen and light bedding—but the nights are cool, so bring an extra blanket or a sleeping bag). No kitchens, but barbeque pits are located outside. A $10 key deposit is required, and it is advisable to reserve space well in advance. Since it is often wet here (4000 foot elevation on the rainy side of Mauna Loa, near Kilauea), the cabins are more popular with hikers than the nearby tent sites. Write: Volcano House, P.O. Box 53, Hawaii Volcanoes National Park, Hawaii 96718; or telephone: 808/967-7321.

In addition to the Namakani cabins, near the Park entrance, the Park maintains a few backcountry cabins accessible only by hiking trails. Two are located in the Mauna Loa backcountry: Red Hill Cabin at 10,035 feet elevation on the Mauna Loa Trail, and Mauna Loa Cabin at 13,250 feet elevation across the Mokuaweoweo Caldera from the Mauna Loa summit. If you're hiking to the Mauna Loa summit, check the availability of these cabins. They are scheduled on a first-come-first-served basis. You must register with the visitor center. Be prepared to share the space with fellow high country hikers.

Halemaumau crater

Hawaiian Visitors Bureau

Additional Park cabins are located in the coastal backcountry region. Pepeiao Cabin is on the Kau Desert Trail, about 5 miles southeast of the Hilina Pali Overlook. Again, it is first-come-first-served, and you must register with the visitor center. Simple camping shelters (not cabins) are located at a few other spots along the coastal backcountry trails (at Kaaha, Halape, and Keahou) (see camping Hawaii Volcanoes National Park under Camping Areas below).

Also located in the Park is the Volcano House Hotel. This is not a cabin, but it has a woodsy atmosphere. It is justly famous for its location on the rim of Kilauea Crater. In addition to the one-of-a-kind view, the hotel is noted for the fire in the lounge hearth—it has been burning nonstop for over half a century. The hotel is worth a splurge (the simple rooms go for $60–$90/night). Contact Volcano House.

In addition to the one-of-a-kind view, the hotel is noted for the fire in the lounge hearth—it has been burning nonstop for over half a century.

State Parks

The state maintains four parks that have cabin shelters: A-frames, housekeeping cabins, or dormitory-type group lodgings. Reservations are required and can be obtained at the Division of State Parks in Honolulu, or in Hilo.

Hapuna Beach State Recreation Area: This is a landscaped beach park located along one of the few remaining undeveloped stretches of sandy beach north of Kona. On 61 acres, it includes picnic sites and a grassy lounge area along the beach front. The simple A-frame lodges in the park can accommodate 4 persons on sleeping platforms in a single room. Hardly luxurious, but it keeps you out of the weather—if that's an issue. The price is right—$7 per night for the entire shelter. It is conveniently situated near the Kohala mountains, the South Kohala coast, and the North Kona district. The park is located a short distance off Queen Kaahumanu Highway (Hwy 19), two and one-half miles south of Kawaihae at the intersection of Highways 19 and 270. Watch for the park signboard.

Kalopa State Recreation Area: Along the rugged north end of the Hamakua Coast, 5 miles southeast of Honokaa, is this lovely state recreation area. It has picnic grounds, an arboretum, a guided nature trail through native rainforest, a 2-mile horse trail, camping, and group cabins that can hold 32 persons (total). Each cabin consists of

Hawaiian Visitors Bureau

Lava Tree State Park, near Hilo, has many odd formations left over from ancient lava flows

several 8-person units complete with beds, bedding, toilet, hot shower, kitchen facilities, and electric heaters (the park is at 2000 feet elevation, so the nights can get chilly). The main problem with the park is that it is often quite wet. When it rains, the lodges are an attractive alternative to the nearby campsites (see the camping section in this chapter). The park is an excellent base for exploring the lush valleys of the Hamakua coast, including Waipio Valley. The park is located 3 miles inland on Kalopa Road, which heads mauka from Hawaii Belt Road (Hwy 19) 5 miles south of Honokaa. Follow the park signboards along several turns and bends in the narrow asphalt road as it winds through ranchlands and eucalyptus groves. The park is at the roadend.

Kilauea State Recreation Area: A lone housekeeping cabin (furnished bedrooms and a kitchen, electric heat) set in a native ohia-tree fern forest provides a peaceful and solitary base for those people exploring nearby Hawaii Volcanoes National Park. If you want to get away, here's a good place. The cabin is located on Kalanikoa Street off Mamalahoa Highway (Hwy 11) one-half mile east of the Hawaii Volcanoes National Park entrance. The cabin is available only on Wednesday through Monday nights.

Mauna Kea State Recreation Area (Pohakuloa Area): The moonlike landscape of the Saddle Road encompasses this state park area. It is often cloudy and cool here, which gives the cabins a cozy feeling. There are 7 housekeeping cabins in the park, each capable of accommodating 6 persons (full kitchen, bath and bedding provided). The location is excellent for exploring the Mauna Kea-Mauna Loa region. The saddle area itself is intriguing—a cindery landscape of cones, lava flows, steppe shrubbery, and high-country vistas. The cabins are generally available; most tourists are deterred by the rental car companies' admonition not to travel on the Saddle Road. The cabins are located at 6500 feet elevation on Highway 200, 35 miles west of Hilo.

State Forest Reserve Cabins

The Division of Forestry maintains five cabins in the Mauna Kea Forest Reserve: Kahinahina, Kanakaleonui, Puu Mali, Kemole, and Puu Laau. They are located on the 4-wheel drive tracks (Kahinahina Jeep Trail and Keanakolu Road) that loop around Mauna Kea from the Saddle Road (Hwy 220). Reserve the cabins at the Hilo office of the Division of Forestry (808/933-4221).

HOSTELS

To meet the need for budget accommodations for active travelers on Hawaii, hosteliers want to strategically locate budget inns around the island so that they are convenient for people on circum-island tours. The proposed hostel locations are at Hilo, on the Hamakua coast, in North Kohala, in the Kona region, and at the volcanoes region. As of this writing, only one hostel exists on Hawaii (see below). Unlike its European counterparts, the Hawaii hostel maintains no strict curfew rules, but it does share the spartan atmosphere characteristic of hostels worldwide.

Kona Lodge and Hostel: This is a budget lodge/hostel located amid an acre of tropical foliage at 1400 feet elevation, above Kealakekua Bay in the sleepy town of Honalo, North Kona. Its location 7 miles south of Kailua-Kona and 6 miles north of Puuhonua O Honaunau National Historical Park makes it a good base for exploring the North and South Kona districts. Bunk rates begin at $14 per night ($12 for AYH cardholders). The dormitory rooms afford little privacy but interesting comradeship—mainly young people on the road. Children are welcome, but smoking and alcohol are not. The proprietor is knowledgeable about the local environment, and he views it as a part of his job to inform his clients about the local environmental opportunities. The hostel is particularly keen on hosting groups of hikers, bikers, and students. For information or reservations, write Kona Lodge and Hostel, P.O. Box 645—Kealakekua, HI 96750; or telephone 808/322-9056 or 808/322-8136.

BED AND BREAKFAST INNS

The number of rural bed & breakfast inns on Hawaii has grown rapidly over the past few years, coincident with the rising popularity of bed and breakfast establishments nationwide. There are now several inns and homes that offer lodging on the island. They vary from simple bedrooms in family homes to full lodges with restaurants. These places are generally low keyed, with fine facilities and a homey atmosphere. The innkeepers can assist you with local information, including the locations of hiking areas and points of natural interest.

Adrienne's Bed and Breakfast: This B&B is conveniently located near Captain Cook in the Kealakekua area of the Kona Coast. Find it near the junction of Hwy 160 and Hwy 11 above Puuhonua O Honaunau. It has an Oceanview Room, a Seashell Room, and a Garden Room, each offering its own amenities at its price. Everyone gets to use the hottub, though. Contact them at: Adrienne's Bed and Breakfast, 85-4577 Mamalahoa Highway, Captain Cook, HI 96704. 808/328-9726.

Banyan House: This former Puna Sugar Plantation residence is located in Keaau, 10 minutes from Hilo airport, along the route to Hawaii Volcanoes National Park or the Kalapana coastal area. Ten acres of tropical gardens surround the lodge, including one of the state's largest banyan trees. It's on Hwy 130 near the intersection with Hwy 11. Contact: P.O. Box 432, Keaau, HI 96749. 808/966-8598.

Champagne Cove: They advertise a romantic hideaway on the blue Pacific, where you can soak up the sun, pick bananas, and feed the friendly sea turtles. Find out for yourself. I include it here because its location near Hilo provides an alternative to Hilo hotels. Be advised that "feeding the friendly sea turtles" constitutes harassment and it is criminally and ecological wrong. Contact them at 1714 Lei Lelua St., Hilo, HI 96720. 808/959-4487.

The Guest House at Volcano: This is a private home, surrounded by 6 acres of fruit orchard and flowering trees, adjacent to upland ohia rainforest in Volcano Village, one mile east of Hawaii Volcanoes National Park entrance. It is a fully furnished home that sleeps five. It's 1½ miles off Hwy 11, on Jade St. Contact: P.O. Box 6, Volcano, HI 96785. 808/967-7775.

Hamakua Hide-Away: A "romantic place" in Kukuihaele village, located above Waipio Valley on the northern Hamakua coast. Hot tub, shower, fireplace and kitchen are parts of the package. Daily and monthly rates are available. The proprieters will inform their clients about the opportunities to explore the Waipio Valley floor. Contact: P.O. Box 5104, Kukuihaele, HI 96727. 808/775-7425.

Island's End Bed and Breakfast: Located upcountry in Waimea, this plantation-era home is situated near hiking trails, historical sites, and the relaxing country scene of Waimea's ranchlands. Contact:

Beautiful Rainbow Falls, near Hilo

Hawaiian Visitors Bureau

Island's End Bed and Breakfast, P.O. Box 2063, Kamuela, HI 96743. 808/889-5265.

Ishigo's Bed and Breakfast: If you're heading to Akaka Falls and you want to spend the night nearby, this place may be for you. The B&B is located in the center of Honomu, 20 miles from Hilo. It occupies the upstairs part of Ishigo's General Store. It has 4 inexpensive rooms. Simple, but clean, and convenient if you're in the area. Contact: Ishigo's Bed and Breakfast/General Store, on the way to Akaka Falls in Honomu. 808/963-6128.

Kilauea Lodge: This is one of the finest lodges on the island, with a good restaurant and an excellent location adjacent to Hawaii Volcanoes National Park. If you plan to stay overnight in the park area, and don't want to camp or to stay at Volcano House, this is a good alternative. The price is high ($80–$100/night). Contact: P.O. Box 116, Volcano Village, HI 96785. 808/967-7366.

The Log House: This bed & breakfast inn is an elegant wooden home tucked into the lush foliage of the upland Hamakua coast. The rates are reasonable and the rooms include use of the downstairs lounge with stone fireplace, a library upstairs, and the kitchen. Its location near Waipio Valley, Waimea, and the rural upcountry makes it a good base for exploring the north part of the windward coast. The inn is located on Mamalahoa Hwy (the alternative route between Waimea and Honokaa, parallel to Hwy 19), in Ahuoloa, approximately 3 miles from Honokaa. Contact: P.O. Box 1495, Honokaa, HI 96727. 808/775-9990.

My Island, Inc.: Rooms are available in the volcanoes region in this century-old home-turned-B&B inn, located on Old Volcano Highway in Volcano Village. Reasonable prices, a good location, and the host's obvious enthusiasm for the Island of Hawaii are their selling points. Contact: My Island, Inc., P.O. Box 100, Volcano, HI 96785. 808/967-7216.

Volcano Vacation: This place has a small 2 bedroom cottage located a few minutes away from Hawaii Volcanoes National Park. With the cottage comes a sauna and a fireplace. Contact: Volcano Vacations, P.O. Box 608, Kailua-Kona, HI 96745. 808/325-7708.

Bed-and-Breakfast Directory: My Island, Inc. operates a directory of noncommercial lodging facilities on the Island of Hawaii. Their list covers many island areas, and it includes a number of small private homes that do not advertise elsewhere. Prices range from $20 to $50, depending upon type of accommodation and location. Contact them for information at: My Island, P.O. Box 100, Volcano, HI 96785. 808/967-7110.

BUDGET HOTELS

The word "funky" has only recently entered the English language, and it has an elusive meaning—somewhere between sleazy and quaint. The term best describes the popular and inexpensive hotels on the Island of Hawaii. They are generally clean places, but they are old and well-worn. What they lack in decor and modernity, they more than make up for in character. The budget hotels have rooms in the $25–35/night range.

Honokaa Club: Located in uptown Honokaa on Mamane Street is this dilapidated hotel that will serve you in a pinch. The rooms are cheap, and while you don't get much for your money, you do get out of the weather. The hotel's restaurant meals are more appetizing than the room decors. Contact: P.O. Box 185, Honokaa, HI 96727. 808/775-0678.

Manago Hotel: This place has a salty character, but it is a cherished institution, nonetheless. Old photos show laborers, truck drivers and traveling salesmen milling around the place in the 1930s and 1940s. It still attracts local workers, but its fame has spread wide and its clientele now includes visitors from throughout the world. Rooms with a common bath are cheaper than those with private bath; ocean-view rooms are a bit more than those with a mountain view (or no

---

There is no vacillation in a person's image of the Island of Hawaii: Some find it ugly, barren and boring; others find it one of the most powerful places on earth.

---

view). At any rate, for Hawaii it's a deal. Contact them at: Manago Hotel, P.O. Box 145, Captain Cook, HI 96704. 808/323-2642. The hotel is located on the makai side of Hwy 11 in downtown Captain Cook.

Shirakawa Motel: Billing itself as "The Southernmost Motel in the U.S.," the Shirakawa is well known for its quaint setting, clean rooms, and budget prices. It is located in Kau district, near the road to South Point. The kindly Japanese woman who owns and runs the places cares for her guests like she does for her flower garden. The motel is situated on the mauka side of Mamalahoa Highway (Hwy 11), about a mile west of Naalehu. Contact them at: Shirakawa Motel, P.O. Box 467, Naalehu, Hawaii 96772. 808/929-7462.

Waipio Hotel: This place has no name, but people in Waipio Valley generally call it the Waipio Hotel. The proprietors, Tom and Sam Araki, run it as an old-style inn. Secluded in Waipio Valley, the hotel is accessible only on foot, horseback, or 4-wheel-drive vehicle. The rooms are clean and cheap ($10/person/night), kerosene-lit, quiet

and picturesque. Its location puts it in the midst of one of the premier
hiking areas on Hawaii. The hotel is generally full, so make advance
reservations by contacting: Tom T. Araki (Waipio Hotel), 25
Malama Place, Hilo, Hawaii 96720. 808/935-7466 (Hilo) or 775-
0368 (Waipio).

CONFERENCE CENTERS AND RETREATS

Several small retreats and conference centers have appeared
recently on Hawaii. These cater primarily to groups, but they also
welcome individuals for a night, a week, or sometimes longer. Most
of these places share a commitment to eastern religions, environ-
mentalism, or social change. The accommodations they offer are
generally quite good, and you need not embrace their philosophy to
be a welcome guest.

Nechung Drayang Ling—Wood Valley Temple: In the early 1900s
Japanese sugar workers in Kapapala/Wood Valley Camp built a
Buddhist temple that was subsequently abandoned in the 1950s,
when workers moved to nearby Pahala. In 1973 the temple was
restored as the residence of Nechung Rinpoche, the Tibetan lama of
Nechung Dorje Drayang Ling Monastery. He attracted a devoted
following in Hawaii. A second temple was moved from Pahala to
Wood Valley to serve as a retreat center for the growing Buddhist
community. In 1980 the Dalai Lama visited and dedicated the
center. The facilities now serve individual travelers, community and
church groups, workshop organizers, and others who seek a quiet
atmosphere. Dormitory rooms and private quarters can accommodate a maximum of 27 persons. The rates are quite reasonable
(around $15/night), the atmosphere is certainly peaceful, and there
are numerous opportunities for involvement in retreat activities
(meditation, yoga, workshops, Hawaiian dance and crafts, etc.). To
reach the temple/hostel, proceed north on the Wood Valley
Camp/Kapapala road, located off Mamalahoa Highway (Hwy 11) in
Pahala, Kau district. The temple is marked by signboards at the end
of the Kapapala Road. Contact: Nechung Drayang Ling, P.O. Box
250, Pahala, Hawaii 96777. 808/928-8539.

Hawaii International Conference Center: Located in the North
Kohala countryside near the village of Hawi, this place has private
and semi-private quarters. They prefer groups, especially students,
but they can accommodate individual travelers. There are kitchen
facilities, a fireplace, a hot tub, workshop space, a library, and
guided tours. Contact: Hawaii International Conference Center,
P.O. Box 13, Hawi, Hawaii, 96719. 808/889-5122 or 889-6343.

Kalani Honua Culture Center and Retreat: "Kalani Honua" means "harmony of heaven and earth". This probably best describes the intent of the founders of this center, who have created a secluded retreat in the Puna district along the coastal road between Kehena and Opihikao. Twenty acres of land and four 2-story wooden lodges, a Japanese style spa, a vegetarian cafe, a crafts center, workshops and seminars, a hiking program, massage, dance classes, and lovely surroundings recommend the center. Individual and group accommodations are available in the lodge; camping is permitted on center grounds. They are located about 45 minutes from Hilo airport: take Hwy 11 south from Hilo to Keaau, turn left onto Hwy 130, pass through Pahoa south to the coastal road (Hwy 137) and turn left. The center is located between mile markers 18 and 17 on Hwy 137. Contact: Kalani Honua, R.R. 2, Box 4500, Pahoa, Hawaii 96778. 808/965-7828.

Botanical Gardens and Parks

There are many fine botanic gardens on the Island of Hawaii. Whether you want to systematically study native or introduced plant species, or simply to stroll through a lovely park, Hawaii's gardens are pleasant places to spend time. The parks described below provide informative and colorful introductions to tropical Pacific flora.

Akatsuta Orchid Gardens: If you're interested in orchids, the Island of Hawaii is the place to be. This garden's collection indicates the tremendous variety of epiphytes that grow on Hawaii. It is located 3 miles east of Volcano Village on Hwy 11. Contact: 808/967-7660.

It's a jungle garden with an eclectic, almost bewildering, array of plants (over 1600 species) growing on 17 acres of land in a lush valley along the rugged Hamakua coast north of Hilo.

Amy Greenwell Ethnobotanical Garden: This low-key garden specializes in native Hawaiian plants, especially those with medicinal or food value. It is located below the Manago Hotel in Captain Cook on the Kona coast. Ask directions in Captain Cook (the roads leading to the garden are unmarked) or call them at: 808/323-3318.

Hawaii Tropical Botanical Garden: This is a widely acclaimed garden spot that has been extensively written about and photographed in the travel literature. It's a jungle garden with an eclectic, almost bewildering, array of plants (over 1600 species) growing on 17 acres of land in a lush valley along the rugged South Hilo coast north of Hilo. Streams, waterfalls, walking trails and visitor amenities complement the lavish tropical plant life collected from around the world and planted here. Palms, bromeliads, gingers, and heliconias mix with ornamentals, medicinals, and rare and endangered Hawaiian species in a somewhat haphazard fashion. Most of the plants are labeled for identification purposes, so one's stroll through the park can also be an education. Mainly, though, the garden is designed to be less of a scientific site and more of a visual feast; anyone who appreciates the beauty of plants will appreciate this lush setting. To reach the gardens, take the 4-Mile Scenic Route off Hwy 19 north of Hilo. The gardens are located across from Onomea Bay just north of Hokeo Point. Open 8:30–5:30, seven days a week. The garden operates as a nonprofit foundation supported by visitor donations and garden memberships. Contact: Hawaii Tropical Botanical Garden, P.O. Box 1415, Hilo, Hawaii 96721. 808/964-5233.

Hilo Tropical Garden: This small (2-acre) garden specializes in orchids and other flowering tropical plants. The atmosphere is commercial: public gardens, nursery, and a visitors center where they sell cut flowers. To visit the garden, take Kalanianaole Ave. (Hwy 12) 2 miles beyond Hilo Airport toward Keokea Point. The garden is on the makai side of the road (watch for the signboard). Open 8:30–5 daily. Contact: Hilo Tropical Gardens, 1477 Kalanianaole Avenue, Hilo, Hawaii 96720. 808/935-1146.

Kalopa Native Forest State Park: This is a natural park in the Hamakua Forest Preserve, offering campsites, rustic lodges, pic-

Guava leaves and fruit

Ron Felzer

nicking, and hiking (see sections on State Parks Cabins, Hiking, and Camping). It also has a premier native forest nature walk and a small arboretum. They are worth a visit even if you don't plan to spend the night. The 4-acre arboretum, established in 1976, contains local Hawaiian plants and Polynesian introductions. All the arboretum species are labeled for identification. The Native Forest Nature Trail is a pleasant walk for anyone (a 0.7 mile loop). The 100 acres of rainforest include ohia (*Metrosideros polymorpha*), kopiko (*Psychotria hawaiiensis*), kolea (*Myrsine lessertiana*), pilo (*Coprosma rhynchocarpa*), hame (*Antidesma platyphylla*), olomea (*Perrottetia sandwichensis*), hapuu (*Cibotium glaucum*), and other native species. The Hamakua District Development Council has prepared a handy little interpretive brochure that guides you through the walk, identifying and explaining plants at various stations along the way. The booklet is available at the trailhead for a small donation. The park is at 2000 feet elevation, and it normally receives about 100 inches of rain a year. Bring an umbrella with you if it looks cloudy below. To reach the park, turn off Hwy 19 south of Honakaa onto Kalopa Road. Follow the signs along the 3-mile stretch of blacktop road that leads up to the park. Contact: HDDC Forest Parks Committee, P.O. Box 637, Honokaa, Hawaii 96727.

Liliuokalani Gardens: This is a rather tame but attractive Japanese-style urban park located along Banyan Drive in Hilo. It has bonsai, bridges over canals, rock gardens, and an elaborate pavilion. Basically, it is a pleasant place to while away some extra time in Hilo. Find the park across from the resort hotels along southwest Hilo Bay.

Nani Mau Gardens: This is primarily a flower garden, but it also contains fruit and nut trees, Its atmosphere is commercial (greenhouse, restaurant, Japanese garden and gift shop). Orchids are their specialty, and since you're on the "Orchid Island," you might want to visit. They are located 3 miles south of Hilo off Hwy 11 on Makalika Street. Open daily 8:30–5. Contact: Nani Mau Gardens, 421 Makalika Street, Hilo, Hawaii 96720. 808/959-3541.

Panaewa Zoo: I include this animal zoo in the section on botanical parks because the zoo's strongest point is not its animals but its plants. It is located in the Panaewa Forest Reserve, and the zoo designers have attempted here a rainforest theme. The usual zoo animals are here, and a few unusual tropical species. If caged animals offend you, skip it. But the ambiance is pleasant and the design seems to meet the animals' need for territory and privacy. To reach the zoo, take Hwy 11 south from Hilo 7 miles toward Volcano village, turn onto Mamaki Street (marked on some maps as Stainback Highway), and proceed one mile to the zoo entrance.

Rainbow Tropicals: This is a nursery that propagates tropical shrubbery, flowers and fruit trees. It is open to the public, and it offers an opportunity to become acquainted with the great variety of domestic and imported species of ornamental plants that are grown on Hawaii. The nursery is 7 miles southwest of Hilo. Take Hwy 11 to Mamaki Street and head mauka to Kealakai Street. Open daily from 8:30–5. Contact: 808/961-2122.

Wakefield Botanic Gardens: This is a funky collection of tropical plants located 18 miles south of Kona at the corner of Hwy 160 and Rodeo Road, near the village of Honaunau. A short walking trail guides you through the garden to a garden cafe, where you can get a light vegetarian lunch. The garden's disheveled appearance gives it a certain nonchalant character that is appealing.

Camping Areas

For its size and the large area of wilderness that it contains, the Island of Hawaii has surprisingly few good camping grounds. The exceptions are Hawaii Volcanoes National Park and Kalopa State Recreation Area—both are premier camping areas. Beach camping, in particular, is hard to come by on Hawaii. Many of the county beach parks that allow camping are unattractive, and some are

---

There are few places on earth where you can witness the tumultuous birth of new land. Hawaii Volcanoes National Park is one such place.

---

dangerous places to stay. In the Puna district, especially, it is inadvisable to camp at the beach parks because of the increased incidence of theft and disturbance reported by park users.

HAWAII VOLCANOES NATIONAL PARK
Hawaii National Park, HI 96718. 808/967-7311.

There are few places on earth where you can witness the tumultuous birth of new land. Hawaii Volcanoes National Park is one such place. Lava fountains, cinder cones, molten rock meeting the ocean, layer upon alternating layer of ash and brittle rock, steaming gaseous vents, moonlike landscapes—all these are here. But the park has more than the fiery power of its volcanoes; it contains the major life zones in Hawaii, and it provides visitors with an unexcelled chance to explore them—despite the bad smell of sulphur, the naked rock that stretches to the horizon in repeated patterns, the days and nights when the rain seems to have come to stay forever. Frequently,

Cinder cones on Mauna Loa's upper slopes

though, exploring here is a quietly moving experience: the music of song birds wafting through the ancient forests of a lava kipuka, mysterious petroglyphs carved centuries ago into smooth pahoehoe lava that seems only a few days old, the afternoon sun casting bent rays through the misty, primordial-appearing ohia forests. To camp and to hike amid these rare landscapes is a privilege.

Park Campgrounds

There are 3 developed camping areas in the park: Kamoamoa, Kipuka Nene, and Namakani Paio; and numerous backcountry campsites.

Kamoamoa: This small campground is near the end of the Chain of Craters Road (2 miles west of the site of the former Wahaula Visitor Center). It occupies a coastal location, and recent volcanic activity along the shore has produced a fine black sand beach adjacent to the camping area. No fees or permits are required; no water is available.

Kipuka Nene: This is one of the Park's most remote developed campgrounds. It is located along Hilina Pali Road, 11.5 miles south of Park headquarters. Take the Chain of Craters Road toward the coast, turn right onto Hilina Pali Road 1 mile past Kokoolau Crater. The campground is at the junction of the road and the Halape hiking trail.

Namakani Paio: This campground is located in a forested area 2.5 miles west of the Park entrance on Mamalahoa Highway (Hwy 11). Picnic shelters, water, and restrooms are near the campsite. No fee or permit is required, but your stay is limited to 7 consecutive days.

Backcountry Camping

All backpackers must register at the Visitor Center. The geological nature of the Park means that earthquakes, volcanic eruptions, and tsunamis are always possible. Rangers need to know the whereabouts of everyone in the backcountry in the event that warnings or rescues are necessary. Use discretion in selecting your backcountry tent site. The Park maintains trail shelters at three coastal locations: Keauhou, Halape, and Kaaha. These are located along the main backcountry hiking trails (see section on hiking). The shelters are small, 3-sided, roofed affairs, with water catchments. They provide little protection during inclement weather. Camping areas are also located along the Mauna Loa Summit Trail. Contact: Division of Interpretation, Hawaii Volcanoes National Park, HI 96718. 808/967-7311.

STATE PARKS

Division of State Parks, Hawaii District, P.O. Box 936, Hilo, HI 96721-0936. 808/933-4200. Street Address: 75 Aupuni Street in Hilo. No fees, but permits are required.

Kalopa State Recreation Area (100 acres): This park and campground is located on the Hamakua coast, south and inland of Honokaa. Head southeast on Hawaii Belt Road (Hwy 19) from Honokaa for 5 miles, turn onto Kalopa Road, and follow it 3 miles mauka to the roadend. The campground is set in a lovely grove of old eucalyptus trees. Restrooms and a covered picnic area with fire pits are nearby. The place receives a great deal of rain, so be prepared with proper gear. An excellent short nature hike leads off from the arboretum below the campsite (see Botanical Parks and Hiking).

Manuka State Wayside Park (13.4 acres): An open-air camping pavilion is located at this park in the Manuka Natural Area Reserve, accessible off Mamalahoa Highway (Hwy 11), 19 miles west of Naalehu. The park is small and the camping shelter consists of poured concrete slabs under a wood-and-tin A-frame awning. Bring a sleeping pad if you plan to spend the night here. Restrooms and firepits are near the shelter. This actually is less a campsite and more an overnight crash site, but its location at the Manuka Natural Area Reserve recommends it for those exploring the surrounding region.

COUNTY PARKS

Department of Parks and Recreation, County of Hawaii, 25 Aupuni Street, Hilo, HI 96720. 808/961-8311. Permits are required; fees are $1/adult/day. Children under 12 are 50 cents. The following county parks allow both tent and trailer camping:

A black-sand beach on the Island of Hawaii

Hawaiian Visitors Bureau

Harry K. Brown Beach Park: Located at the black sand beach in Kalapana, in Puna district, off Hwy 137. Not recommended for visitors because of recent confrontations between local residents and outsiders.

Kapaa Beach Park: This is a fairly popular place to camp. There is good snorkeling offshore when the seas are calm. Located on Akone Pule Highway (Hwy 270), north of Mahukona.

Keokea Beach Park: Located near Niulii village in North Kohala District, between Kapaau and Polulu Valley (off Hwy 270). This is a nice spot.

Koleloke Beach Park: This lovely park is located on the Hawaii Belt Road (Hwy 19), a mile north of Honomu. It is very close to Akaka Falls State Park.

Laupahoehoe Beach Park: This park and camping area is situated on a spectacular peninsula affording splendid views of the rugged north Hilo coastline. The park is fairly remote and quiet. The peninsula is remembered for the tragedy that struck a group of Boy Scout hikers in 1946: they were swept to their deaths by a tsunami that struck the peninsula. The park is located off the Hawaii Belt Road (Hwy 19), at the end of a short turnout road that descends the bluffs below Laupahoehoe village.

Mahukona Beach Park: Not recommended for overnight camping, but the daytime snorkeling is excellent. Located off Akone Pule Highway (Hwy 270), north of Lapakahi State Historical Park.

Milolii Beach Park: This park is located in an Hawaiian village at the end of a remote side road off Highway 11. It probably doesn't need more *haoles* (white foreigners) camping out; not recommended.

Onekahakaha Beach Park: Not recommended for overnight camping because of its proximity to Hilo. Located off Highway 137 in east Hilo.

Punaluu Beach Park: The park is at the end of Punaluu Road, off Mamalahoa Highway (Hwy 11), between Naahelu and Pahala. It has a nice black sand beach. Quiet on weekdays; on weekends the park is heavily used by local residents; it is one of the few swimming beaches in the Kau district.

Samuel M. Spencer Beach Park: Not recommended; the park has been taken over by local residents who work at the Waikoloa resort and live on the beach for lack of nearby affordable housing.

Whittington Beach Park: The park is 3 miles north of Naalehu on Mamalahoa Highway (Hwy 11). Campsites are under coconut palms next to a rocky lagoon. Nice enough, and quiet.

PRIVATE CAMPING AREAS

The Kona Lodge and Hostel (P.O. Box 645, Kealakekua, HI 96750; 808/322-9056) has a camping area. They charge $7/night. The Lodge is located on Kuakini Highway (Hwy 11) in Honalo village. The Kalani Honua Culture Center and Retreat (R.R. 2, Box 4500, Pahoa, HI 96778; 808/965-7828) permits camping on their grounds. It is probably the best place to camp in southern Puna district.

OTHER CAMPING AREAS

Backcountry camping is allowed in the state forest reserves at Mauna Kea and Mauna Loa. Contact: Division of Forestry, Hilo Office, Hilo, HI 96721. 808/933-4221.

An excellent camping area is at the mouth of Waipio Stream in Waipio Valley on the Hamakua coast. Park your car at the Waipio Valley Overlook (at the end of Hwy 220) and walk down to the valley floor. (Four-wheel-drive vehicles can make it down the steep dirt track that descends to the valley floor.) It provides a good base from which to explore Waipio valley and the areas beyond, to Waimanu Valley.

For other, less-known camping spots, contact the Moku Loa Group of the Hawaii chapter of the Sierra Club (P.O. Box 1137,

Hilo, HI 96721), or one of the nature guides described in the section on nature tours.

Environmental Groups

There is a special urgency to the environmental movement on the Island of Hawaii. The island is a stronghold for anti-development activists on the one hand, and the target for massive resort development on the other. The tension between the two is far from reconciled and, in fact, is heightening. By virtue of its size and sparse land-

---

The residents of the Island of Hawaii are hardly inured to the negative aspects of large-scale development.

---

scape, the Island of Hawaii has retained extensive undeveloped regions. But development nodes in Kona and South Kohala, particularly, threaten extensive coastal areas with their extravagant forms of commercial amusements.

The residents of the Island of Hawaii are hardly inured to the negative aspects of large-scale development. Yet resorts mean jobs. The economic rewards of tourism, however, are not evenly distributed throughout the island. A geographical tension is developing between the sunny Kona coast, where resorts and associated employment are booming, and the rainy Hilo region, which is largely bypassed by the major tourism ventures.

Obviously the disparity has a good deal to do with the climate and the amenities of the land. The environment and development tangle with economic realities on Hawaii in a highly charged political arena. In this cloudy morass of issues, political agendas, and emotions, community environmental groups are working to make sense out of the conflicts and effect some kind of responsible path for development on the Big Island.

The groups mentioned below are based on the Island of Hawaii, and most of them deal with local island issues. They also supplement the statewide environmental groups based on Oahu.

Epicenter-Hawaii: This is a Kona-based organization that pursues and networks permaculture activities on the Island of Hawaii. They are also involved with appropriate technology, creating landscapes of edible plants, bioregionalism, and reforestation programs. In addition, they serve as a networking agency for organic farmers and grocers. Contact them at: EPICENTER-HAWAII, P.O. Box 2428, Kailua-Kona, HI 96745. 808/322-3106.

Hamakua District Development Council, Inc. (Forest Parks Committee): These are the folks who maintain the excellent nature study facilities at Kalopa State Park. Their programs involve trail maintenance, exotic plant control, native plant propagation, and interpretive guide service. All their work is voluntary and they get their funds from small donations by park users. The council is a good example of a grassroots effort to promote sensitive use of the natural environment in a specific place—in their case the native forests of Hamakua. They have been doing their job since 1962, while volunteers come and go. Contact: Forest Parks Committee, Hamakua District Development Council, Inc., P.O. Box 637, Honokaa, HI 96727.

Na Ala Hele: This nonprofit organization got started in 1979 by seeking to preserve a coastal walking stretch along the South Kohala/North Kona shoreline. Since then, they have advocated trail preservation, sponsored hikes, conducted political campaigns, and mobilized members for various service trips (usually shoreline clean-up projects, which sometimes involve camping). Members are notified of upcoming projects by mail. Its a no-frills outfit. Contact: Na Ala Hele, P.O. Box 1572, Kealakekua, HI 96750.

Save Hawaii Foundation: This fledgling organization publishes an informative newsletter (when funds are available) that covers conservation issues throughout the island. Their agenda includes identifying environmental issues and bringing these to the public's attention. Contact: Save Hawaii!, P.O. Box 888, Captain Cook, HI 96704.

Sierra Club—Moku Loa Group: This is the Island of Hawaii group of the Hawaii chapter of the Sierra Club. They are involved in a variety of Sierra Club-type of issues, and they serve as the local representative of the state and national organization. Contact: P.O. Box 1137, Hilo, HI 96721.

Heiaus

The Island of Hawaii has about 200 surveyed heiaus. Most of them are along the dry leeward coast, from the North Kohala peninsula to South Point, and in the Puna district south of Hilo. The significance of the Island of Hawaii in the cultural history of the Hawaiian Islands is indicated by its large number of heiaus, many of which are sizeable and in very good shape.

Ahuena: On the north side of Kailua Bay along the outskirts of Kailua off Hwy 11 is this large (120' by 150') platform heiau. It is located between the King Kamehameha Hotel and the beach, and is accessible through the hotel grounds. Walk down to the shoreline and follow it to the obvious heiau location. A fort once occupied this site, and the associated heiau was initially restored by King Kamehameha I. It is now maintained by his namesake hotel.

Hikiau: This multitiered heiau, 190' by 100', is located beside Kealakekua Bay at Kealakekua Bay State Underwater Park in Captain Cook. It is known mainly as a ceremonial place frequented by Cook, and is near the site where Cook was killed in 1779.

Kalalea: This fishermen's heiau is at the end of South Point Road off Hwy 11. Some ancient canoe moorings are adjacent to the heiau. The bluffs and grassy slopes that border the rocky coastline at South Point near the heiau provide good coastal hiking, and you might consider combining your heiau visit with a walk (see hiking section). The water here is crystalline and plummets to great depths only meters offshore. The site remains a favored spot for local fishermen, who cast their lines from the cliffs above the sea. Ti leaf offerings seen at the heiau suggest that contemporary fishermen still rely on the blessings of the gods to complement their modern fishing technology.

Ke-eku: At a coastal location near the Lagoon Hotel in Kahaluu is a large heiau of first rank—a *puuhonua,* or "place of refuge". Nearby petroglyphs recount the coastal life of early inhabitants who resided near the heiau site. The heiau is likely to also have been a temple for human sacrifice as well as a refuge and sanctuary during wartime. Pass through the hotel grounds to the shoreline access; the heiau is readily visible.

Mookini Luakini: Near Upolu Point in Kohala is the 1500 year old Mookini heiau—Hawaii's oldest and most sacred site. King Kamehameha the Great's birthing rituals were performed here, and it was the early focus of religious life in Kohala. The Mookini family descendants have served as *kahuna nui* (guardian priests) of the heiau for generations, and the present *kahuna nui,* Momi Lum, has been instrumental in developing the site as a place to learn about Hawaii's past. She lifted the *kapu* that had kept the heiau closed to all but the Hawaiian *alii,* and the site is now a National Historical Landmark open to the public. To get there from Kailua-Kona, follow Hwy 270 (Akone Pule Hwy) north to Kohala and turn off near Hikapoloa toward the ocean at Honoipu Landing (sign says COAST GUARD). Alternatively, from Hawi, take the road heading makai off Hwy 270 that is signed UPOLU AIRPORT. Either way, the road leading to the heiau becomes little more than a dirt track that skirts the ocean and the pasture. This impressive heiau receives relatively few visitors, and the site usually remains undisturbed and silent. The massive stone walls, altar, grass kahuna hut, and large sacrifical stone evoke a presence that is strong and immediate. Best time to visit is late afternoon/early evening when the low sun angle enriches the site with much texture and color. Information about the heiau can be obtained by writing Mrs. Leimomi Mookini, P.O. Box 7125, Honolulu, HI 96821.

Puako Petroglyphs: The Mauna Lani Resort at Puako in South Kohala district has developed a park where an extensive field of petroglyphs had been carved in the pahoehoe lava. Resort planners named it Kalahui Puaa Historical Park with the purpose, ostensibly, of educating visitors and of stimulating interest in the natural and cultural history of the area. More likely, it was designed to appease community concern over the potential loss of this historical area. About 3000 carved symbols here compose the most extensive cluster of petroglyphs in Hawaii. The park area includes numerous ancient settlement features in addition to the petroglyphs, and provides a unique record of how the Hawaiians lived. Besides the numerous rock carvings of people, animals and activities, the area contains 800-year-old house sites, fishponds, several small heiaus, plazas, and sports fields. Its location on the resort grounds also shows the incongruous nature of commercial development along this booming South Kohala coast. The intentions of the Park developers may well be fine, but it is disconcerting and baffling to dodge golf balls and to skirt tennis courts while following the historical trails.

A Puako petroglyph

Perhaps a better bet is to hike to the petroglyphs at the end of the Puako road near Lae o Panipou Point. At the roadend are a small turnout and a wooden sign indicating a walking trail heading mauka through scrub kiawe to the petroglyph fields. You will pass several sets of carvings along the trail, but the best are at the very end, after a half-hour stroll. More petroglyphs are found along the lava shoreline near the roadend. Next to some tidal pools, they are highlighted by whitish salt accumulations that clearly display the carved symbols in the black-lava rock.

Puhina o Lono: Across Kealakekua Bay from the Hikiau heiau is the site where Captain Cook was killed. To reach this heiau, you must walk down the trail to Captain Cook Monument from the turnoff along Hwy 11. The shoreline site is well marked and frequently visited. The gruesome details aside, this is where the Hawaiians discovered that their white god Cook was mortal and killed him during a short battle at the beach. Even when dead, Cook still was considered to have great mana, and it evidently was thought to be shared by those who reportedly feasted on his body. Accounts of Cook's death vary, making it difficult to say precisely how Cook died and whether his body was cannibalized. The conviction of many historians is that, although his murder was committed in battle, his body was ritually prepared and eaten by his conquerers.

Puuhonua o Honaunau Heiau: Formerly called the City of Refuge, this heiau now bears its Hawaiian name. It is the island's most famous and most frequently visited historical site. It became a national historical park in 1961, and it has an excellent interpretive center. The place originally was a sanctuary for those who had violated the sacred laws, called *kapu,* that governed the relations between chiefs and commoners, and regulated the entry into and use of certain natural areas. Refugees from war and defeated warriors also gained asylum by entering the compound. After the *kahunas* performed the necessary absolutions, the *kapu* violaters and the refugees were free to re-enter society. Near the refuge are the old palace grounds of the ancient chiefs, several smaller heiaus, canoe landings, fishponds, and other settlement features. The extensive site is an authentic and well-preserved monument to early Hawaiian life. To visit, follow the signs along Hwy 11 between Keokea and Honaunau in South Kona. Its location south of Kealakekua Bay is well marked on most travel maps.

Wahaula Heiau: At the end of the Chain of Craters Road in Hawaii Volcanoes National Park, near the former Kalapana park entrance (which has been blocked in recent years by lava flows), is one of

Hawaiian Visitors Bureau

Puuhonua o Honaunau Heiau

Hawaii's most sacred places—the Wahaula Heiau, Temple of the
Red-mouthed God. Constructed in the 13th century under the direction of the *kahuna* Paao, this heaiu was dedicated to Chief Ahaula
and traditionally off-limits for commoners. After the heiau was
annexed to Hawaii Volcanoes National Park, a visitor center was
established with an interpretive service for heiau visitors. On the
afternoon of June 22, 1989, I watched the Visitor's Center ignite and
burn to the ground under the advance of a lava flow from Kilauena.
The heiau, situated on a 30 foot rise, was spared. During the summer of 1989, rangers battled the rising lava with fire hoses and
helicopters to save the heiau while archeaologists worked furiously
to map and record the site in case it too succumbed to Pele's grip.

On the afternoon of June 22, 1989, I watched the Visitor's
Center ignite and burn to the ground under the advance of a
lava flow from Kilauea.

Waikaloa Historical Site: Once an ancient land division (*ahupuaa*)
of the Kingdom of Kohala—home of Kamehameha the Great—later
a part of the Parker Ranch, Waikaloa is now a resort community in
the hands of developers who are constructing one of the world's
premier tourist destinations. The Hyatt Regency, with its lavish recreation of a watery tropical fantasyland, dominates the scene. The
hotels built at the resort site occupy the grounds of an extensive
historical area that includes important and endangered anchialine
ponds—rare natural ecosystems of brackish water formed by tubes

and depressions in the lava field that link groundwater with the ocean.

To their credit, the developers have included some of the natural and cultural history in the resort landscape: the Kahapapa and Kuualii fishponds, the anchialine ponds (Anchialine Pond Preservation Area), and various settlement sites. But like the Mauna Lani Resort complex mentioned previously, the result is a disconcerting mix of natural ecosystems, resort amusements, and historical markers. The anchialine ponds are sandwiched among the golf course fairway numbers 3, 4 and 17; the petroglyph field is along number 7; and the Ala Mamalohoa (King's Trail) skirts the number 8 tee before lining up with number 15 green.

Hiking Areas

Hawaii Volcanoes National Park

The Island of Hawaii is the youngest island in the Hawaiian Archipelago. It is situated closest to the "hot spot" in the ocean floor that is responsible for the volcanic formation of the entire Hawaiian Island chain. This explains why the island appears so different from

Boardwalk through devastated area in the national park

Hawaiian Visitors Bureau

the others—it is still erupting and growing, and the erosional forces
that have worked over many millions of years to sculpt the older
islands have had less time to carve the terrain of the Island of
Hawaii. It is composed actually of five great volcanoes. In the north
is the oldest, Kohala. To the south of this is Mauna Kea, whose last
eruption occurred 4500 years ago. West of Mauna Kea is Hualalai,
which erupted once in historical time, in 1801. Mauna Loa and
Kilauea are the southernmost volcanoes and the youngest of the five,
and both are still active. The southwest part of the island is of most
recent geological origin. Much of the southern landscape is barren,
because plants have yet to set root and to prosper in many areas of
the recent lava flows. But in older places, luxurious native forest
grows.

To walk through this landscape is an unsettling experience;
there is a primitive power here that bespeaks the origins of
life.

At Kilauea, volcanoes continue to erupt as they send flows of
new lava down the mountainsides. The remnants of former
eruptions—calderas, pits, cinder cones and tubes—and the additions of current eruptions are dominant landscape features. In fact,
as current lava flows continue to enter the sea, they create new land.
Much of this awesome landscape was set aside by Congress in 1916
to become Hawaii Volcanoes National Park. Today the Park
preserves the natural setting of Hawaii's volcanic activity, and it
serves as a refuge for native plants and animals.

To walk through this landscape is an unsettling experience; there
is a primitive power here that bespeaks the origins of life. Hikers in
the area invariably leave with not only new images of the land, but
also new imaginings of how our earth came to be. All visitors to the
Park should first check in at the visitor center; open daily 7:45–5.
Hourly films, interpretation programs, trail guides, maps, a museum,
and knowledgeable park rangers will orient you to the Park and will
highlight the diverse opportunities there. Hikers headed for the backcountry are informed of current conditions in the various Park
regions.

There is a tremendous variety of hiking opportunities in the Park.
You can climb to the 13,677-foot summit of Mauna Loa and stand
amid deep snow on the earth's second tallest mountain. The neigh-
boring volcano, Mauna Kea, visible to the north, is the highest at
13,796, in that both mountains extend below the ocean surface for
another 18,000 feet. Or you can walk at sea level on a black-sand

beach that may be only a few weeks or days old. There are hikes that tunnel through lava tubes, pass ancient petroglyphs, or wind among craters, fissures, calderas, and cinder cones. Here we divide the Park hikes into four groups: alpine, caldera, lava desert, and coast.

Alpine Hikes

Mauna Loa: The premier alpine hike on Hawaii goes to the summit of Mauna Loa. The summit can be reached by two routes: the Observatory Trail from the north, and the Mauna Loa Summit Trail from the south. A third route, the Ainapo Trail, is not recommended unless you go with someone familiar with the trail. The trailhead for the Observatory Trail is at the end of the Observatory Road, which heads off the Saddle Road (Hwy 200) one-half mile east of the Mauna Kea Road junction (adjacent to the Kipuka Ainahou State Nene Sanctuary). The trailhead for the Mauna Loa Summit Trail is located at the end of the Mauna Loa Road, which leaves Mamalahoa Highway (Hwy 11) about 2 miles west of the Park entrance. The Observatory Trail is the shorter of the two routes (6 miles one way), but geologically it is less interesting. Since you begin at 11,000 feet after driving up the Observatory Road, you also will have had less time to acclimate to the elevation, and the likelihood of altitude sickness is therefore greater. The Mauna Loa Summit trail is the recommended route. It is 18.3 miles one-way, and it will require 3–4 days

Steam vents in Hawaii Volcanoes National Park

minimum. The weather conditions at the summit are often extreme, and this hike should be attempted only by experienced, properly equipped backpackers. In the winter, the trail is often closed by heavy snow; check at the visitor center for current conditions.

Kipuka Pualu: Visitors call this place Bird Park, a fitting appellation for the ancient meadows-and-forest land. A kipuka is an island in lava, an old lava surface surrounded by recent flows. The Hawaii kipukas support some of the richest concentrations of native Hawaiian life, making them evolutionary as well as geological islands. Kipuka Pualu is traversed by a self-guided nature walk (1-mile loop) that takes the hiker through meadows and forests containing some of the world's rarest plants and birds. The trail is located 2 miles up the Moana Loa Road, which turns off Hwy 11 about 2 miles west of the Park entrance (the same road that leads to the Mauna Loa Summit Trail).

Caldera Hikes

The Kilauea shield volcano is one of the earth's most active volcanoes. It is the showpiece of the Park, and a popular hiking area. The caldera trails have easy access from the visitor center. They take you into the 4-mile caldera, across lava flows, past steaming vents, and through fern forests and lava tubes. The most recent eruptions in the caldera of Kilauea's 4000-foot summit occurred in the fall of 1979. The current volcanic activity is centered on the lower slopes of Kilauea in what is known as the East Rift Zone. Today the caldera does not contain the lake of molten rock observed in the 19th and early 20th centuries, but it does contain the fire pit of Halemaumau, steaming gas vents, and brittle and bare lava surfaces. Everywhere are eerie reminders of recent volcanic episodes. The main trails in the caldera area are the Crater Rim Trail (11 miles), Halemaumau (6.4 miles), Kilauea Iki (5 miles), Thurston Lava Tube (0.3 mile), and the Devastation Trail (1.2 miles). For trail descriptions, check with the visitor center.

Lava Desert Hikes

The greatest number of lava flows in the Park originate from the eruptions of Mauna Loa's summit caldera, Mokuaweoweo. Many of the flows that compose the lava desertlands of the Park are historical, having occurred during the past century. Forests have not had time to develop on these recent flows; the landscape remains bare and sparse, and extremely arid. The lava underfoot takes two forms: Aa and Pahoehoe. The first, aa, is rough and brittle, often described as "clinkery". This lava type was formed from vigorously-stirred molten rock that trapped irregularly-shaped bubbles of gas.

Pahoehoe (left) and aa (right) lava

The cooling process left sharp rock fragments, accretionary lava balls, and rough, angular surfaces. The second lava type, pahoehoe, cooled in the absence of vigorously-stirred gases and the emitted lava was more fluid than the aa type. The resulting smooth, billowy rock surface contains many curious formations caused by the liquid rock flowing around obstacles in the land. The lava desert hikes traverse extensive areas of both lava types and you will quickly learn to distinguish between them.

Kau Desert: Many of the hikes in this region traverse an area known as the Kau Desert. This bleak landscape is located between Hwy 11 and the Chain of Craters Road, south of the Kilauea caldera and north of the abrupt palis (cliffs) that descend to the coast (Hilina Pali, Polio Keawe Pali, and Holei Pali). The trails here are hot, dry, and shelterless. They provide solitude and an austere landscape. Popular trails in the Kau Desert include the Kau Desert Trail (19.9 miles), the Mauna Iki Trail (8.8 miles), the Halape Trail (7.2 miles), and the Keauhou Trail (8 miles). These trails all require that you bring water, wear strong shoes, and have proper sun gear. The Kau Desert Trail leads to the cabin at Pepeiao, and then loops over to the Hilina Pali Overlook at the end of Hilina Pali Road. The Mauna Iki Trail begins at Hwy 11, about 9 miles west of the Park entrance, proceeds past some enclosed prehistoric footprints, and loops around to intersect with the Kau Desert Trail near the Mauna Iki Lava Shield. The Halape Trail begins at the Kipuka Nene Camp-ground and descends to a camping shelter at Halape Beach. The Halape area was the sight of a devastating earthquake-triggered tsunami that stuck the coast in 1975, killing two campers. The shelter area has since been rebuilt, new coconut palms have been planted, and the beach camp is again a popular destination. The infrequently used Keauhou Trail descends from the Chain of Craters Road, over the Polio Keawe Pali, and down to a camping shelter on the coast. Check at the visitors center for current conditions and trail descriptions.

Maunu Ulu and the East Rift Zone: A second set of desert trails traverses the area around Maunu Ulu, Makaopuhi Crater, and Napau Crater. The landscape here is more varied and interesting than in the Kau Desert region. The hiking routes in the area include the Napau Trail (7 miles), the Naulu Trail (a 2-mile connecting route between the Kalapana Trail and the Chain of Craters Road), and the Kalapana Trail (9.2 miles). A third, short trail, the Puuloa Trail (0.5 mile), located near the bottom of the Chain of Craters Road, takes you to a fine set of petroglyphs. Certainly the most interesting of the first three routes is the Napau Trail. It leads you through a varied volcanic terrain of craters, cinder cones, lava shields, and inter-esting *pahoehoe* lava surfaces. These trails are accessed via the Chain of Craters Road.

Coastal Hikes

The Park coastline is a remote, harsh area of bare rock and crashing surf. If you're interested in solitude and an almost transcen-dental landscape, you will enjoy this region. Several beach camp shelters are located on the coast, at the terminus of the main desert backcountry trails (Kaaha Shelter, Halape Shelter, and Keauhou Shelter). These shelters are available on a first-come-first-served basis. Water is available only at the specificed trail shelter areas; be sure to carry plenty with you. Fishing is prohibited along the coast, and swimming spots should be cautiously selected; do not swim in the open ocean, as these waters are rough, with strong currents. Trails are marked by cairns (stone piles), so please stay on them. The Kalue Trail (6 miles) begins at Pepeiao Cabin, crosses the Kukalaula Pali, and proceeds along the coast to the Kaaha Shelter, where it links up with an access trail to the Hilina Pali Trail. The Puna Coast Trail (9.7 miles) begins at the Keauhou Shelter and goes along the coast to the Chain of Craters Road at the Puuloa Parking Area. This is a remote stretch of coastline, offering plenty of privacy and quiet. It traverses bleak country—the recent lava flows of the Mauna Ulu episode (1969-73).

Other Hiking Areas

Apart from Hawaii Volcanoes National Park, the Island of Hawaii affords relatively few hiking opportunities. Much of the upcountry land along the slopes of the main volcanoes is private ranchland, and off-limits to the public. A few of these areas provide guided tours for a price. The Parker Ranch in Waimea, for example, occasionally organizes hikes on ranchland. Much of the island's best shoreline is also off-limits to the general public because it is privately held by resort developers.

The island's state parks contain a few short hiking trails. Akaka Falls State Park has a 0.7 mile guided loop through a planted forest of gingers, bamboos, orchids, azaleas, tree ferns, hibiscus, and numerous other introduced and native species. At midpoint along the trail is the park centerpiece—420-foot Akaka Falls. The Park is located off the Hawaii Belt Road (Hwy 19), 15 miles north of Hilo. Turn mauka onto Hwy 220 at Honomu, and follow this to the Park at the roadend.

Another hiking area is in Kalopa State Park, located 5 miles south and 3 miles inland from Honokaa. Take Kalopa Road off Hawaii Belt Road (Hwy 19) 3 miles *mauka* to the roadend. There are a picnic area and an arboretum near the parking lot. Beyond the arboretum is the trailhead for a 0.7 mile guided nature walk that passes through a lovely native rainforest (34 stations are marked and discussed in an interpretive guide available at the trailhead for a small donation). The trail maintenance and the guide booklet are the work of the Honokaa District Development Corporation Forest

Hawaiian Visitors Bureau

Akaka Falls

Parks Committee. (Contact the HDDC at: P.O. Box 637, Honokaa, HI 96727).

A hike not to be missed is the trail to the Puako petroglyphs (see section on heiaus). This 1-mile route traverses kiawe scrubland to reach the petroglyphs, which were carved in the *pahoehoe* rock by the ancient Hawaiians. The best set of carvings is at the end of the trail. The petroglyph trail is at the end of Puako Road. To get there, head north from Kona on Queen Kaahumanu Highway (Hwy 19); after 30 miles turn *makai* onto Puako Road, and follow it to the roadend.

One of the premier wilderness hikes on the Island of Hawaii is the Waipio-Waimanu Valley Trail (8 miles). The route follows the rugged sea cliffs and deep valleys of the windward Kohala coast, ending at remote and wild Waimanu Valley. This is a 2-day hike at minimum, and you likely will want to spend some time exploring in Waimanu Valley. The trail begins in Waipio Valley. You can see the trail switchback up the north valley wall from the Waipio Valley Overlook at the end of Highway 240. To reach the trailhead, proceed from the overlook down the dirt track to the valley floor and follow the well-marked trails across the valley. The Waimanu Trail begins near the beach at the far valley wall.

Several coastal trails exist on the leeward side of the island. One begins at the Waikoloa Resort Complex, off Highway 19 in South Kohala, and more or less follows the coast for about 5 miles to Kiholo Bay. Much of the trail traverses the 1859 lava flow, so the trail is hot and dry. Another trail begins at Milolii Beach County Park in South Kona and follows the coast south 4 miles to Niuou Point. A third route begins at South Point (located at the end of South Point Road off Mamalahoa Highway (Hwy 11) and follows a 2-mile trail east along the coast to a green sand beach. This is a windy and wild section of coastline, and is an excellent place for beachcombing and exploring the tidal pools.

For guidance to the island's more remote hikes, contact the Na Ala Hele hiking and environmental group (P.O. Box 1572, Kealakekua, HI 96750) or the Moku Loa Sierra Club group (P.O. Box 1137, Hilo, HI 96721).

Natural Foods

Two important and related issues for the Island of Hawaii are the problem of food self-sufficiency and the land abuses perpetrated by the plantation agriculture industry. The island's environmental diversity can support a wide array of local agriculture, but economics have traditionally supported the monocrop sugar and plantation-fruit industries. This is no longer as true of Hawaii as it once was, because plantation agriculture requires cheap land and labor. The consumption of sugar in the American market also has fallen off, reducing the demand for sugar-cane products. But the years of intensive land use, neglect, and chemical additions to the soils and groundwater still threaten Hawaii's land. Recently, several small organic growers

Hawaiian Visitors Bureau

Beach at mouth of Waipio Valley (zigzags on mountain are part of a trail)

began providing fresh farm produce for the natural food markets on Hawaii. They conduct sustainable agriculture that produces nutritious food. Natural-food stores carry items in bulk form, and they usually have on hand a variety of dried foods. If you plan to do some hiking on the island and you need to stock up on backpacking foodstuffs, the natural food groceries are handy places.

Abundant Life Natural Food: Located at 90 Kamehameha Avenue in Hilo, across from the bay. 808/935-7411.

Big Island Natural Foods: Upcountry's natural food place in Waimea (Kamuela) at the Parker Ranch Shopping Center. 808/885-6323.

Golden Son: Located in downtown Honokaa on Mamane Street. 808/775-0043.

Keaau Natural Foods: In Keaau near the junction of Hwy 130 and Hwy 11, on the way to Volcano Village. 808/966-8877.

Kona Healthways: The leeward coast's most extensive natural food grocery, located at 74-5588 A Palani Road in the Kona Coast Shopping Center, Kailua-Kona. 808/329-2296.

Ohana O Ka Aina: A food cooperative and natural grocery located in Kealakekua on Hwy 11. Behind the grocery is the Ohana Cafe, serving vegetarian foods to eat in or to go. 808/323-3600.

Pahoa Natural Groceries: Located in Pahoa off Hwy 130, Puna district. 808/965-8322.

Farmer's Market: Every 1st and 3rd Sunday of the month a farmer's market is held in Volcano Village at the Cooper Center on Wright Road. Early mornings are the best times.

Kuoloa Farm: Specializes in organic produce. Contact: P.O. Box 452, Kurtistown, HI 96760. 808/966-7792.

Nature Tours and Outdoor Excursions

There are numerous ways to enter the natural areas on the Island of Hawaii. The most common way is by foot. Refer to the hiking and camping sections for specific information on this mode of travel. But alternatives exist, including bicycles, kayaks, horses, and submarines. The following section describes commercial operators who lead environmentally designed tours on the island. I have omitted references to helicopters, zodiacs, parasailing, van tours and other motorized forms of transport (except the submarine—because it has no peer—and the Mauna Kea summit tour by jeep—because the place is so extraordinary and the road leading to it is for 4-wheel drive-vehicles, although I've done it in a rental car). The mechanized modes of travel regularly infringe upon the more natural and quiet modes. This is especially true in places like Waipio Valley, where the roaring 4-wheel-drive tour industry has rutted the dirt lanes and disrupted the quiet of the valley floor. You will find here, in contrast to the more commercialized and conventional tours, references to the more low-key ways of exploring the natural areas.

BICYCLING

Whether you go alone, or with a tour group, the Island of Hawaii is one of the best Hawaiian Islands for bike touring. The long and winding roads are generally quiet. The obvious exceptions are the roads in the Hilo and Kona regions. The road grades range from flat to steep, and lead to various exciting options: the lush coastal Hamakua road; the upcountry lanes of North Kohala, which look to be in northern Scotland; the desolate moonscape of the Saddle Road; and the hot, dry, straight Kona stretch. Bicycle touring allows you the chance to take in the countryside at a leisurely pace, or to pump your heart out on the uphill stretches.

Rentals and Repairs

If you wish to avoid the organized cycling tours, rent a bike on the island or bring your own. It now costs about $30 to ship a bike to Hawaii from the mainland ($20 for the interisland flights from

Honolulu). Below is a list of bicycle shops on the Island of Hawaii
that either rent or repair bikes.

B&L Bike and Sports: 74-5576 B Pawai Place in Kona. 808/329-
3309.

Big Island Mountain Bike Headquarters: In Waimea Village
Shopping Center. 808/885-5005.

Competitive Edge Triathlon Center 75-5744 Alii Drive in Kailua-
Kona. 808/329-8141. 808/885-2115 in Waimea.

Cycle and Surf: In downtown Waimea. 808/885-5005.

Dave's Triathlon Shop: 75-5626 Kuakini Hwy Bay 12 in Kam
Square, Kailua-Kona. 808/329-4522 They rent mountain bikes.

Hawaiian Pedals: Located in Kona Inn Shopping Village in Kailua-
Kona. 808/329-2294.

Mid-Pacific Wheels: 1133 C Manono Street in Hilo. 808/935-6211.

Bike Tours
    There's a new outfit on the island called Hawaiian Eyes-Big
Island Bicycle Tours. They lead journeys by bike to various parts of
the island, including a trip down Mauna Kea. The Bike Down a
Volcano experience takes you from 13,796 feet to sea level in a
matter of hours. It's all downhill; they initially take you to the volcano summit in a van. Other guided journeys include the scenic
country lanes that wind through the rolling grasslands of Kohala; the
sweeping volcanic landscape of the Saddle Road; and the ocean
coastline and sugar-cane fields of the Hamakua Coast. Touring distances range from 10 to 52 miles, and prices range from $35 to $90.
Contact: Hawaiian Eyes-Big Island Bicycle Tours, P.O. Box 1500,
Honokaa, Hawaii 96727. 808/775-7335.

HORSEBACK RIDING
    The Island of Hawaii has a rich ranching history, and the exten-
sive pasturelands and upland forests on the island are crisscrossed
with horse trails. Much of the land is privately held by the large
ranches, including Waimea's 225,000-acre Parker Ranch, the
largest private ranch in the U.S. A number of tours now operate on
the island that take small groups by horse into rural or wild lands,
including the ranchlands. Listed below are several groups that lead
rides into diverse island settings. All rides provide similar amenities, such as country lunches, relaxation time, and lessons if necessary. Most trips last a half-day. The prices average around $50.
Personally tailored excursions are available from most of the outfits.
Ironwood Outfitters: Located in upcountry Waimea, they specialize in leading groups through the high pasture country of Kohala

district on a "top of the mountain trail ride." The elevation of this area averages several thousand feet above sea level, and cool temperatures and clear skies prevail much of the time, permitting magnificent vistas of the Kohala mountains, Mauna Kea, and the leeward coast. The feel here is of high steppe and pasture, and the horseback tours offered at Ironwood Outfitters take advantage of the upland environment. Contact: 808/885-4941.

Kings' Trail Rides O' Kona: Trails in the Kealakekua Ranch take riders through a working cattle ranch, fern forests and the Hualalai mountains. Some tours include a coastal segment near Kealekekua Bay on the south Kona coast. Dry conditions generally prevail, except at the higher elevations. Contact: Kings' Trail Rides O' Kona, P.O Box 1366, Kealakekua, HI 96750. 808/323-2388.

Waipio Na Alapa Trail Rides: For a different experience, this outfit leads small groups by horseback into the back of the lush Waipio Valley. The operators are long-time residents of the valley, and the tours are informative adventures through rainforest, past taro fields, across ancient settlement sites, and up to the base of valley waterfalls. Contact: Waipio Na Alapa Trail Rides, P.O. Box 992, Honokaa, HI 96727. 808/775-0419.

Waipio Valley Wagon Tours: If you want to leave the driving to them, check out Waipio Valley Tours. A mule-drawn covered wagon takes visitors into the valley on a leisurely and comfortable narrated tour. If at first it seems a little hokey, let the creaking wooden wheels and the informative driver persuade you otherwise. The 2-hour tours depart several times daily from Kukuihaele village, located above the valley; 4-wheel-drive shuttle service transports passengers to the valley floor. Cost is $25/person; children are half price. There is a 20% discount for Hawaiian Island residents (*kamaainas*). Contact: Waipio Valley Wagon Tours, P.O. Box 1340, Honokaa, HI 96727. 808/775-9518.

Parker Ranch Tours: The 225,000-acre Parker Ranch recently began tours of the ranchland and facilities. This is cowboy country, and if you're interested in the way things work on a Pacific cattle ranch, you might want to saddle up with them. Contact: the Parker Ranch, P.O. Box 458, Kamuela, HI 96743. 808/885-7655.

NATURALIST GUIDE SERVICE

Persons or groups interested in arranging personally tailored excursions to the Island of Hawaii may want to contract for the services of a professional naturalist guide. These guides are particularly useful for small student groups that seek to explore the Hawaiian environment in a structured way, but anyone would benefit from the knowledge and experience of the Island's naturalists. The most informed and experienced nature guide on the island is Bobby Camara, who leads tours for Wilderness Travel when he is not involved in his own guide services. Bobby is an island son, born in Honokaa, and he has devoted his life to the study of Hawaii's natural and cultural history. With years of experience leading individual and group tours, he knows how to translate his knowledge and love of the island into an authentic and unique experience for his clients. Contact: Bobby Camara, Naturalist, P.O. Box 485, Volcano, HI 96785. 808/967-7787.

OCEAN TOURS

Atlantis Underwater Tours: A high-tech 43-passenger, 3-crew, Atlantis submarine takes visitors to depths of up to 150 feet in the clear waters along the Kona Coast. The one-hour voyages open up a vast undersea world of coral reefs and marine life, and if you're not a diver, this may be your only way to see life at these depths. A small shuttle boat takes you out to the submarine, where you lock down for the below-water excursion. Divers accompany the vessel, and at prescribed feeding stations they will attract legions of rainbow colored reef fish. Both day and night trips are offered. Located off the Kailua Pier adjacent to the King Kamehameha Hotel. Contact them at: Atlantis Submarines Hawaii, L.P., Shop "L", Hotel King Kamehameha, 75-5660 Palani Rd., Kailua-Kona, HI 96740. 808/329-6626 or 329-6625.

SNUBA—Big Island: This new enterprise conducts marine exploration tours using a device somewhere between a snorkel and scuba tanks—"snuba ". It essentially involves a float with attached airhose. The device combines the security of being tethered to a surface float and air supply with the freedom of prolonged underwater stays at depths of up to 25 feet. This is an affiliate of the SNUBA group on Oahu, and they share a conservationist approach to marine adventure. Contact: SNUBA-Big Island, P.O. Box 4388, Kailua-Kona, HI 96745. 808/326-5444.

SUMMIT TOURS

Hawaii's tallest mountain, Mauna Kea, rises 32,000 feet above the ocean floor and towers 13,796 feet above the ocean surface—making it the worlds' largest mountain massif. Once glaciated, now snow-covered in the winter, the summit of Mauna Kea is an extraordinary place. Several international observatories are located here which give the ethereal summit a stellar look. The journey up the mountain takes you through a remarkable cross section of life zones—from the tropical lowlands through the temperate midlands to the arctic-like highlands. The road leading to the summit is

Snow on Mauna Kea

normally passable only by high-clearance 4-wheel-drive vehicles. Under excellent weather conditions, it is possible to take a regular automobile (although beware, all rental-car drivers—it'll cost you $500 if you need to be rescued by the company). If you wisely choose not to drive your own vehicle, you can enlist the services of the summit tour agency. They charge $65/person for the 6-hour narrated trip. Contact: Summit Tours, P.O. Box 5128, Kukuhaele, HI 96727. 808/775-7121.

MISCELLANEOUS

Painting in Paradise: Here's a new twist on an old theme: capture nature on a canvas to take home with you. Artists lead small groups to Waipio Valley, the Hamakua coast, Mauna Kea, Onomea Valley, and other island destinations. Explore your talent on canvas while you explore your surroundings. They charge $125 for a one-day trip. The price includes painting materials and a smock. Contact: Aloha Aina Arts, P.O. Box 2066, Kamuela, HI 96743.

Outdoor Equipment and Supplies

The Island of Hawaii has a poor selection of stores for camping equipment. It's best to gear up before visiting the island; Honolulu is the closest good source of backcountry supplies. The stores mentioned below have the largest selections of outdoor gear on Hawaii. They are all in Kailua-Kona; Hilo has no camping gear outlet.

Gaspro: Located at 74-5598 Luhia in Kailua-Kona. 808/329-7393. Only a limited selection here.

J&J Sporting Goods: This place has the best selection of gear. They also sell stove gas. 74-5539 Kaiwi St. in Kailua-Kona. 808/329-2610.

Kona Surplus: Army surplus stuff here. 74-55960 Pawai Place in Kailua-Kona. 808/329-5056.

Pacific Rent-All: They rent some camping equipment. 1080 Kilauea Ave in Kailua-Kona. 808/935-2974.

Basically Books: They stock a variety of useful Hawaii maps and hiking guidebooks. 169 Keawe Street in Hilo. 808/961-0144.

Snorkeling and Surfing

Most of the beaches on the Island of Hawaii lack the protection of an offshore reef, and the waters are potentially dangerous, subject to strong currents and high surf. The exceptions are the coves and lava reefs along the leeward coast. These areas provide some of the world's best snorkeling. Rich coral, rocky bottoms, and diverse marine life make for spectacular underwater exploring, suitable for beginners through experienced snorkelers. The surfing sites on the island are best left to experts, though. Strong currents and rocky shores prevail, and when the surf is up so is the danger level.

SNORKELING
Hilo Area
Onekahakaha Beach Park: A boulder breakwater protects a shallow cove for snorkelers. Accessible from Kalanianaole St., 3.5 miles east from downtown Hilo.

James Kealoha Park: Summer snorkeling is fine here, especially near Scout Island in the eastern part of the rocky bay. The park is 4 miles east of Hilo, on Kalanianaole St.

Richardson Ocean Center: Snorkeling is popular in the shallow bay fronting the interpretive ocean center here. On Kalanianaole St., next to Leleiwi Beach County Park, 5 miles east of Hilo.

Leeward Coast
Honaunau Bay: A cove adjacent to Puuhonua o Honaunau National Historical Park in South Kona. It offers some of the most spectacular undersea terrain in Hawaii. Accessible off Mamalahoa Highway (Hwy 11) by following the signs to the national park (see Heiaus).

Kealakekua Bay: Below Captain Cook is this large bay with spectacular snorkeling. The entire cove is the Kealakekua Bay State Underwater Park, and it provides premier snorkeling for beginners through experts. Accessible from Hwy 11 in Captain Cook by following the signs to Napoopoo Beach Park.

Kailua-Kona: Several beach parks exist along Alii Drive south of downtown Kailua-Kona. The best for snorkeling is Kahaluu Beach Park, 3.5 miles from town.

North of Kailua-Kona are several beach parks that offer splendid snorkeling when the ocean is calm. These include Hapuna Beach State Recreation Area, Lapakahi State Historical Park, and Mahukona Beach Park. All are accessible off Queen Kaahumanu Highway (Hwy 19) heading north from Kailua-Kona by following the signs.

SURFING

When the surf is up, the coastal waters are dangerous. There are no surf spots for novices. Practiced surfers should check with local lifeguards for local conditions. Beach parks offering rideable surf include James Kealoha Park and Honolii Beach Park near Hilo, Kahaluu Beach Park near Kailua-Kona, and Anaehoomalu Beach in Waikaloa, near the Waikaloa Sheraton resort.

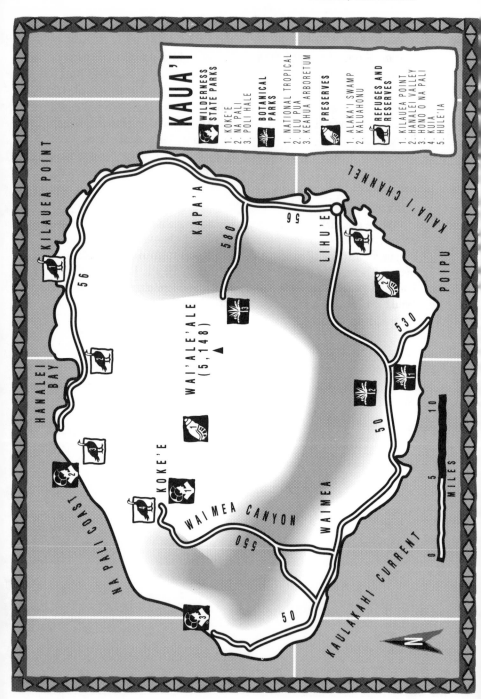

KAUA'I

WILDERNESS STATE PARKS
1. KOKE'E
2. NA PALI
3. POLI HALE

BOTANICAL PARKS
1. NATIONAL TROPICAL
2. ULU PUA
3. KEAHUA ARBORETUM

PRESERVES
1. ALAKA'I SWAMP
2. KALUAHONU

REFUGES AND RESERVES
1. KILAUEA POINT
2. HANALEI VALLEY
3. HONO O NA PALI
4. KUIA
5. HULE'IA

KILAUEA POINT

KAUA'I CHANNEL

KAPA'A

LIHU'E

580

56

56

POIPU

530

HANALEI BAY

WAI'ALE'ALE
(5,148)

50

KOKE'E

WAIMEA

WAIMEA CANYON

550

10

5

MILES

0

NA PALI COAST

50

50

KAULAKAHI CURRENT

N

Chapter Four

Kauai

Background

The island of Kauai often is called the "Garden Island." Indeed, the lush green mountain slopes, the profusion of flowering trees and bushes, the many waterfalls, and the sheer abundance of tropical life suggest that this is an appropriate name. But the highest recorded rainfalls in the world have been measured on Kauai, near the summit of 5148-foot Mt. Waialeale (485) inches per year). The waters that drain Kauai's interior mountains have carved spectacular, 2750-foot-deep Waimea Canyon, a 14.5-mile-long chasm that is called the Grand Canyon of the Pacific, and the equally magnificent but more remote Wainiha Gorge (11 miles long). They have also contributed to the formation of the 3000-foot sea cliffs along the northern Na Pali coast. These areas are anything but gardenlike. They are wild places that create awe and a sense of the primordial in visitors who see them.

Kauai is the oldest of the main inhabited islands of the Hawaiian chain. Geologists agree that the single great volcanic shield that makes up the island began forming about 4–6 million years, and the last volcanic activity ceased over 1 million years ago. The caldera of the Kauai shield volcano roughly corresponded in location to the present-day Alakai Swamp Wilderness Preserve—a magnificent bog located in a wet depression below Mt. Waialeale. Presumably, the epoch of volcano-building included numerous eruptions alternating with quiet times, which would account for the complex geology of the island.

Because Kauai is older than its southeastern neighbors, the forces of erosion have had more time to scrape, chip, and wash away the surface. The northerly location of the island puts it into the path of cyclonic storms as well as trade winds, and both contribute to the high rainfall on the island. The rivers and streams fed by this rainfall have created a magnificent landscape of jagged and spiny cliffs, steep-walled valleys, and alluvial terraces. This landscape, softened

by lush vegetation, together with the abundant waterfalls, the
numerous sandy beaches, and the absence of a large human
population give Kauai its unique character.

There is little night life on the island, a dearth of commercial
amusements, and no large city. The entire island has a resident
population of less than 40,000. The tourist hotels are concentrated
around Poipu Beach along the south coast. Elsewhere on the island,
small inns and a few marginally successful resorts accommodate
visitors. The pace of life on the island is slow. It complements the
island's weathered terrain. Residents are attuned to this tempo, and

---

But the highest recorded rainfalls in the world have been
measured on Kauai, near the summit of 5148-foot Mt.
Waialeale (485 inches per year).

---

visitors either adjust or they leave out of boredom to seek the heady
entertainment of Oahu or Maui. Kauai's rewards as a travel destination require close attention to the land. Of course, it is possible to
cruise at highway speeds along the coastal roads (Hwy 50 and Hwy
56) or on the short feeder roads to tourist sights, and to see the
famous landmarks: Niihau Island off Barking Sands Beach, Wailua
Falls in Kawaihau, the Sleeping Giant (Nounou Ridge) near
Wailua, Waimea Canyon, the Kalalau cliffs, and Lumahai Beach—
made famous in the movie "South Pacific." But to plumb the depths
of the place, it becomes necessary to explore farther afield than the
roadside. Hike the steep trail to Kalalau along the Na Pali Coast,
slog through thigh-deep muck in the Alakai Swamp in search of rare
native plants and birds, scamper down dizzying trails into Waimea
Canyon, sit quietly for a sunset at Polihale, or slowly explore the
delights of one of the island's botanic gardens. These experiences
reveal Kauai to be a place of exquisite beauty. For its small size
(553 square miles) it offers a great deal of natural beauty and many
areas of remote backcountry. This chapter helps you to explore the
natural opportunities on Kauai.

Alternative Lodging

BED AND BREAKFAST INNS

Many of the bed-and-breakfast establishments on Kauai do not
advertise; they are simple rooms in private homes that can be
located only through the statewide B&B directory services discussed in the Hawaiian Islands chapter. There are a few inns, however, that do not rely on any state-wide directory. These cater to a
local clientele.

Kilauea lighthouse is at the northernmost point of Hawaii

House of Aleva: Located on the ridge above the Wailua River, this private home offers rooms for $50/night double and $35/night single. It is conveniently located near Opaekaa Falls, a few miles inland from Kapaa in Kawaihau district. Contact: 5509 Kuamoo Rd., Kapaa, Kauai, HI 96746. 808/822-4606.

Kay Barker's Bed and Breakfast: The home is located behind the Sleeping Giant mountain, with views of Mt. Waialeale and the state Waialeale Forest Reserve. Hiking trails begin behind the house. Room rates start at $25/night. Contact: Kay Barker, P.O. Box 740, Kapaa, Kauai, HI 96746. 808/822-3073.

Keapana Center Bed and Breakfast: Keapana Center is a spiritual retreat located in the hills above Kapaa. They arrange a variety of outdoor activities, conduct meditation retreats, provide wellness workshops, and offer B&B facilities for visitors. Room rates start at $50/double. Contact: Keapana Center Bed and Breakfast, 5620 Keapana Road, Kapaa, Kauai, HI 96746. 808/822-7968 or toll-free 800/822-7968.

Poipu Bed and Breakfast Inn: On the south shore of the island, amid the resorts at Poipu, is this luxurious and expensive B&B inn, a graceful old place built in 1933. For a splurge, it is a better choice than the nearby Poipu resorts. The inn is located on Hoonani Road,

3 minutes from old Koloa town. Contact: 2720 Hoonani Road, Koloa, Kauai, HI 96756. 808/742-1146 or call toll-free 1-800-552-0095.

CABINS

Bob and Cindy's Hale by the Sea: The cabins here take full advantage of the serenity and the outstanding scenery of the north shore near Haena. Rooms rent for $40/night. Contact: Bob & Cindy's, P.O. Box 1697, Hanalei, Kauai, HI 96714. 808/826-6828.

Camp Naue: This YMCA camp is located on the north shore, near Haena Beach Park, at the northwest end of Kuhio Highway (Hwy 56). The cabins are located on the beach in a shady grove of ironwood trees. They rent for $10/person/night. Camping is allowed on the nearby grounds and on the beach for $8/tent. The camp is located at the intersection of Aleale Road and Hwy 56, a mile or so east of Haena Beach Park. You can arrange to stay simply by showing up before 6 p.m. If you want to reserve a place in advance, contact the Kauai YMCA office in Lihue at P.O. Box 1786, Lihue, Kauai, HI 96766. 808/246-9090.

Kahili Mountain Park: Tucked into a quiet valley below Kahili Peak in the Koloa district of Kauai's south coast is 215-acre Kahili Mountain Park, owned and operated by the Seventh-Day Adventist Church. This is not a commercial park; in fact, it's not a park at all but a collection of cabins and cabinettes strung across the valley floor on private grounds that include a small school, a swimming pond, and gardens. The cabins rent for $20–35 per night (3–6 persons). To ensure a spot, you will need to make reservations well in advance, since they often book up 3–4 months ahead. Cancellations frequently occur, though, so check with them even if you haven't made advance arrangements. The camp is located one mile mauka off Kaumualii Highway (Hwy 50) on an unmarked gravel road; look for the sign that reads *Kalihi Mountain Park* one-fourth mile west of the intersection of Hwy 50 and Maluhia Road (the tree tunnel road that goes to Poipu). Contact: Kahili Mountain Park, P.O. Box 298, Koloa, Kauai, HI 96756. 808/742-9921.

Kokee Lodge: I cannot recommend this place too highly. The Kokee area is a premier hiking area, with access to Waimea Canyon, the Alakai Swamp, and the Na Pali ridge hikes. If you want to get out of the weather (which can often be cool and rainy), and relax beside a warm fire, then the lodges at Kokee are the place to stay. They are situated at 3600 feet elevation in 4345-acre Kokee State Park. (See Camping Areas and Hiking Areas for descriptions of the park and the surrounding area.) Kokee Lodge is privately run,

Cabin at Kokee Lodge

although it is in the state park. They maintain 12 furnished cabins that sleep from 3–7 persons. Rates äre $35 and $45 per night per cabin, with a maximum 5 day stay. Reserve well in advance, several months if possible. Kokee Lodge is on Kokee Road (Hwy 550) above Waimea Canyon in Kokee State Park, one-half hour up the mountain from Waimea. Contact: Kokee Lodge, P.O. Box 819, Waimea, Kauai, HI 96796. 808/335-6061.

Botanical Gardens and Parks

Keahua Forestry Arboretum: The upland site of Keahua Arboretum is adjacent to the state Waialeale Forest Reserve, west of the Wailua reservoir in Kawaihau district. To visit the arboretum, drive mauka on Hwy 580 from Wailua to the roadend. Four-wheel drive vehicles can proceed across the stream at the end of the road, but others will have to park at the turnout.

Several walking trails wind through the arboretum forest, passing groves of painted gum trees (*Eucalyptus deglupta*) and scattered ohia lehua (*Metrosideros collina*), and skirting dense tangles of the yellow-flowered hibiscus known as hau (*Hibiscus tiliscus*). Next to the trails are thickets of the pesty malbar melestoma (*Melestoma malbathricum*)—a pink-flowering plant which was introduced from India as an ornamental but which has spread from private gardens into the forest reserves. The state forest area extends beyond the arboretum to Waialeale, a distance of 5½ miles across lush, wet terrain. The views of Waialeale on a clear day from high points in the arboretum are extraordinary. The arboretum is the starting point for the scenic 2.1 mile Kuilau Trail (see hiking section). A picnic area and a stream swimming pool are also located in the arboretum.

Kukui Lono Park: This incongruous little garden is set on top of a
rise in the middle of a golf course. At first glance it appears to offer
little in the way of botanical study. However, the Japanese design,
the native Hawaiian plant collection, and the splendid ocean views
make it worth the short detour off Kaumualii Highway (Hwy 50).
Look for the signboard on Hwy 50 in Kalaheo that marks the turnoff;
follow the signed road for 2 miles to the top of the nearby ridge. The
park is located at the roadend.

National Tropical Botanical Garden: Formerly called the Pacific
Tropical Botanical Garden, this is a nonprofit educational and
scientific center that was chartered by Act of Congress in 1964. As
the premier tropical botanical research garden in the U.S., its mandate is to collect and preserve endangered plant life from throughout
the tropics. The 186-acre garden is located in Lawai village, near
Kauai's south shore. The garden is open only to guided tours
arranged through the visitors center. The tours are offered Monday
through Friday at 9 a.m. and 1 p.m., on Saturdays at 9 a.m., and on
Sundays at 1 p.m. They last approximately 2–3 hours and cost
$15/person. You must make advance reservations; contact: National
Tropical Botanical Garden, P.O. Box 340, Lawai, Kauai, HI
96765. 808/332-7361.

For those unable to make the longer guided tour, there is a short
self-guiding walking tour of the plants at the visitors center. The
center is open Mon.–Fri. 7:45–4. The garden is at the end of
Hailima Road, 0.7 mile makai of the junction of Hwy 530 (Koloa
Road) and Hwy 50 in Lawai. In addition to the main garden at
Lawai, the National Tropical Botanical Garden maintains a satellite
garden in Limahuli Valley on Kauai's north shore. This wet-site
garden specializes in rare native Hawaiian plants. You can arrange a
visit through the Lawai visitor center. To become a member of the
National Tropical Botanical Garden, which entitles you to receive
their numerous publications as well to participate at no cost in
regular garden tours, pay annual membership dues of $35.00 (Asso-
ciate) or $10.00 (Student). Write them at the above address.

Olu Pua Botanical Gardens: The gardens contain a large collection of flowering plants, intended for people seeking more an
aesthetic than an educational experience. The gardens are at the end
of a short gravel road heading mauka from Hwy 50 in Kalaheo,
Koloa district. The gravel road has no sign, but the gardens are indicated by a signboard at the turnoff from Hwy 50, next to a large
macadamia orchard. Open Monday through Saturday, 9:30–3.

Hanalei Valley in northern Kauai

Camping Areas

Kauai's camping areas include state parks, county parks, private parks, and backcountry forest reserve sites. As is true on all the islands, the camping regulations on Kauai vary considerably according to the type of campsite. Competing jurisdiction and related differences in regulations can make the process of obtaining the proper permits cumbersome. For some of the most popular camping areas, permits must be secured well in advance. In less popular areas, permits are easily obtainable or not even required. Most areas are restricted to tent camping, but trailer camping is permitted in Kokee and Polihale state parks. To rent a trailer or for information on trailer camping elsewhere on Kauai, contact: Beach Boy Campers, P.O. Box 3208, Lihue, HI 96766. 808/245-9211. OR Holo Holo Campers, Inc., P.O. Box 1604, Lihue, HI 96766. 808/245-4592.

STATE PARKS

Permits are required and must be obtained in advance. Contact: Division of State Parks, Kauai district, P.O. Box 1671, Lihue, HI 96766. 808/245-4444. Street Address: 3060 Eiwa St. in Lihue. You may also obtain permits at the Division of State Parks in Honolulu.

Kokee State Park

This is an outstanding state park, with plenty of opportunities for high quality camping and hiking. A developed campground is tucked into the Ohia forest located across the meadow from the Kokee

Natural History Museum. The campground includes restrooms, cold-water showers, and picnic areas. According to local lore, the meadow was once a thick forest inhabited by an ogre who attacked passing travelers. The Hawaiian diety Kanaloa cleared the forest, dispelled the frightful spirit from Kokee, and struck the place forever clear of trees. The meadow now is an excellent place for daytime picnics and moonlight strolls.

Kokee adjoins Waimea Canyon State Park, 15 miles north of Kekaha on Kokee Road (Hwy 550). It is situated at the 3600-foot elevation level; camping can be wet and cold here anytime of the year, so be properly equipped.

In the morning you will inevitably be roused by a wandering moa—the scarlet red jungle fowl (*Gallus gallus*) that descended from the fighting cocks introduced to Hawaii by the Polynesians many centuries ago. The lack of natural predators here in Kokee has allowed these colorful birds to survive and mulitiply, and they now parade through Kokee like a band of colorful minstrels, sounding their early morning call to the delight or the chagrin of campers.

The camp at Kokee is as an excellent base for hikes into the surrounding 4345-acre wilderness area. Several natural area reserves, wilderness preserves, forest preserves, and wilderness state parks join at Kokee in a dazzling array of natural areas: the jagged cliffs along the Na Pali-Kona Forest Preserve, the dizzying trails of Waimea Canyon, the lush stream hikes in the upland Ohio rainforest, and the muddy tracks of the primordial Alakai Swamp. The forests of Kokee are extraordinary places. The number of native species is large, and in places like the Alakai Swamp and along the Awaawapuhi Trail, you will find intact extensive areas of old-growth forests.

New life, though, has invaded these old forests. The celebrated Kauai Methley plum trees (*Prunus cerasifera* × *salicina*), introduced from South Africa and now flourishing in the Kokee forests, used to draw big crowds from the coasts during the picking seasons, but they now quietly grow old in the forests, unattended and largely forgotten. The brilliant pink flower that hangs from vines in the forests is the banana poka (*Passiflora tripartita*), a plant introduced to Kauai in 1920 as an ornamental. It now grows wild, strangling native trees as it spreads its color through the green forests. Pigs were first introduced to the area by the Polynesians, who used them for sacrificial offerings, food, and boar's-teeth jewelry. These small (50–60 pounds) beasts interbred with pig species brought by Westerners, became feral, and grew wily, mean and big. Many now top 200 pounds, with long tusks and bristly hair. They are terrible rooters, destroying vast tracts of vegetation as they dig for the tubers that sustain them. Watch for wallows of mud and rooted bushes along the hiking trails, clear indicators of the damage these beasts can wreak in the forests. The pigs now are favorite prey for local hunters who stalk them with specially trained dogs in the dense tangles of forest.

Less dangerous and more attractive prey in Kokee are the rainbow trout that yearly entice fishermen to the cool streams of the mountains. First planted in the 1920s, the trout now inhabit 8 highland streams, growing to quite large sizes in the remote stretches. The record caught is 6 lbs, 4 oz and 23 inches. Each year trout eggs are flown to Honolulu from California. They are incubated on Oahu and the fry are then backpacked or helicoptered

---

Less dangerous and more attractive prey in Kokee are the rainbow trout that yearly entice fishermen to the cool streams of the mountains.

---

into the Kauai mountains. And each year many of the trout are taken during the fishing season that lasts in Kokee for 16 days, beginning on the first Saturday of August. During these weeks, the camps and lodges are full; reservations are made a full year in advance.

The Kokee environment contains both natural beauty and wilderness conflicts. Historically, efforts to make the area a national park have been consistently voted down by the local people, who fear the loss of their traditional use rights—hunting, fishing, plant-collecting. The range of habitats, from dryland shrub to lush rainforests and bogs, supports a multitude of native plants and animals. Many of these are in danger of extinction. The world's rarest bird—the oo bird—has been sighted only four times since 1982 and is now presumed to be gone forever. To camp in the developed camping area near the lodges, you will need a permit from the Division of State Parks. Additional, more remote camping areas are located in the surrounding backcountry, some of which is accessible only by hiking (see Hiking Areas). Other backcountry campsites can be reached by 4-wheel-drive vehicle (see Forest Reserve Campsites below).

Na Pali Coast State Park

This 6175-acre wilderness area is Kauai's showcase wilderness park, and it retains its authenticity and integrity by remaining one of the most inaccessible places in the Hawaiian Islands. Indeed, you can visit only by walking or by boat. While it is true that less adventurous souls can take a luxury cruise along the park's coast without ever setting foot on land or even getting wet, they experience only a surface veneer of the Na Pali wilderness. The depth of the place is grasped only by walking along the contours of the cliffs, resting against their flanks when weary, and, when hot with sweat, bathing in the streams that cascade from the mountaintops. Most people who hike along the Na Pali Coast go no farther than the first valley, 2 miles from the Kee Beach trailhead. This is an easy dayhike. But the trail eventually goes to Kalalau Valley, where it ends at a spectacular cliff-and-beach setting.

There are 4 camping areas along the Na Pali: Hanakapiai, Hanakoa, Kalalau, and Milolii. Hanakapiai Valley is the first valley you reach, and the camping area there is located in the valley near the beach. In the winter months the ocean currents sweep most of the sand away. Hanakoa is the second major valley, 4 miles beyond Hanakapiai. A camping area is located along the trail near the Hanakoa stream crossing. Some hikers spend overnight here, to

Hanakapiai Valley on the Na Pali coast

allow time to explore the upper valley, but the camping area is usually wet and often thick with mosquitos. It is wise to continue the additional 5 miles into Kalalau, where you will find the third Na Pali camping area. Kalalau is a magical place of tropical pandanus and planted fruit trees, sea caves, knife-edge ridges, waterfalls, bathing pools, and rich sunsets. You will want to spend a few days here. The final Na Pali Park camping area is at Milolii, accessible only by boat. The site is at the west end of the state park, along an isolated coastal stretch. The quiet and the vivid sunsets recommend this place for those who want to get away from things. Camping permits for Milolii are restricted to a 3-night maximum.

The maximum for camping in Na Pali Coast State Park is 7 nights. You will need a permit for each of the camping areas, obtainable at the state parks office in Lihue or Honolulu.

Polihale State Park

Where the Na Pali coast ends, Polihale begins. Southwestward, the cliffs recede and a broad, long stretch of white sand beach separates the shoreline from the inland fields of sugar cane and the kiawe scrublands. The 137-acre park is located at the end of a 5-mile dirt road, well-graded and easily passable, off Kaumualii Highway (Hwy 50) at the west end of the island. The primitive camping area contains several secluded tent sites amid the coastal dunes. Picnic areas, restrooms and water are conveniently near the campsites. The park can be extremely hot and dry during much of the day. The scrub kiawe that shelter the camping areas provide little relief in the full sun of midday. When the trades are strong, the winds can whip the sand into a nasty blast that ruins the outdoor experience. At more peaceful times, the wild coastline to the north, the overwhelming quiet, and the colorful sunsets that silhouette the forbidden offshore island of Niihau combine to make Polihale a rare and pleasant escape. Summers provide calm water for swimming and fishing. In the summer, you may want to sightsee elsewhere during the day and return to the Park in late afternoon to enjoy the cool and the color of the approaching evening. Secure camping permits in advance at the state park office in Lihue.

COUNTY PARKS

The County of Kauai maintains 8 parks that allow camping, all of them along the coast; there are no inland parks. The county beach parks vary considerably in size, the seclusion they offer, and the surrounding sights. Some of the parks, such as Lucy Wright Park in Waimea town, are next to major highways and provide little in the way of natural camping. Other parks, such as Anini Beach Park, provide quite nice and fairly private camping along lovely stretches of coast. The county parks do not compete with the state parks for excellent camping and hiking, but they serve as convenient areas to spend the night for those who want to stay out of hotels.

Tents and permits are required to camp at a county park. Information and reservations can be made in advance by writing, but permits must be acquired in person from the Parks Permit Section, Division of Parks and Recreation. Look for the building behind the Convention Center off Rice Street at the west end of downtown Lihue. Office hours are 7:45–4:30 weekdays. Permit fees are $3/person. After business hours, permits can be obtained at the Kauai Police Department, 3060 Umi Street in Lihue. You are limited to 8 consecutive days per month, and a maximum monthly stay of 12 days. If it is impossible to secure a permit in advance, it may be possible to pay the park attendant who daily checks for permits. They generally arrive at the park in the early morning. A $5/person charge will be assessed against anyone caught camping without a permit.

Haena Beach Park: This is one of the prettiest county parks on Kauai, located west of Hanalei, past the village of Haena, on Hwy 56. Tent sites occupy a grassy knoll above a wide beach. Rip currents prohibit swimming in the winter, but on calm summer days the swimming is fine. Firepits, restrooms, and outdoor showers are conveniently located on the five acres of parkland surrounding the tent sites. One of the main attractions of the Park is its proximity to the Na Pali coast trailhead. The Park itself contains some interesting features: the Maniniholo Dry Cave is located across the road from the tent area, and the stretches of beach west and east of the campground provide excellent areas for morning and evening strolls. Trailer camping is permitted at Haena Park.

Hanalei Beach Pavillion: Near the wharf on Hanalei Bay, a few minutes north of the village, is this beach park, which occasionally allows camping. The view across the bay toward the Na Pali Coast is nice, but the Park is not really recommended for overnight camping. It is close to town and it lacks privacy. Camping rules for this park also change frequently, and tent camping is often prohibited.

Anini Beach Park: In many ways, this is the nicest county park on Kauai. While it lacks the spectacular scenery of Haena Park, its quiet, secluded beach and the large offshore lagoon are quite lovely, particularly in the light before dawn. The tent sites are under shady ironwood trees next to the beach. A large grassy area between the campsites and the road is good for picnics and games. At low tide, most of the lagoon can be waded. (Wear tabies—the Japanese fishermen's shoes—or sneakers for protection on the sharp coral.) The Park's two and one-half acres contain picnic shelters and firepits. The location of the Park is fairly remote: travel on Kuhio Highway (Hwy 56) west of Kilauea village, cross the big bridge that spans the Kalihiwai River 2 miles beyond Kilauea, turn *makai* on Kalihiwai Road and then take a quick left onto Anini Road. Follow this to the roadend.

Anahola Beach Park: Along the north windward coast of the island, between Kapaa and Kilauea, is this small beach park that has a few camping areas. It is not recommended. Local homeless folks have taken over the park, and visitors (particularly *haoles*) are not welcome.

Hanamaulu Beach Park: This park, located near Lihue, gets the traffic and sometimes the trouble of a city park. The camping site is located at the end of Hanamaulu Road, off Hwy 56 in Hanamaulu village. Trailer camping is permitted.

Niumalu Beach Park: The park's location adjacent to Nawiliwili Harbor makes it convenient for visitors to Lihue. Elsewhere in the world, it would be a splendid place, but on Kauai it is only mediocre. To reach the park, travel on Rice Street (Hwy 50) south from Lihue for 2 miles. Turn right onto Mokihana Street near the boat harbor. Stay on this street past the coral fill and the small bridge until you reach the campsite at the far end of the picnic pavilion. Trailer camping is permitted.

Lucy Wright Park: You must be pretty desperate to camp here. The park is located only a few feet from Highway 50 in Waimea town, where the Waimea River enters the ocean. There is little about this park to recommend it for camping.

Salt Pond Beach Park: The best developed camping area on Kauai's south shore is here. To reach it, turn left onto Lele Road off Kaumualii Highway (Hwy 50) in Hanapepe, then right onto Lolo Kai road for one-quarter mile. Past the dry salt ponds is the beach and the camping ground. The waters offshore from the 6-acre beach park provide good winter swimming and summer surfing conditions.

PRIVATE CAMPING PARKS

There are two private camping parks on Kauai—the Camp Naue YMCA park and the Kahili Mountain Park. These have been described in the section on alternative lodging—cabins. In addition to the lodges, both parks provide tent sites for a small fee. Their privacy, security, and convenient location recommend them as camping sites. Camp Naue is located off Hwy 56 less than one mile east of Haena Beach Park (808/246-9090). Kahili Mountain Park is located in Koloa district one mile mauka off Hwy 50 beginning one-fourth mile west of the intersection of Maluhia Road and the highway. Watch for the sign that reads *Kahili Mountain Park*. 808/742-9921.

FOREST RESERVE CAMPSITES

There are several established campgrounds in state forest reserve backcountry regions. In most areas, backcountry camping is allowed 300 feet and more off the trail. Check the signboard at the trailhead for current restrictions—natural conditions change frequently, as do the policies regarding overnight use of the forest reserves. Some of the established campsites are accessible by 4-wheel-drive vehicle, others can be reached only by hiking some distance. The forest reserve camps that are the most accessible and those that are frequently used by hunters and fishermen may be badly trashed. It is disappointing to come upon these areas after hours spent in the pristine forest. They tell their own story of wilderness conflicts on Kauai. Many of the campsites, however, remain clean, and are stunning in their isolation and location. Several are simply set amid the most beautiful scenery in the world. Most forest reserves on the island are managed for day use only. Exceptions are in the Kokee forests and at the bottom of Waimea Canyon, where several back-country camping sites are located. To camp in one of the forest reserve campgrounds, you must first secure a permit, available free in person at the Division of Forestry office, located in the same building as the county parks permit office. Or write the Hawaii Department of Land and Natural Resources, Division of Forestry, P.O. Box 1671, Lihue, HI 96766. Camping is limited to 4 nights within a 30-day period, and no more than 2 consecutive nights at one campsite.

Kokee Area

There are three campgrounds in the Na Pali—Kona Forest Reserve adjacent to the Kokee State Park. In addition to their proximity to state park hiking trails, the campgrounds are near the Alakai Wilderness Preserve—a superior wildland. Kawaikoi Camp and Sugi Grove campsite are both located near the trailhead of the Kawaikoi Stream Trail. The Sugi Grove campsite is the better of the two, with tent sites tucked into a lovely hemlock forest situated above broad and clear Kawaikoi Stream. This is a lovely place, cool due to its upland location (3500 feet), with a smell reminiscent of the north woods. A third campsite is Camp 10, near Mohihi Falls at the trailhead of the Mohihi-Waialae Trail. All three Na Pali-Kona campgrounds are accessible by 4-wheel-drive vehicles. During hunting season (hunting days are subject to change—check with the Division of Forestry and Wildlife) and trout fishing season (the first half of August), these campgrounds are full of enthusiastic sportsmen. Plan your trip to avoid these peak times, or stick to the weekdays.

Waimea Canyon

There are 5 campgrounds near or at the bottom of Waimea Canyon, in the Puu Ka Pele Forest Reserve. Wiliwili Camp is located at the bottom of the Kukui Trail. This is a popular day hike area, so the campsite is not very private, but its location is convenient for those exploring the canyon floor. Three quarters of a mile south of Wiliwili Camp, along a short jog off the Waimea Canyon Trail, is Poachers Camp. This site is frequented by hunters in 4-wheel-drive vehicles who travel up from Waimea along a private canyon-floor jeep road. Avoid it, if possible. A third campsite, the Kaluahaulu Camp, is located at the junction of the Waimea Canyon Trail and the Koaie Valley Trail, about one-half mile up the Waimea

Waimea Canyon, "Grand Canyon of the Pacific"

Hawaiian Visitors Bureau

River from the end of the Kukui Trail. The other 2 campsites in Waimea Canyon are both located along the Koaie Stream, on the Koaie Canyon Trail. These are the best sites in the canyon for seclusion and a wilderness feeling. They are accessible only by foot, and they remain in primitive condition.

OTHER CAMPING AREAS

Many local residents know their island well, and they know about spots to camp that visitors can only dream about: those special, out-of-the-way places that only insiders get to. The camping areas described above are official and well-established. But let your imagination take you to the other places. Check around with local hikers and outdoorspersons to find alternative spots. One place that has become popular for both local residents and visitors is a stretch of secluded beach near Kilauea called Secret Beach. It is secret no longer, and on road maps it is called Kauapea Beach. It is one of the last of Kauai's hippie beaches, attracting counterculture types, nudists, and campers who want to slip through the bureacracy of the parklands. The setting is superb: a mile of crescent sand beach hemmed in by green cliffs and blue ocean, bounded on the east by the Kilauea National Wildlife Refuge and on the west by steep cliffs. To get to the beach, take the road to the Kilauea National Wildlife

---

Kalalau is a magical place of tropical pandanus and planted fruit trees, sea caves, knife-edge ridges, waterfalls, bathing pools, and rich sunsets.

Refuge, and pass through Kilauea village to Kauapea Road. Take this road to the left for exactly 0.3 mile and look for a trail to the beach along the fence on the makai side of the road. You can park on the roadside.

Environmental Groups

1000 Friends of Kauai: This is the most comprehensive environmental action group on Kauai. Founded in 1979, its members work on land use issues, environmental preservation, education, and community involvement in environmental affairs. Specific programs address aquaculture development, sustainable farming, recycling, freshwater stream research, and beach access rights. The group relies on a network of volunteers for its grants program, workshops, and community work. It also regularly publishes a newsletter, *Ka Leo Hoaaloha* (Voice of a Friend), that goes to members. Contact: 1000 Friends of Kauai, P.O. Box 99, Hanalei, HI 96714.

The Alliance: A loose network of conservation-minded folks whose agenda includes lobbying in local and state government for environmental causes. Contact them at: P.O. Box 399, Koloa, HI 96756. 808/742-7477.

Heiaus

Along the southern shores of Kauai are many heiau sites. Only a few of these can be visited, though, because most are on private property. Several heiaus exist at spectacular sites elsewhere on the island, such as on the west coast at Polihale, along the east coast at the impressive Wailua complex, and on the north shore near Kee beach.

Haena Heiau: At the end of Hwy 56 on Kauai's north shore, beyond Hanalei, is Kee Beach in Haena State Park. This is the beginning of the hiking trail along the majestic Na Pali coast, and a rare hula heiau is located here. The terraced platforms at the base of a steep cliff command an outstanding view of the ocean, the coastline and the northern skies. The broad, level platform in the center of the heiau near the cliff face is known as Lohiau's Dancing Pavillion. Lohiau was legendary chief of Kauai and lover of Pele. Myth connects the dance initially performed here with the epic journey of Pele and her younger sister Hiiaka through the Hawaiian archipelago, before their falling out over Lohiau. Indeed, the heiau still is actively used by hula dance groups, called *halaus*. The site is blustery with salt spray and bordered by lush vegetation—a lovely place, particularly at sunset.

Hoahi Heiau: Two miles west of Poipu along the coastal road over Waikomo Stream, adjacent to Hoai Bay, this heiau marks the birthplace of Prince Jonah Kuhio Kalanianaole—one of Kauai's most renowned royal persons. The site has five platforms built upon pahoehoe lava and includes a fire pit and stone worship items. Fishponds, a fishing shrine, house sites, sports grounds, and agricultural terraces occupy land around the heiau.

Kihouna Heiau: A wall-enclosed temple complex along the shoreline, probably a fishing shrine according to local legend, is located at Kihouna Point, Poipu, in Koloa district. Two hotels—Poipu Beach Hotel and Waiohai Hotel—currently border the heiau and more or less maintain it. It is accessible by passing through hotel grounds to the shoreline.

Nualolo Kai Heiau: Accessible only by boat, this heiau is the most impressive one along the remote Na Pali coast. It was most likely an agricultural heiau, used for planting and harvest celebrations by the large farming and fishing community that resided here about 600 years ago. The heiau, composed of three terraces at the base of a steep cliff face, sits among other reminders of the past: enclosures, walls and mounds, house platforms, and trails. The fringing reef offshore supplied the early residents with fish and shellfish, coral for implements, and the gonads of sea urchins—a delicacy eaten with poi.

Polihale Heiau: At the west end of Kauai, where Hwy 50 appears to fade into the sun setting over Niihau, Polihale State Park is set amid sand dunes and a long stretch of beach (called on many travel maps Barking Sands Beach because of the squeaking sound the fine-grained sand makes when you walk on it). At the north end of the beach, past the picnic pavilions, is Polihale Heiau, a 4-terraced structure situated at the base of Polihale cliff below Puu ka Pele Forest Reserve. The site is in good shape, with sturdy walled enclosures, and is paved throughout with coral and iliili—small, round, water-worn pebbles. The function of the heiau is unknown, although it clearly played an important part in religious observances of local residents.

Wailua Complex of Heiaus: One of the most important prehistoric sites in the Hawaiian Islands and the most sacred place on the island of Kauai, residence of former *alii* and now designated a national historical landmark, the complex of heiaus at Wailua is simply outstanding. Take Hwy 56 north of Lihue to Hwy 580, then go a short distance mauka along the Wailua River to Wailua River State Park. There are a number of heiaus and other settlement sites along the way. The cultural complex at Wailua has direct legendary connections to Polynesia, mentioned in accounts of the epic voyages between Hawaii and the Society Islands in the 12th and 13th centuries. The last major dynasty of Hawaiian royalty, including Queen Liluokalani, came from Wailua. A commercially reconstructed Hawaiian settlement with village houses, meeting halls, taro fields, and shrines is located in the valley along the Wailua River. If this commercial fabrication puts you off, avoid it, but the Wailua complex of heiaus mentioned below is well worth a visit. You'll need to explore a bit on your own here; not all the heiaus are well-marked.

One heiau in this complex is Hikinaakala ("rising of the sun") heiau. The ancient name for this seaside heiau is Hauola (lit., "dew of life"), a place of refuge in times of war. The structure covers one acre and includes a series of petroglyphs visible at low tide. It is exceptional for being the only heiau of the Wailua complex that is adjacent to the ocean.

At Kapaa in eastern Kauai

Holoholoku Heiau: North of the Wailua River on the south side of Kuamoo Road just beyond Coco Palms Hotel is a *luakini* temple (a place of human sacrifice) that also served as a place of refuge. Nearby are large sacred birthstones upon which the *alii* mothers bore their children. The ancient name of the heiau is Ka Lae o Ka Manu, meaning crest of the bird. The site includes a sacrificial stone and the enclosed birthing sanctum, where kings and chiefs were born, attended by majestic ceremony, chants, and the playing of drums.

Malae Heiau: The largest surviving heiau on Kauai, covering over 2 acres, is located a short distance inland on the south side of the river in a cane field across Highway 56 from Lydgate State Park.

Poliahu Heiau: Situated high on the precipitous north bank of the Wailua River, 1.5 miles upstream from Holoholoku Heiau, this heiau commands an impressive view of the other heiaus. It was a luakini temple, used for human sacrifice, and the site includes altars, an oracle tower, house sites and platforms.

Hiking Areas

The established hiking trails on Kauai traverse a wide range of environments: coasts, mountains, foothills, and canyons. Some hikes take a few hours, others take several days. The hiking regions described below have been selected because of their uniqueness, because of the opportunities that they present to enjoy and learn about different wildlands, or because of the beauty they make accessible. They are organized according to type of environment: mountain, canyon, foothills, or coast. On the windward north-east shores, the land is wet and wild, and the weather is often windy and usually cloudy or rainy. The forests are lush and the trails are often muddy. On the leeward shores, conditions are much drier, sometimes desertlike, and it is hot during midday. Drought-tolerant plants and barren landscapes are common. When selecting a region to hike in, keep in mind these general conditions and remember that the terrain is varied and the weather changes rapidly.

In the mountains around Kokee, conditions depend on elevation and upon exposure to the rain-bearing trade winds. The mountain trails in the upland forests are cool and quiet places, a contrast to the blustery coastal trails. Waimea Canyon presents yet another environment. In many places it is bare of vegetation. The rocky ledges and deep ravines are desertlike in appearance, and the pastel cliffsides resemble the mainland Southwest enough to warrant, along with its depth, Waimea Canyon's title as the "Grand Canyon of the Pacific".

To plan a hike, a guidebook is helpful. This chapter refers you to Kauai hiking areas, but it does not present complete trail descriptions, nor does it refer to every trail that exists. Several guides are available. The newly-updated *Hawaiian Hiking Trails* by Craig Chisholm includes a chapter on Kauai trails, with 10 hiking routes described and mapped. *Hiking Kauai*, another recently-revised book, includes 14 hiking areas, and describes several dozen trails. A new series of pocket guidebooks by Magic Fishes Press includes Hawaiian hiking guides and camping information. *The Kauai Guide to Hiking* by Kathy Valier is an excellent little guide to less traveled trails. In addition to travel directions the book includes sections on the natural and cultural history of the hiking regions. Wilderness Press is publishing a new Kauai guide by Kathy Morey in 1990. Hawaii Nature Guides publishes trail pamphlets for the Kokee and Na Pali hiking regions. These brief, interpretive trail maps can be ordered directly from Hawaii Nature Guides, P.O. Box 70, Kealia, HI 96751.

Mountain Hiking Areas

Most of Kauai's premier mountain hikes are in Kokee State Park, in Waimea Canyon State Park, in the adjacent forest reserves above the coastal mountains (Na Pali-Kona Forest Reserve), or in the forest reserves above Waimea Canyon (Puu Ka Pele Forest Reserve). You can expect cool temperatures due to the elevations. In Kokee the wind chill factor can bring winter day temperatures down to 40 degrees F., and winter nighttime temperatures regularly drop to the mid-30s. The northeast upland trails are wetter than those to the south, and on many days the higher areas will be socked in by clouds. Do not let these wet conditions deter you. The hiking trails lead through majestic forests of native plants and birds, and the frequent mists lend further appeal to these primordial settings. But be prepared with raingear, a hat, good walking shoes or boots, and sunscreen (for the spaces between the clouds).

The base for the mountain hikes is Kokee State Park. Trail guides and maps are available at the natural history museum (open daily from 10–4). At the ranger station near the Park center you can obtain information on current trail conditions.

In Kokee the wind chill factor can bring winter day temperatures down to 40 degrees F., and winter nighttime temperatures regularly drop to the mid-30s.

Along the trails in this mountain section, you will hike through stands of native Hawaiian trees and communities of introduced species. The trail elevations range from 2400 feet to over 4000 feet. The natural distributions of forest plants correspond to the elevational differences and to unique local habitat conditions. Native upland ohia-koa forests (*Metrosideros polymorpha—Acacia koa*) occur along the ridgetops and upper valley slopes. These trees form the upper canopy beneath which grow a profusion of small trees, bushes, ferns and flowers. Tangles of uluhe fern (*Dicranopteris linearis*) often form impenetrable thickets in disturbed areas near the trails. The maile vine (*Alyxia oliviformis*), found along the forest floor, is a favorite plant of the Hawaiians, dedicated to the hula goddess Laka, and used to make fragrant leis for special occasions. Like the colorful, sweet-smelling plumeria, the maile is a member of the periwinkle family.

As you walk through the Kokee forests, notice where native species are dominant and where the invaders have made strong inroads. The redwood trees and sugi cedars that grow near the Kawaikoi stream were introduced in the 1930s by the Civilian Conservation Corps to reforest clear-cut slopes. Local gardeners brought to Kokee ginger, nasturtium, and banana passion fruit to plant around house sites. These plants escaped into the forest, where they now compete with native Hawaiian plants.

Kokee's forests contain some most unusual plants. For example, the silversword-related iliau (*Wilkesia gymnoxiphium*), is a plant with sword leaves and silvery hairs that grows on the dry ridges above Waimea Canyon. It blooms once in its life and then dies. The intriguing Naupaka kuahiwi (*Scaevola procera*), blooms with only a "half-flower". Legend suggests that it is betrothed to the Naupaka kahakai (*Scaevola taccada*), also with a half-flower, that grows on the sands of distant beaches.

The forests of Kokee harbor a delightful community of birds. The apapane fills the forests with its song as it scurries from ohia tree to ohia tree in search of nectar from the salmon-colored flowers. The iiwi has a loud, harsh, and squeaky voice, offsetting like a rusty hinge the melodious song of the apapane. The rasping scream of the white-tailed tropic bird is often heard in Waimea Canyon. The flute song of the oo bird in Alakai Swamp has not been regularly heard since 1977, and the bird may be now extinct. *Hawaiian Forest Plants* by Mark Merlin is a good guide to plant identification. *Hawaii's Birds* is a useful field guide for birders.

Kokee State Park Hiking Areas

There are 10 hiking trails in the state park that are maintained for visitors. They vary from half-hour nature walks to full-day journeys (allowing for rest breaks and a leisurely pace). Most of them traverse gently rolling to moderate terrain.

Black Pipe Trail: 0.4 mile. An access off Halemanu Road to the Canyon Trail, the trail traverses the upper canyon rim, through koa forest and past native hibiscus and iliau.

Canyon Trail: 1.7 miles. Follows the canyon's north rim from the Cliff Trail to the Kumuwela Lookout. Good views all the way to the ocean.

Cliff Trail: 0.1 mile. A short walk off Halemanu road to a canyon lookout.

Ditch Trail: 3.5 miles. The longest single trail in the park, connecting Kumuwela Road and Camp 10-Mohihi Road. Views of Poomau Canyon through the upland forests.

Halemanu-Kokee Trail: 1.2 miles. A self-guiding nature trail through native koa and ohio-lehua forest, and the Waineke Swamp. A popular, easy stroll.

Kaluapuhi Trail: 2.0 miles. When plum-picking was popular in Kokee, this was a heavily used trail because it leads to a plum-tree grove. The trailhead is on Hwy 550 between the state park and the Kalalau lookout.

Hawaiian Visitors Bureau

Honopu Beach in northwest Kauai, one of the most inaccessible beaches in the world

Kumuwela Trail: 0.8 mile. An access trail off Camp 10 Road, leading to the Canyon Trail and the Ditch Trail.

Nature Trail: 0.1 mile. A short loop through the native forest behind the state park museum and picnic areas.

Puukaohelo-Berry Flat Loop: 2.0 miles. A forest trail through native ohia-lehua and koa, and redwood and sugi pine. It is a popular loop off the Camp 10-Mohihi Road.

Waininiua Trail: 0.5 mile. A forest trail used mainly as an access route between the Kokee State Park camping area and the hiking trails near Kumuwela Ridge.

Forest Reserve Trails

Six good trails lead through the forest reserves adjacent to Kokee State Park. A seventh, the Nualolo Trail, is closed at this writing. Check the ranger station at Kokee for current trail information.

Alakai Swamp Trail: 3.5 miles. This is a premier wilderness trail that leads through the swamp of the Alakai Wilderness Preserve—a primordial forest bog that sits on the floor of a huge, ancient caldera. Its elevation (4000 feet) has kept out disease-bearing mosquitoes, so the native bird life is luxurious here. Numerous swamp-adapted native plants grow here in the absence of foreign species, and they give the place an otherworldly look. Wet conditions prevail; thigh-deep mud is to be expected, so wear raingear and appropriate

clothing. The Alakai Swamp trailhead is off Camp 10—Mohihi Road
at the Alakai Picnic Area. Alternatively, you can intersect the Alakai
Trail from the Pihea Trail, which begins at the Hwy 550 roadend.
The trail ends at Kilohana—a viewpoint from which, on clear days,
you can just about see forever. Certainly the views of Wainiha Valley
and Hanalei Valley are outstanding.

Awaawapuhi Trail: 3.1 miles. The trail begins on Hwy 550, one
mile north of the Kokee State Park campgrounds. The trailhead is
clearly signed. The trail traverses upland dry forest before descending to 2400 feet at the coastal overlook. Panoramic views of
Awaawapuhi and Nualolo valleys reward you at the end of the trail.

Kawaikoi Stream Trail: 1.7 miles. This easy loop trail along
Kawaikoi Stream and through the adjacent upland forests is one of
the most picturesque trails in the mountains.

Mohihi Waialae Trail: 4.0 miles. This trail begins at the end of the
Camp 10—Mohihi Road, and skirts the southern edge of the Alakai
Swamp Wilderness Preserve. It's only marginally maintained, and in
rainy weather the dangerous stream crossings close the trail.

Pihea Trail: 3.7 miles. This trail into the Alakai Swamp begins along
the Kaunuohua Ridge, below the Puu o Kila lookout at the Hwy 550
roadend. It skirts the back of Kalalau Valley, providing splendid
views, before heading into the swamp and linking up with the Alakai
Swamp Trail.

Poomau Canyon Lookout Trail: 0.3 mile. A short walk from Camp
10—Mohihi Road to a canyon lookout.

Canyon Hiking Areas

Waimea Canyon is famous for its resemblance to the Grand
Canyon of Arizona. It is a river-eroded chasm, formed by the
Waimea River and its tributaries. A trail system descends through
the dizzying heights of the gorge and then follows the Waimea River
and the smaller streams that feed it. The hikes are through generally
dry, rocky terrain, but they afford superb views of the canyon walls,
streams, and waterfalls.

Iliau Nature Loop: 0.3 mile. A self-guiding nature trail that traverses native upland scrub vegetation. Excellent views of Waimea
Canyon and the tributary Waialae canyon.

Kukui Trail: 2.5 miles. This is the main trail into the canyon. It
begins off Hwy 550 near the Iliau Picnic Shelter, and descends 2000
feet to the canyon floor, where it links up with the Waimea Canyon
Trail at the Wiliwili campground.

Koaie Canyon Trail: 3.0 miles. The trail begins at the Kaluahaulu campground along the Waimea Canyon Trail. It follows Koaie Stream through a scenic canyon to the Lonomea campground. During rainy weather high water in the Waimea River may close the trail.

Waimea Canyon Trail: 8 miles. Most of this trail is on private property. The upper part is in Waimea State Park, easily accessible via the Kukui Trail. The lower section, leading to the coastal town of Waimea, requires a special permit. Inquire at the ranger station in Kokee State Park.

Windward and North Coast Foothills Hiking Areas

The ridgelines between Mt. Waialeale and the east and north coasts provide good hiking areas. Many of these are fair-weather hikes; when its raining, the trails are muddy and unpleasant, with no views.

Hanalei-Okolehau Trail: 2.3 miles. This route provides panoramic views of Hanalei Valley and the north shore area, including the Hanalei National Wildlife Refuge. To reach the trailhead, take Ahiki Road (intersects Highway 56 at the iron bridge below Hanalei National Wildlife Refuge overlook) up Hanalei Valley to the cemetery. Park below the cemetery and follow the powerline-maintenance trail up the slope. At the top, the trail follows the ridge to the Kaukaopua lookout.

Kalepa Ridge Trail: 2–4 miles. Offers panoramic views of east Kauai, from Mt. Waialeale to the coast. This is the driest of the

---

This landscape, softened by lush vegetation, together with the abundant waterfalls, the numerous sandy beaches, and the absence of a large human population give Kauai its unique character.

---

windward coastal trails, with no major stream crossings. Permission to cross private land is required from the Lihue Plantation Co., (P.O. Box 751, 2973 Kele St., Lihue, HI 96766. 808/245-7325). The trail begins near the town of Hanamaulu, 2 miles north of Lihue. With permit in hand, proceed to Peter Rayno Park on Kuhio Highway (Hwy 56), where you must park your car. Walk for a few minutes down Hulei Road. Cross the cemetery and follow the paved cane haul road to the lower crest of Kalepa Ridge. The hiking trail begins at the ridgetop.

Kalalau Beach—end of the trail

Kuilau Trail: 2.1 miles. This hiking trail begins at the Keahua Forestry Arboretum (see section on botanic parks), near the end of Hwy 580 (this is the road that follows the Wailua River to Opaekaa Falls). The trail offers splendid views toward Mt. Waialeale of the windward mountains.

For other, less-traveled hiking trails along the windward and north coast areas, refer to *The Kauai Guide to Hiking* by Kathy Valier.

Coastal Hiking Areas

Short hikes along the coast at Polihale State Park and Anini County Beach Park are pleasant diversions. The main coastal hiking trail is along the north coast cliffs from Kee Beach to Kalalau Valley, called the Na Pali or Kalalau Trail.

Kalalau Trail: This hiking trail is in a class by itself. From the trailhead at Kee Beach in Haena State Park, the trail skirts the majestic Na Pali Coast, a dramatic landscape of towering sea cliffs and deep valleys, for 11 miles to Kalalau Valley. The Kalalau Trail, an ancient Hawaiian route, is the only land route along this rugged coast, crossing 5 valleys and skirting numerous precipitous cliffs. Although it is well-maintained, much of the trail is steep and narrow, and a few difficult passages should be approached cautiously. The first section of the trail, to Hanakapiai Beach (2 miles one way), is a popular day hike for fit walkers. The stretch between Hanakapiai and the next major valley, Hanakoa (4 more miles), requires more strenuous hiking, with numerous stream crossings and steep switchbacks. The final 5 miles to Kalalau are the most beautiful, and they reward the hiker with outstanding views of the 4000-foot-high fluted cliffs of the remote Na Pali. At the end of the trail is Kalalau Valley—an exquisite area with numerous opportunities to explore lush forests, ancient Hawaiian settlement sites, caves and coasts. The entire 11 miles to Kalalau can be covered in a day by good hikers. Many people divide the hike into two days by stopping at either Hanakapiai or Honokoa. Camping permits, required for all Na Pali coast campsites, can be obtained from the Division of State Parks in either Honolulu or Lihue. During the summer, when the weather is good, you will need to make a reservation well in advance. The Kalalau Trail has become very popular in recent years.

The entire 11 miles to Kalalau can be covered in a day by good hikers.

This trail is covered in detail in the Hawaii hiking guidebooks. For an excellent companion book, see *On The Na Pali Coast* by Kathy Valier. It provides a wealth of detail about the natural and cultural history of this coastal region.

Miscellaneous Attractions

Kilohana: If you want to glimpse a bit of Kauai's agricultural past, this tourist attraction might interest you. It is a 35-acre historical showcase of rural life based on the sugar economy. The grounds contain a working farm, a century-old plantation camp, flower gardens, and various commercial enterprises including retail shops and art galleries. But is it authentic? Probably. A stroll through the estate gives one a feel for the way life must have been among the landed wealthy during Kauai's sugar heyday. The Wilcox family owned the estate, which in the 1930s included 26,000 acres of sugar cane. Kilohana is located along Hwy 50 (Kaumualii Highway), 1.5 miles west of Lihue. Admission is free and the plantation is open daily at 9:30 a.m. For information, call 808/245-5608, or write: Kilohana, P.O. Box 3121, Lihue, HI 96766.

Natural Foods

Hanalei Health and Natural Foods: They stock a good supply of bulk foods for the hippies in Hanalei, the yuppies in Princeville, and backpackers heading for Kalalau. Open daily 8 a.m.–9 p.m.; located in the Ching Young Village shopping plaza in Hanalei. 808/826-6990.

ırtin Farm Fresh Fruit Stand: Delicious fresh fruits are available at the roadside stand on Kilauea Road between Kilauea village and the national wildlife refuge. They use the honor system at the counter—you select your items and then you put your money in the bucket.

Nature Tours and Outdoor Excursions

The splendid environmental opportunities on Kauai support a growing number of persons who lead excursions into the wilderness, including kayak outfitters, trail guides, hunting and fishing guides, and others. Some of the programs they offer simply cannot be duplicated on your own, because of difficult logistics, bulky equipment needs, or restricted entry into natural areas.

KAYAK TOURS

As on many of the other Hawaiian islands, kayaks have become a popular way of exploring Kauai's remote coastal wilderness. On Kauai, they are used also to explore the otherwise inaccessible parts of Hanalei, Wailua, and Huleia rivers. The various tour agencies on Kauai that specialize in kayak excursions offer competitive prices and similar equipment setups but they vary in destinations and in quality of guides. The coastal sections of Kauai vary tremendously in terms of difficulty of travel, water quality, wildlife, and beaches. Research the many options to select the journey that suits you best.

Hawayaking: A new twist on an old design, the "hawayak" is a glass-bottom, hard-shell kayak vessel that holds one person. Luana of Hawaii leads hawayaking tours into the Hanalei National Wildlife Refuge. It's a bit gimmicky and not well thought-out (most of the refuge sights are above water). The same company offers kayak trips exclusively for honeymooners. Contact: Luana of Hawaii, P.O. Box 1008, Hanalei, HI 96714. 808/826-9195.

Island Adventure: They offer tours of the Huleia National Wildlife Refuge, which includes the Huleia River, the Menehune Fish Pond, and the filming site for "Raiders of the Lost Ark." Apart from Indiana Jones' fantasies, the tour allows you access into the 240-acre Huleia Wildlife Refuge. The excursions last about 3 hours and cost $32/person. Island Adventure is located at the Small Boat Harbor in Nawiliwili Harbor, Lihue. Call: 808/245-9662.

Kayak Kauai: The folks who own and operate Kayak Kauai are the kayaking professionals on the island. Together they have over 20 years of kayaking experience along the island's coasts, and they know the coasts as few others do. If you want to go alone, they rent a variety of kayaks: Metzelers, Scuppers, Puffins, Chinooks, and Sea Scape IIs. Rentals cost $35–$75/day.

What they do best, however, is guide tours along the Na Pali and other coastal wilderness areas. The guided coastal treks vary from day trips ($95/person) to 5-day excursions ($625/person), all inclusive. In addition to the Na Pali Coast, kayak treks are available for many other coastal areas, including the Kilauea National Wildlife Refuge and the remote Kipu Kai region on the south shore (good for winter months, when the north shore closes during storms and heavy surf). They also guide trips to the Hanalei National Wildlife Refuge, to inland rivers, and to remote barrier reefs. Kayak Kauai also offers occasional 5-day kayak trips to Molokai ($650/person). They have two stores: downtown Kapaa on Hwy 56 (Kuhio Hwy) near the Aku Road intersection (808/822-9179); and in Hanalei, on Main Street (808/826-9844); or write them at P.O. Box 508, Hanalei, HI 96714.

Outfitters Kauai: Sea kayaking tours along the south shore can be arranged through Outfitters Kauai, in Poipu. Three-hour tours of the south shore near Poipu cost $38/person. Contact: P.O. Box 1149, Koloa, HI 96756. 808/742-9667.

BICYCLING

Kauai's roads vary in quality for cycle touring. The windward coastal road (Hwy 56) between Lihue and Hanalei traverses spec-

Lumahai Beach, on Kauai's north shore

Hawaiian Visitors Bureau

tacular terrain, but the traffic is heavy and the road shoulders are narrow. Most of the time your view is limited to the pavement in front of your bike or to the front tire. The Kokee road (Hwy 550) is a steep uphill grind, but the views are outstanding and the road is wide enough to allow cyclists the chance to relax occasionally and enjoy the vistas. Highway 50 between Waimea and Polihale State Park is a wide, level stretch of road that is excellent for biking, except for the last 2 miles of gravel road that lead into the Park, which are more suited to mountain bikes than touring cycles.

Bicycles Kauai: Bike sales and service are available here, as well as a limited selection of tour and mountain bike rentals. They provide accessories for touring cyclists. Located in Kapaa at 1379 Kuhio Hwy (Hwy 56). 808/822-3315.

Bike Cruise and Snorkel: Guided bike tours of the north shore, with options for snorkeling, are arranged by North Shore Bike Cruise and Snorkel Inc. They are an all-day affair that includes a beach barbeque and swimming. They provide a shuttle service and full equipment. Contact: P.O. Box 1192, Kapaa, HI 96746. 808/822-1582.

HIKING

There are no fulltime guide services to accompany backpackers on Kauai, but several are in the works. Outfitters Kauai and Jungle Bob's (see Outdoor Equipment and Supplies) can help you plan an itinerary. Hawaii Nature Guides publishes a series of small, informative nature and hiking guides that will lead you into the backcountry. They cover both coastal and mountain destinations, providing insights into the cultural and natural history of the places, as well as giving clear trail descriptions. For a listing of available guides, contact: Hawaii Nature Guides, P.O. Box 70, Kealia, HI 96751.

HORSEBACK RIDING

Two stables provide trail rides on Kauai, one on the south shore and one on the north shore. They offer quite different experiences for the rider.

CJM Country Stables: They lead riders along the coast east of Poipu to secluded beaches, panoramic headlands, and secluded forests. Rides vary in length from 1-hour ($25/person) to 3-hour breakfast rides ($55/person). Contact: 5598 Tapa Street, Koloa, HI 96756. 808/245-6666.

Pooku Stables: Coastal and inland valley rides on Princeville Ranch are arranged by Pooku Stables. Rates vary from $23/person for 1-hour valley rides to $70/person for a 3-hour waterfall picnic ride. Contact: P.O. Box 888, Hanalei, HI 96714. 808/826-6777.

OCEAN TOURS

The wilderness coasts of Kauai are accessible by means other than kayaks and swimming. An entire flotilla of cruise ships ply the coasts, particularly the Na Pali section. These ships compete with the gentler ways of journeying to the remote spots. There is a great deal of controversy over the regulation of motorized boat access to different spots along the north coast. Conservations want to maintain this region as wilderness for both ecological and aesthetic reasons. On the other side are the charter catamarans and zodiac rafts that operate out of Hanalei. These boats take passengers on cruises along the Na Pali coast, regularly dropping people off at secluded beaches.

Captain Zodiac's was the first of the rubberized raft expeditions. In the past decade, numerous outfits have arisen, creating problems for coastal wildlands by exceeding the carrying capacity of some natural areas and endangering wildlife habitats—and thus threatening the "wilderness experience" for those who enter the area by nonmechanized means. Nonetheless, the zodiacs are the only practical way for many persons to see the coast, and the battle between coastal preservationists and commercial cruise operators will likely continue. If you choose to take a zodiac or a charter cruise—and there is no doubt that they are exhilarating experiences—you might consider the implications of doing so.

Captain Zodiac: They are the originator of the Cousteau-style Na Pali zodiac cruises, and their itinerary has grown to include a variety of half-day and full-day excursions, whale-watching tours, backpacker/hiker drop-off services along the Na Pali, snorkeling expeditions, and land-sea combinations that allow you to stretch your feet on coastal walking trails. Visit them at their office in Hanalei, on Kuhio Highway (Hwy 56) near the Ching Young Village shopping center, or contact: Captain Zodiac, P.O. Box 456, Hanalei, HI 96714. 808/826-9371.

Na Pali Adventures: They use catamarans for a faster, smoother trip. If that is what you're after, contact them in Hanalei on Kuhio Highway (Hwy 56), adjacent to Aku Road; or call 808/826-6804.

Pacific Safari: They are exceptional in offering moonlight cruises that include a night dive to see the dark reef mysteries. Seasonal specials include whale-watching excursions. Contact: Safari Cruises, Ltd., P.O. Box 1287, 3483 Weli Weli Road, Koloa, HI 96756. 808/742-7033.

Fishing Guides: Kauai's inland waters offer freshwater bass fishing. Two popular outfits conduct fishing tours on the inland reservoirs and private lakes.

Bass Guides of Kauai: P.O. Box 3525, Lihue, Kauai, HI 96766. 808/822-1405.

Cast and Catch Fresh Water Bass Guides: P.O. Box 1386, Koloa, HI 96756. 808/742-7548 or toll-free, 800/443-9180.

There are numerous ocean fishing charters on Kauai. Check the harbors at Hanalei and Nawiliwili for excursion boats.

AIRBORNE TOURS

There are numerous helicopter tours on Kauai. I recommend none of them for the simple reason that they ruin the wild for others' enjoyment, with their low-flying tactics and noisy copters. There is an alternative way to see part of the island by air: Tradewinds Glider Flights can take you on an aerial tour of south and west Kauai by quiet glider. The price is $45/person for a 20 minute ride. Their office is located next to the Green Gardens Restaurant on Kaumualii Highway (Hwy 50) in Waimea, or contact: P.O. Box 2099, Lihue, HI 96766. 808/335-5086 or toll-free, 800-2-GLIDER.

FOUR-WHEEL DRIVE TOURS

It's risky to recommend an off-road vehicle tour in a book on natural opportunities, but the roads in Kokee State Park that are travelled by Kauai Mountain Tours are designed for jeeps and trucks with 4-wheel drive. They take you to the back of Waimea Canyon and into outstanding forests of eucalyptus, redwood, pine, koa, and ohia. The tour provides time for leisurely nature walks and picnicking. Contact: P.O. Box 3069, Lihue, HI 96766. 808/245-7225.

Outdoor Equipment and Supplies

A few new shops selling backcountry supplies have opened on Kauai. They service both the north and south shores.

Jungle Bob's: This is the first retail store on Kauai to consistently maintain a wide selection of backcountry equipment and supplies. They have a well-informed staff who can assist you with your preparations for hiking and camping on the island. In addition to name-brand gear sales, they rent backpacks, tents, stoves, coolers and other smaller items. Fuel for camp stoves can be purchased in bulk. Open 7 days a week. They have 2 locations—one in Hanalei at Ching Young Village shopping plaza (808/826-6664), and one in Kekaha at the Waimea Canyon Plaza (808/337-9331.

Outfitters Kauai: This is a new outfit that serves a wide range of backcountry needs. They rent mountain bikes for $25/day, including helmet, water bottle, maps, and car racks that fit rental cars. Name-brand backpacking gear is available, as well as maps, stove fuel and freeze-dried foods. They also rent kayaks for both river and ocean journeys, and they lead kayaking tours along the Na Pali coast and on the navigable inland rivers (see Kauai Kayak Tours). Located at the Kiahuna Shopping Village in Poipu. Contact: Outfitters Kauai, P.O. Box 1149, Koloa, HI 96756. 808/742-9667.

Pedal-n-Paddle: They rent canoes, kayaks, bicycles, snorkeling gear, and other water sports equipment but mainly "play toys"; not serious backcountry gear. Prices vary according to length of rental. Contact them at Ching Young Village shopping plaza in Hanalei. To reserve equipment in advance, write Pedal 'n Paddle, P.O. Box 1413, Hanalei, HI 96714. 808/826-9069.

Snorkeling and Surfing

Kauai has many of the most scenic beaches in the Hawaiian Islands. Unfortunately, the offshore waters are often dangerous due to steep bottoms, lack of a protective reef, and strong currents. Winter conditions of high surf preclude water activities for all but expert surfers. Summer months bring calmer water, but snorkeling is limited by uninteresting undersea terrain. At all beaches, safety varies with the season. Check with locals before venturing into unknown waters. The snorkeling and surfing spots listed below are the most popular, but they require caution.

SNORKELING
Poipu Beach Park: Many people snorkel here because it is usually safe, but water quality and undersea scenery are marginal. Accessible off Poipu Road, 5 miles south of Kaumualii Highway (Hwy 50), via Maluhia Road (Hwy 520).

Anini Beach: The longest fringing reef in Hawaii protects nearshore waters even during winter storm swells. The snorkeling here is some of the best you'll find on Kauai. Accessible off Kuhio Highway (Hwy 56), via Anini Road. (see Camping).

Kee Beach: Patches of reef protect the nearshore waters, which make for very good snorkeling. Accessible at the end of Hwy 56, where the Kalalau trailhead is located.

SURFING
Winter brings huge swells to the north shore, and popular surfing spots for expert surfers exist at Haena Beach, on Hwy 56. Surf breaks off Wailua on the east coast are popular with locals. Summer swells occasionally roll onto Kauai's south shore.

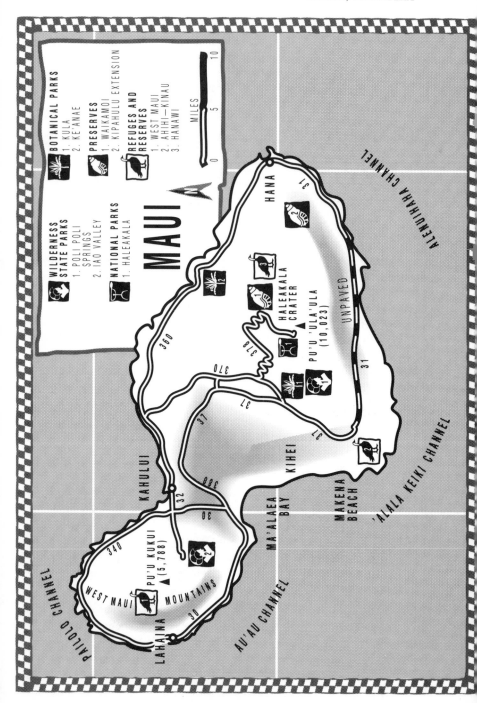

Chapter Five
Maui, Lanai, and Molokai

Background

This chapter contains information about three islands: Maui, Lanai, and Molokai. The information on Lanai and Molokai is insufficient to constitute a separate chapter for each, so they are combined here with Maui. Together with the uninhabited island of Kahoolawe, these islands constitute the County of Maui (with the exception of Kalaupapa Peninsula on Molokai—the state-administered hospital settlement located there constitutes its own county, Kalawao). With some local differences, the administration of many natural areas and parks adheres to the county political division. More fundamental to the three islands' unity is the fact that they are part of the same volcanic massif, so they share origins in the same volcanic epoch. The parent island, Maui Nui, consisted of 3230 square miles—about half the size of the Island of Hawaii. It contained six major volcanoes. Most of the low-lying areas between the volcanic mountains are now flooded, and so shallow seas separate the present-day islands of Maui, Kahoolawe, Lanai, and Molokai.

Two major volcanoes and an intermediate lava plain (the Maui Isthmus) make up the land mass of Maui. The larger and younger of the two volcanoes is Haleakala (10,023 feet). Much of the mountain is now in Haleakala National Park. The showpiece of the mountain and the Park is the huge summit crater, a magnificent landscape of volcanic and erosional origin. Across the Maui Isthmus from Haleakala are the West Maui mountains. These attain a maximum elevation of 5788 feet at Puu Kukui. The West Maui shield caldera at one time was about 5 miles across. Subsequent eruptions, collapses, and stream erosion have reshaped the caldera. A prominent feature of West Maui is Iao Needle—an erosional remnant of the ancient caldera.

Across the Auau Channel from west Maui is the island of Lanai. The high point of the island, Lanaihale (3370 feet), represents the summit of the single shield volcano that built the island. The Palawai Basin, across which traverses the Manele Road leading from Lanai City to the campsites near Manele Bay at Hulopoe Beach Park, is the remains of a volcanic caldera. Wave, wind, and stream erosion have all played significant roles in shaping the contours of present-day Lanai. They contribute to Lanai's most precious export (but one for which it receives no compensation)—topsoil lost to the ocean.

Northeast of Maui, across the Pailolo Channel is the volcanic doublet island of Molokai. Two big shield volcanoes—West Molokai and East Molokai—dominate the island's physical geography. A third, much smaller basaltic shield volcano is at Kalaupapa Peninsula. The interior highlands and the north coast of Molokai contain some of the most spectacular landscapes, remote wilderness, and unique natural communities found in the Hawaiian Islands. The east Molokai mountain reaches its maximum elevation at Kamakou (4960 feet)—a lush, forested area that is now a centerpiece of The Hawaii Nature Conservancy Kamakou Preserve. The northern slopes of the east Molokai mountain have been eroded by streams and by waves to form a coastline of magnificent sea cliffs, some over 3500 feet, and several huge amphitheater valleys (Halawa, Wailau, Pelekunu). The West Molakai landscape lacks the dramatic relief of the eastern part of the island. At the west end of the island is Papohaku Beach, one of the longest white sand beaches in the Islands, providing excellent camping.

Wave, wind, and stream erosion have all played significant roles in shaping the contours of present-day Lanai. They contribute to Lanai's most precious export (but one for which it receives no compensation)—topsoil lost to the ocean.

The diverse terrain of these islands contains a wide range of habitats for communities of native plants and animals. Many of these areas are maintained as wilderness preserves: Kipahulu on Maui—a splendid scientific reserve; Haleakala on Maui—a national park; and The Nature Conservancy Preserves on Molokai at Kamakou, Pelekunu Valley, and Moomomi Dunes; as well as numerous state natural area reserves, national wildlife refuges, state forest reserves, and other parklands. Many other habitats have been significantly modified by humans, creating new arrangements of plant and animal life. These have their own beauty, but one fashioned by the people that inhabit them. The landscape descriptions and travel information contained in this chapter will guide you to many of the environmental opportunities that exist on the triplet islands of Maui, Lanai, and Molokai.

The smallest of the islands in the Maui group is Kahoolawe (116 square kilometers). I omit it from the book for the simple but important reason that access to the island is restricted because it is a military bombing site. The island is a desert, denuded across much of its surface—the result of wind erosion on soils laid bare by wave action, of overgrazing by sheep and cattle, and of U.S. Navy bombing practices. It is currently uninhabited, with the important exception of regular visits by members of the "Protect Kahoolawe Ohana" ("Ohana" means "family"). This community group rallies to the call of "Aloha Aina" (love of the land), and it has been battling inside

Molokai waterfall and swimming hole

and outside of the state and federal courts to return Kahoolawe to the Hawaiian people.

It is possible to visit Kahoolawe on one of the Ohana excursions to the island. These are not tourist ventures. They are spiritual and ecological journeys organized for persons who are committed to the ideals of land preservation. For information on the Kahoolawe problem or excursions to the island, contact: Protect Kahoolawe Ohana, P.O. Box H, Kaunakakai, Molokai, HI 96748.

Alternative Lodging

BED AND BREAKFAST INNS

Bed and Breakfast Maui Style: This is a B&B directory that has 15 listings throughout the island. The majority of the rooms are in private homes, and they vary in price from $40 to $55/double. The directory organizes its listings in 5 zones: (1) Kahului, (2) West Maui, (3) Kihei, (4) Upcountry, and (5) Hana. You should be somewhat acquainted with the island in order to select the location that matches your interest. Briefly: Zone 1: Center of commerce and trade, port city. Zone 2: Kaanapali/Lahaina resort area with hotels, restaurants, beaches and golf courses. Zone 3: Sun and sandy beaches with calm waters for snorkeling. Zone 4: Mid-slope of Haleakala with ranchland, rainforests, cool nights and bright days, close to good hiking. Zone 5: Lush and wet Hana coast with a dramatic shoreline and splendid forest hikes. Contact: P.O. Box 886, Kihei, HI 96753. 808/879-7865.

Haikuleana Bed and Breakfast Inn Plantation Style: This is a 130-year-old plantation house on the north shore between the Hana Highway (Hwy 360) and upcountry Makawao. It is situated amid pineapple trees and pine trees along Haiku Rd. south of Pauwela. $65/night. Contact: 69 Haiku Road, Haiku, HI 96708. 808/575-2890.

LODGES

There are several lodges on Maui, but its seems that most island accommodations are tailored to the fashionably wealthy. Where you find simplicity, it is likely to be a fashion. Nonetheless, a couple of lodges exist that refrain from the trendiness, and backwoods cabins are located in a few of the state parks and state forest reserves.

Heavenly Hana Inn: When you walk through the entrance to this inn, you enter a peaceful and gentle place. Japanese gardens, a reading room, a lanai, and comfortable bedrooms grace the inn. The owners also rent a beach cottage on Hana Bay and a family cottage in Hana village. Prices are reasonable for Hana: $75/double at the inn; $85/double at the beach cottage; $60–90 for the family cottage depending on the number of persons. If you want to relax in a contemplative environment, or to be close to Hana hiking areas, this is a good place to stay. Located on Hwy 360 (Hana Highway), one mile north of Hana village. Contact: P.O. Box 146, Hana, HI 96713. 808/248-8442.

Iao Valley Lodge and Springs: The lodge is situated along Iao Stream next to Kepaniwai Heritage Gardens (less than a mile below Iao Needle State Park). Rates are $65/double. Contact: RR1, Box 518, Wailuku, HI 96793. 808/242-5555.

Kula Lodge: Few places in the world have a view that matches that from Kula Lodge. The Isthmus of Maui, the West Maui Mountains, and the islands of Lanai and Molokai are in clear view from the lodge, located at 3200 feet elevation on Haleakala. Outstanding sunsets add to the evening view. The lodge is on Route 377, about 20 minutes' drive from Kahului. The lodge maintains rustic chalets, each with a private lanai and a fireplace for the cool evenings. Prices: $80–125/chalet depending on size and amenities. Contact: RR1, Box 475, Kula, HI 96790. 808/878-2517.

CABINS

Camp Pecusa: Six miles southeast of Lahaina on Highway 30, near the small village of Olowalu, is this rural camp owned by the Episcopalian Church. In addition to tent sites, the camp has several cabins that they rent to tourists for $7/night. The cabins are spartan but clean. The camp is located at a quiet spot on Hekili Point, with a nice beach and good views of Haleakala. Watch for the Camp Pecusa signboard on the *mauka* side of Highway 30 as you near Olowalu. The camp entrance is 200 yards off the highway. Contact: Camp Pecusa, 800-Olowalu Village, Lahaina, HI 97671. 808/661-4303.

Haleakala National Park: The Park maintains three backcountry cabins in the crater—Holua, Kapalaoa, and Paliku. Each is equipped with minimal cooking equipment, a wood-burning cooking stove, a pit toilet, and a limited supply of water and firewood. Maximum capacity is 12 persons. You must supply your own sleeping bag and other personal gear. The rates are $5/person/night for adults and $2.50/child under 12, with a $15/night minimum. These cabins are so popular that the Park has turned to a lottery system to determine who gets them. Make your reservations several months in advance—6–8 months is recommended. Send a $15 deposit with your reservation request to Haleakala National Park. Include names

Haleakala Crater is 19 square miles in area, 21 miles in circumference, with a rim more than 10,000 feet above sea level (Mauna Kea and Mauna Loa in distance)

and social-security numbers of all persons in the party. Give alternative dates if possible. If you get a cabin, pay the balance and pick up the key at Park Headquarters upon arrival. (Note: Cabin reservations are often canceled, and you may be able to get one by asking at Park headquarters.)

Poli Poli Spring State Recreation Area: This is one of Maui's most remote parks, situated at 6200 feet elevation in the fog belt of the Kula Forest Reserve. There is only one cabin in the park, but it is rarely used. Reserve the cabin at either the Honolulu or the Wailuku office of the Division of State Parks. A maximum of 6 persons can stay at the cabin. The cost is $7/person for a double (a single person can reserve the entire cabin for $10). To reach the park and the cabin, drive up Waipoli Road 9.7 miles from Highway 377 (Kekaulike Avenue) in Kula. The last few miles of the road are rough. In wet weather a 4-wheel-drive vehicle is recommended. Check with the Division of State Parks for current conditions.

Waianapanapa State Park: There are 12 furnished cabins at Waianapanapa, with a capacity of 6 persons each. The rates vary according to the number of persons, beginning at $10/night for one person, up to $30/night for 5 adults ($2.50 for each child under 12). Maximum stay is 5 nights. The cabins are clean and comfortable, with full kitchens and outdoor barbeque pits. The Hana coast region is quite popular, so you will need to make reservations for the cabins in advance by contacting the Honolulu or Wailuku state park office.

Botanical Gardens and Parks

Helani Gardens: While it is advertised as "Hawaii's only drive-thru botanical park," you needn't and you shouldn't limit your tour through the garden to your vehicle; the entire concept is a bit ludricrous. The park has an eclectic blend of native and introduced species, aesthetically pleasing but lacking scientific design. They have a nice picnic setup, and the park makes a good spot for lunch. Admission is $3/adult, $1/child; open 10–4 daily. The garden is 1 mile north of Hana on Hwy 360, on the *mauka* side of the road.

Kahuna Gardens: One of Maui's best scientific gardens, it is a satellite park of the National Tropical Botanical Garden (see Kauai Botanical Gardens and Parks), located on a verdant 120-acre parcel of land along Maui's wet east coast. It is owned and maintained primarily for scientific research purposes, but it also offers public tours. Their specialty is ethnobotany; the garden holds extensive collections of food and medicinal plants gathered throughout

Polynesia. It is open 10–2 Tuesday through Saturday; admission is $5 (free for members). Contact: 808/248-8912. The garden is on Ulaino Road, 1.5 miles *makai* of Hana Highway (Hwy 360) at Kalahu Point.

Kula Botanical Gardens: For casual visitors, this is probably Maui's finest botanical park. It is situated on 23 acres of land (5 acres of public access) along the western flank of Haleakala in the "upcountry" Kula region. The garden was established in 1968 as a place to both enjoy and learn about Hawaiian flora. Native Hawaiian and introduced Pacific species grow in the well-laid out gardens and arbors. Admission is $3/adult; 50 cents/child. The garden is located about one-half mile from the junction of Kekaulike Rd. and Kula Highway (Hwy 37). Contact: RR 2, Box 288, Kula, HI 96790. 808/878-1715.

Maui Enchanting Gardens: For flower-lovers, the Kula area is unsurpassed on Maui. Flower farms abound here, painting the rolling landscape with vibrant colors and soft pastels. In the midst of this intoxicating landscape is the Maui Enchanting Gardens, a lovingly attended floral garden of 8 acres. It's almost too cute, with its quaint and colorful layout, cobbled pathways, and aphoristic signposts. $3/adult admission. Located on Kula Highway (Hwy 37), 2 miles south of the junction of Highway 37 and Highway 377. Contact: RR1, Box 696-B, Kula, HI 96790. 808/878-2531.

Keanae Arboretum: Located midway along the Hana road, near Keanae Peninsula and the village of Keanae, is this elaborate arboretum. White ginger, impatiens, philodendron and elephant-ear taro border the trail that leads into the park. The shaded valley of the arboretum contains 6 acres of well-tended ornamentals, timber, and food plants. The meandering arboretum walk terminates at a taro propagation farm. Most plant species in the arboretum are marked and identified with labels. To reach the arboretum, follow the Hana Highway (Hwy 360) east from Kaumahina State Wayside Park 4 miles. The arboretum is well-marked with a signpost.

Kepaniwai Heritage Gardens County Park: On the way to the famous Iao Needle are the less-famous Kepaniwai Heritage Gardens. They blend the Orient with the Pacific along Iao stream, in a quiet setting hemmed in by the steep Iao Valley walls. Japanese gardens and oriental pavilions intermingle with tropical plants and Polynesian thatched homes. There are places to wade and to swim in the stream, and the nearby picnic facilities make it a nice spot to lunch. Follow the Iao Valley road (Hwy 32) 3 miles west from downtown Wailuku; the Park is located on the south side of the road, well-marked with a signpost.

Tropical Gardens of Maui: This is a commercial garden located along the route to Iao Needle. It features wishing wells, schools of colorful carp swimming in concrete ponds, a garden-kitchen restaurant, a gift shop, and—oh yes—plants. Admission is $3/adult, $1/child admission. Located on Haahumanu Road (Hwy 32), 1 mile west of its junction with Honoapiilani Highway (Hwy 30).

Upcountry Protea Farm: In the Kula region many farmers grow a flower, called protea, that looks almost like an animal. Native to South Africa and Australia, the protea is named after the Greek god Proteus, who was known for changing his shape. The upcountry Kula region has a climate similar to the plant's native areas, and the rich volcanic soils here provide an excellent habitat for these exotic blooms. The Upcountry Protea Farm welcomes visitors to its two and one-half acre farm, located 1 mile up Kimo Drive off Haleakala Highway (Hwy 377) in Kula. Contact: Rt 1, Box 485F, Kula, HI 96790. 808/878-2544.

Camping Areas

Many of the developed campgrounds on Maui are in Haleakala National Park or in a state park. On Molokai, there is one state park campground and one county park campground. On Lanai, there is one private campground.

MAUI CAMPING AREAS
Haleakala National Park

Park headquarters are located 2 hours from Kahalui, on Haleakala Highway (Hwy 378). A visitors center located near the crater summit also provides information on camping and hiking in the park. The 28,000-acre park is divided into two sections: the Haleakala crater region, and the coastal region around Kipahulu and Oheo Gulch. Both areas contain campsites and splendid hiking trails.

Hosmer Grove Campground: This is a small campground at the 6800-foot elevation, 1.3 miles below Park headquarters. A self-guiding nature walk through the nearby forest begins at the campground. The campground can accommodate 25 persons, but it is usually quite empty. The tent sites occupy a grassy area, with picnic tables and fire pits nearby. No reservations or permits are required, but campers are limited to 3 nights per month. Trailers are permitted in the parking area.

Crater Campsites: There are two backcountry campsites in the crater—one near Paliku cabin and a second near Holua cabin. Drinking water is available at these sites. The maximum capacity of each campsite is 25 persons. Permits are required, and can be obtained at Park headquarters upon arrival (open 7:30–4 p.m. daily). To reserve a spot (the campsites often fill up on weekends), write in advance to Park headquarters. Specify the preferred site and the numbers of campers. There is a limit of 2 consecutive nights at one campground, with a maximum of 3 nights/month in the crater. The crater campgrounds are generally used by those on extended backpacking trips through the crater (see hiking section) There are no other camping areas in the crater; the closest alternative spots are at Hosmer Grove and in the Kipahulu-Oheo Gulch campground.

Kipahulu/Oheo Gulch Campground: This is a primitive campground located in the Kipahulu section of the Park, off Highway 31 near the Oheo Gulch pools. These pools are erroneously called on some travel maps, "Seven Pools," but there are many more than 7 pools along this beautiful stretch of Oheo Stream. No permit is required, but you are limited to 3 nights/month. The camping area is marked by a signboard 100 yards beyond the Oheo Gulch visitor's parking area. The tent sites are situated along a grassy ridge above the ocean, protected by a windrow of ironwood and lauhala trees.

State Parks

Division of State Parks, Maui District, P.O. Box 1049, Wailuku, HI 96793. 808/243-5354. Street address: 54 High St. in Wailuku.

Waianapanapa State Park: This 120-acre park includes a small campground. The tent sites are located in a grassy area adjacent to the cliffs along Pailoa Bay. There is not much privacy in the camping area, but the hiking trails nearby offer splendid opportunities to explore the wild, isolated coastline for which the park is famous. Sea stacks, blow holes, arches, caves and tidal pools line the coast in both directions. There is no camping fee, but you must obtain permits at the Division of State Parks office in Honolulu or Wailuku. On weekends, the campground fills up, so make an advance reservation. The park is located off Hana Highway (Hwy 360), 3 miles west of Hana, makai of the village of Kaeleku—watch for the Waianapanapa signboard on the highway.

Poli Poli Spring State Recreation Area: This 10-acre state park, located in the Kula "upcountry" region, has a remote campground (as well as a cabin—see section under lodging). The park lies in a fog belt above the 6000-foot elevation, surrounded by the Kula and Kahikinui Forest Reserves, totalling about 12,000 acres. It contains non-native but nonetheless beautiful forests of sugi pine, eucalyptus and redwood. From the campground, an extensive trail network

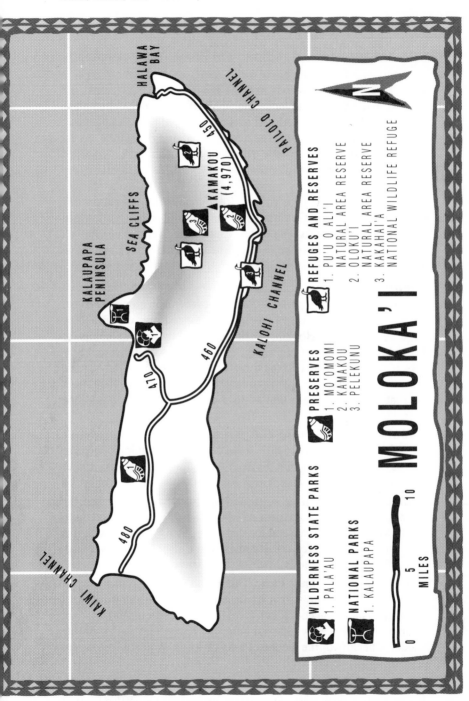

branches out into the surrounding forest reserve (see hiking section). The park is popular with local residents, who use it on weekends. Weekdays remain quiet, with few visitors. When the park is empty, you feel much alone amid some of Maui's most pristine wilderness. The deep woods and the magnificent vistas across the isthmus to the West Maui mountains make the spot a treasured place to camp and to hike. In addition to the developed park campground, camping is allowed in the adjacent Kula and Kahikinui forest reserves. Trailside shelters for overnight camping are located along several of the hiking routes that traverse the forest reserves (see hiking section).

To reach the park, take Waipoli Road mauka from Highway 377 near Kula Botanical Gardens. For several miles the road winds through upland pasture. The last few miles are over dirt and gravel; during very wet weather the road can be impassable due to mud and deep ruts.

County Parks

There are 7 county parks on Maui, most of them along the coast. Only 2 allow year-round camping—Baldwin Park and Rainbow Park. A third park, Hookipa Park, occasionally permits camping. The other 4 county parks prohibit camping. Reservations and permits are required (and a $3 fee for out-of-state visitors). They can be obtained by writing or by visiting the Department of Parks and Recreation. Campers are limited to 3 consecutive days in any one park.

Baldwin Park: This beach park is located off the Hana Highway (Hwy 360), near the funky little town of Paia. The campground is in a grassy fenced-off area, not far from the highway. It is not a particularly pleasant place to camp, and you would do well to avoid it.

Rainbow Park: The park is located between Paia village and the cowboy-turned-New Age town of Makawao. It's fairly private and quiet; if you're in the area and looking for a place to set up a tent, this park will do. Watch for the Rainbow Park signboard midway between the two towns on Baldwin Ave. (Highway 390).

Hookipa Beach County Park: This is the world's premier boardsailing spot. Persistent strong winds and frequently large winter surf combine to make the conditions ideal for practiced windsurfers. Tent camping is periodically allowed here; the regulations vary with the season. Check with the County Parks office in Wailuku for current policies.

Private Campgrounds

There is only one private campground on Maui—Camp Pecusa (see also Alternative Lodging). Located along Honoapiilani Highway (Hwy 30), 6 miles southeast of Lahaina, the private park is owned by the Episcopalian Church, which maintains it as a quiet, unimproved visitor's park. They charge $3/night for each tent, with no established day limit. The place is peaceful, with a nice beach and beautiful sunrises. It is also conveniently located for those visiting Lahaina, and it is the only place to camp in the Lahaina district. Watch for the Camp Pecusa signboard on the makai side of Hwy 30. Contact: Camp Pecusa, 800 Oluwalu Village, Lahaina, HI 997671. 808/661-4303.

Other Camping Areas

Check with the Maui Sierra Club group or other local hiking groups (see Hiking) for information on alternative camping areas. A popular spot in the past was Makena Beach, located near the end of Wailea Alanui Road south of Kihei. A few hundred yards south of the prominent cinder cone at Nahuna Point, look for dirt tracks that head toward the ocean, ending at an undeveloped parking area. Until recently, this lovely stretch of undeveloped beach was a favorite camping site of local residents and visitors. It is now near a major tourist resort and it has consequently lost its appeal for camping. Some folks still camp there; you may want to check it out.

Several of the more remote county parks that do not allow camping are nevertheless used by campers desperate for a place to stay. You can car-camp (i.e., sleep in your car) at these spots. Many beaches are private enough to set down a sleeping bag for a night. Use discretion if you decide to stay in nonestablished campsites.

MOLOKAI CAMPING AREAS

Molokai has 3 official campgrounds. In addition to these, numerous remote camping areas are located in the interior mountain forests and along the north coast at Wailau Valley. These areas are accessible only by strenuous backcountry travel. Significant wilderness areas on Molokai are managed as nature preserves; camping is not allowed in these areas.

Palaau State Park: This 233-acre park, located at the end of Kalae Highway (Hwy 47), is most noted for its phallic fertility stone. A quiet campground is located in an ironwood grove in the Park. No fees are required, but you need to obtain a permit from the Division of State Parks office in Honolulu or in Wailuku, Maui.

Papohaku Beach: A long stretch of isolated beach is located at the west end of Molokai. Calm swimming waters, sunshine, and shady shores prevail here. At the north end of this beach is the Kaluakoi Resort, but at the south end of the beach, well away from the resort, is a primitive campground at Papohaku Beach County Park. There are no amenities here, but it nevertheless is an excellent spot to tent camp. No fees or permits. Follow Highway 460 west from Kaunakakai to Kaluakoi Road, and take it to its end.

One Alii Beach County Park: This is a small beach park on the island's south coast near Kaunakakai that allows tent camping. No fees or permits. The park is located off Kamehameha V Highway (Hwy 450), 3 miles east of Kaunakakai.

Halawa Beach County Park: There is no established campground here, but many people nevertheless camp in this lovely valley. An excellent hiking trail heads up the valley to Hipuapua Falls. There is no drinking water available, so be fully self-contained.

Forest Reserve Campsites: Camping is permitted in the state forest lands at Waikolu Pavilion and Wailau Valley. These both are back-country sites; for information, contact the Division of Forestry and Wildlife, P.O. Box 1015, Wailuku, HI 96793. 808/243-5352. (Also see Hiking section).

West Molokai mountain stream

LANAI CAMPING AREAS

The natural areas on Lanai are fast succumbing to the tourism demands for destination resorts. There is only one place to camp on the island—near Manele Bay on the south shore, at Hulopoe Beach. To stay there requires a permit from the Koele Company—a subsidiary of Castle and Cooke Company, which owns most of the island. There is a camping registration fee of $5/person/day, with 7 days maximum. Write for permits well in advance: Koele Company, P.O. Box L, Lanai City, Island of Lanai, HI 96763. 808/565-6651. At this writing Manele Bay is being developed for tourism, and a huge generator now hums constantly, destroying the former quiet and solitude of the place. As a result, the bay is less attractive as a camping spot. If you plan to visit Lanai, I recommend that you stay at the inexpensive Lanai Hotel in Lanai City, and dayhike to the island's natural areas (see Hiking section).

Environmental Groups

Environmental activism is not particularly strong on Maui, but some of the groups involved in the conservation effort are effective also in providing educational opportunities for the community.

Pacific Whale Foundation: Whale harrassment in Hawaii generally is not the problem it is elsewhere (for instance, off California), primarily because the whales traditionally come close to the shore here. People for generations have been watching the whales cavort in the warm and clear near-shore waters without resorting to flotillas of whale-watching vessels. But the fleet of charter boats is growing, and the potential for serious harassment exists despite the regulation of whale watching.

The Pacific Whale Foundation conducts research on the ecology of whales and other marine animals for conservation and management purposes. They have been doing humpback whale research on Maui since 1980. During the past decade they specifically have been monitoring the impacts of whale-watching tours. As a nonprofit organization, they offer educational whale-watching tours to enlist support for their activities. The tours are led by naturalists, and the focus is on marine education. The Pacific Whale Foundation also offers intern opportunities for those interested in combining marine education with hands-on skills development in ocean research. Nine research teams include interns in their humpback whale ecology studies. For information about their activities and programs, contact: Pacific Whale Foundation, Kealia Beach Plaza, Suite 25, 101 N. Kihei Road, Kihei, HI 96753. 808/879-8811.

Whale Aid: This is a group of concerned citizens and businesses on Maui, staffed by volunteers, that organizes community support for whale research and education. Their activities extend scientific knowledge about whales to the community through education seminars, student grants, school presentations, and visitor services. They also provide educational whale watches for residents and visitors. Contact: 808/667-9425.

Sea Shepherd Conservation Society: This is a nonprofit marine mammal protection agency that conducts educational whale watching tours led by marine specialists. The fares help support the work of the society. Contact: P.O. Box 2147, Kihei, HI 96753. 808/874-6072.

Heiaus

There are many heiaus scattered along Maui's coastline, and a few in the interior. Most of these are on private land, however. The following heiaus are the most accessible as well as the most nearly intact.

Halekii—Pihana Heiau: Located on a sand dune ridge overlooking the mouth of Iao Stream, one-half mile from Wailuku, is this double heiau complex of terraces, walkways, platforms, pits and walled enclosures. It was used for ritual ceremonies prior to battle, and apparently is still in use, as evidenced by the regular offerings of flowers and ti leaves found at the site. It is a state monument and is easily accessible along the beach road one-fourth mile inland from Nehe Point.

Kanekauila Heiau: Past Hana on Hwy 31, beyond the Oheo Gulch pools but before the village of Kipahulu, is this platform heaiu above the ocean. It commands a majestic view of the coastline and the Island of Hawaii to the south. Its function is uncertain, but its more recent historical association is with a nearby grave site. Look for the heiau along the grassy slopes a short distance west of the Kipahulu primitive camping area in Haleakala National Park.

La Perouse Bay: A large site situated between an extensive *aa* lava flow and the ocean, this heiau probably had importance for fishing, since the surrounding settlements were primarily fishing villages. It is not, however, a typical *koa,* or fishing shrine. The unique, notched heiau walls enclose large courtyards paved with the small water-worn pebbles called iliili. To reach La Perouse Bay, head south on Hwy 31 through Kihei, past the recent despoilage at Makena (some call it development), past lovely little Keawalai Church, and across Maui's most recent lava flow (ca. 1790) to Keoneoio where the road gets bad and then ends (on most rental car maps the last part of the road is marked off-limits). The coastline here is rocky, but a meandering path through the lava field allows you to stroll the length of the embayment on part of the Hoapili (King's) Trail that once encircled the island.

Waianapanapa State Park: The proper name for this heiau is Ohala, a low platform heiau of considerable size (110' by 75'). Its early function is unknown, although archival references to the site mention that "drums are said to be heard from this heiau on certain nights." It is located in Waianapanapa State Park, which you will certainly want to visit anyway while you're traveling this Hana Road section of Maui. The heiau is located at Paina Point, along the coastal trail some 45 minutes walk from the park campground. Pounding seas, sheer black cliffs, and lush green pandanus groves border the trail. If you walk through the gate enclosure onto the private cattle lands, you've gone too far: the heiau is on the state park side of the fence on a low hill above the trail.

Molokai

There are heiaus on Molokai too numerous to mention, but the sites are either on private property or so utterly remote as to be almost inaccessible. So they remain locked in Hawaiian history and spirit, and out of reach for all but the most determined—who can probably find them without the aid of this book. Along the rugged northern coast, which can be visited only by boat, there are plenty of remote coastal heiaus. If you travel this coastline (see Molokai Nature Tours and Outdoor Excursions), keep a sharp eye out.

Hiking Areas

The natural landscapes of Maui, Molakai, and Lanai contain a wide range of hiking environments, including the sparse, moonlike landscape of Haleakala, the lush rainforests near Hana, the summit bogs on Molokai, and the upland dry forests on Lanai. The trails through these natural areas provide diverse experiences, ranging from short nature walks to backpacking trips that last several days.

MAUI HIKING AREAS
Haleakala National Park

Open 24 hours/day. Entrance fee is $3/car. Park headquarters is open from 7:30–4. The House of the Sun Visitors Center at the summit is open from sunrise to 3 p.m. A popular time in the park is sunrise, when hundreds of people who have ascended the mountain in the pre-dawn hours are at the top when the sun first strikes the mountain. From Kahului take Highway 37 to Highway 377, then

turn up Haleakala Crater Road (Hwy 378). Haleakala Crater is at
the end of the road, 2 hours driving time from Kahului.

Much of the 10,023-foot volcanic summit of Haleakala (lit.,
"House of the Sun") was set aside in 1916 as a national park. Stream
erosion and scattered volcanic activity in the caldera of the massive
volcano created the crater's landscape. The 19-square-mile crater
floor lies one-half mile below the crater rim, and it contains 36 miles
of hiking trails. Austere lava landscapes in the crater and wet upland
forests along the rim and the sides of the mountain provide habitat
for a wide range of native plant and animal species. The native
Hawaiian goose, or nene (*Nesochen sandvicensis*), is the state bird.
It and the Hawaiian dark-rumped petrel, or uau (*Pterodroma
phaeopygia sandwichensis*), are two of the state's unique and
endangered birds found in the crater. The crater is the world's only
home for the Haleakala silversword (*Argyroxiphium sandwicense*),
a majestic plant that grows in the dry cinder rock, reaching a height
of several feet, with blossoms over 3 feet tall. The park is a magnificent wilderness area, designated as an International Biosphere

The rare silversword plant blooms once in its lifetime

Hawaiian Visitors Bureau

Reserve by the United Nations. The volcano is now dormant; the last eruption occurred in 1790, on the southwest slope.

Crater Trails

The hiking routes in Haleakala crater traverse a moonscape of intriguing volcanic landforms, with delicate pockets of vegetation that support rare communities of plants and birds. The environment is fragile, so please stay on the designated trails. Weather conditions can change rapidly, and the high elevation means that night temperatures can be cold. Temperatures of 32 degrees F. and below are common, and backpackers should be well-equipped with cold-weather gear. There are 3 main hiking routes in the crater, with shorter connecting trails. These take you from the rim to the crater floor, across the crater, and back up the rim. They vary in distance

---

A popular time in the park is sunrise, when hundreds of people who have ascended the mountain in the pre-dawn hours are at the top when the sun first strikes the mountain.

---

and grade; to cover the entire trail system would require at least one overnight camp. Dayhikes are popular, and they are entirely feasible along any of the routes if you carefully assess your own hiking ability and the distance you can cover in a day. Illustrated hiking guides are available at Park headquarters.

Halemauu Trail: 10 miles. The trail begins about 3.5 miles above Park headquarters, at the 8000-foot level. The first 1.5 miles are along gently rolling terrain near the outer crater rim. The trail then descends steeply for 2 miles to the crater floor, and reaches Holua Cabin after another mile of hiking. The trail terminates at Paliku Cabin on the east side of the crater.

Kaupo Gap Trail: 9 miles. This is used primarily as an exit trail to the Kipahulu coastal region. It begins at Paliku Cabin (6400 feet) and goes across the east crater rim before descending to the park boundary at 3800 feet. The remaining 5.5 miles are along a private jeep road (public access requires no permit) until you reach Highway 31. At this point you are 9 miles east of the park's Oheo campground at Kipahulu.

Sliding Sands Trail: 8 miles to Oili Puu. The trail begins below the summit at 10,000 feet, near the House of the Sun Visitor Center. The first 4 miles are a steep descent on loose gravel before you level out on the crater floor. The trail passes Kapalaoa Cabin before intersecting with the Halemauu Trail at Oili Puu. The return is not easy because of the long uphill grade. A pleasant alternative is to exit the crater via the Halemauu Trail, allowing you to see a different part of the crater, with a shorter uphill climb.

Other Park Hikes

In addition to the crater hikes, Halealaka National Park maintains hiking trails that traverse the crater rim, the outer slopes of the volcano, and the lush rainforests near the coast at Kipahulu.

Hosmer Grove: 0.5 mile. A short, self-guiding nature walk begins at the campground and meanders through a forest of eastern red cedar, Douglas fir, and lodgepole pine. These trees were planted in 1910 for slope-conservation purposes on denuded cattleland. They now provide a pleasant environment for short hikes.

Crater Rim Walks: On weekends and on most weekdays, the Park Service conducts nature walks along the crater rim. The 2–3 hour hikes are led by a Park naturalist. The hiking schedule varies with the season; check with Park headquarters for current programs.

Waikamoi Preserve: The Nature Conservancy manages, in cooperation with the National Park Service, a stretch of rainforest and subalpine scrubland near the upper north slope of Haleakala. Hikes into the preserve are restricted, but they can be arranged through the Preserve Manager, Waikamoi Preserve, 895 W. Kuiaha Road, Haiku, HI 96708. 808/575-2747. The park also conducts bird watching expeditions into the preserve on Monday, Thursday, and Friday mornings. The 2.5 hour hikes begin at 9; meet at the Hosmer Grove Campground.

Kipahulu Area: In 1969 Haleakala National Park expanded to add the Kipahulu District, an internationally recognized pristine rainforest containing numerous rare and endangered plants and animals. The district is reached by driving 62 miles southeast of Kahului via the Hana Highway (approximately 3 hours). The lower part of the district, near the coast, includes the popular Oheo Pools. More than 20 pools exist along one mile of Oheo Stream—a popular place for hiking and swimming, but be wary during rainy periods when flash floods are common. The stone walls located amid the grassy slopes above the pools were built by the early Hawaiians as part of an ancient settlement. Please do not disturb these sites. The hiking trail at Kipahulu begins at the Oheo parking area and leads first to Makahiku Falls overlook (0.5 mile) before continuing up the south side of Oheo Gulch 1.5 miles to the base of Waimoku Falls. The trail passes through forests of native kukui (*Aleurites moluccana*) and introduced varieties of ginger, breadfruit, mango, and monkeypod before reaching extensive areas of exotic bamboo forest. Beyond

Oheo Gulch pools in Kipahulu area

Waimoku, the upper Kipahulu rainforest is closed to the public. It is designated as a scientific reserve to protect native birds and plants.

West Maui Hiking Areas

There is limited hiking opportunity in the West Maui mountains. The Waihee Ridge Trail (3.0 miles) climbs the windward slope of West Maui to an overlook above Wailuku. The trail begins at the Boy Scout camp at the end of Maluhia Road off Kahekili Highway (Hwy 34) northwest of Kahului, and ends at the border of the West Maui Natural Area Reserve. The trail is in good condition, but the weather is usually wet and windy. On a clear day, the views are spectacular in all directions. Another access trail to the West Maui mountains is in Iao Needle State Park. The park is at the end of Kaahumanu Avenue (Hwy 32) west of Wailuku. From the Iao Needle overlook, the trail heads up the ridge above Iao Stream. The back part of the valley borders the West Maui Natural Area Reserve—Panaewa Section. The trail tapers off after a couple of miles and ends near the steep valley walls.

La Perouse Bay Hiking Area

At the end of Kihei Road (Hwy 31) is the Ahihi-Kinau Natural Area Reserve, bordering on La Perouse Bay and the King's Highway Coastal Trail. (The last part of Hwy 31 is very rough and rental cars are not allowed on it.) The hiking route follows the coast for 5.5 miles, from La Perouse Bay to Kanaio Beach, passing interesting lava formations and tidal pools. The ancient trail continues beyond this point, but it traverses private property and is closed to the public. The region is usually hot and dry, and no water is available.

The Iao Needle is close to Wailuku

Kula and Kahikinui Forest Reserve Trails

The Poli Poli Springs State Recreation Area serves as the base for several trail networks that extend into the nearby forest reserves. This is a remote area on the southwest slopes of Halealaka, above 6000 feet. The forests lie in the fog belt, so conditions are often wet and cool, but the forests are lovely, and this hiking area provides a wonderful sense of wilderness. If you are looking for the quiet of a remote upland forest where the hanging mist dampens even the sound of the rustling trade winds, this place is for you. Poli Poli is reached by taking Waipoli Road mauka from Hwy 377, near Kula Botanical Gardens. The last few miles of Waipoli are over dirt and gravel; during very wet weather the road can be impossible due to mud and deep ruts. Trailhead markers are located at various points in the park. Tents are prohibited, but bedroll camping is permitted in the forest reserve, and trailside shelters are located along several hiking trails. This is the backcountry, and persons on extended hikes need to be properly equipped. The Poli Poli trail system is outlined below; for trail maps and descriptions, contact the Division of Forestry and Wildlife, Maui Office, P.O. Box 1015, Wailuku, HI 96793. 808/244-4352. The hiking guidebooks also include descriptions of many of these trails.

Boundary Trail: 4.0 miles. Native scrub forest and planted stands of eucalyptus, pines, and cedars.

Kahua Road Trail: 3.5 miles. Popular with hunters, accessible by 4-wheel-drive vehicles.

Haleakala Ridge Trail: 1.6 miles. Spectacular views in all directions; trail shelter for overnight camping.

Plum Trail: 1.7 miles. Planted forests of ash, sugi pine, and cedar. Plum trees bear fruit in summer.

Poli Poli Trail: 1.6 miles. A short loop through the Park.

Redwood Trail: 1.7 miles. Dense groves of planted redwoods; trail shelter for overnight camping.

Skyline Trail: 6.5 miles. Rugged and barren, traverses cinder-cone landscapes and native scrubland; spectacular views.

Tie Trail: 0.5 mile. Connects Redwood Trail and Plum Trail.

Upper Waiakoa Loop Trail: 3.0 miles. Native scrub vegetation, good views. Natural cave shelter for overnight camping.

Waiakoa Loop Trail: 3.0 miles. Native scrub vegetation, with some planted pines.

Waiohuli Trail: 1.4 miles. Grassland and planted stands of ash, redwood, and cedar. Trail shelter for overnight camping.

Hana Highway Hiking Areas

There are few places in the world where one can approach a wilderness experience from the window of an automobile. The Hana Road is one such place. This tortuous, narrow road winds through lush rainforests, past waterfalls, and along dramatic coastal cliffs. There are many places to stop and pause, to walk into the woods, or to explore a streambed. The spots described below have short nature walks that are well worth the time to stretch your thoughts along with your limbs.

Waikomoi Ridge Trail: 0.8 mile. Starts at Hana Highway (Hwy 360), 3.5 miles past Kailua village (watch for the signboard). The trail heads up the ridge on the *mauka* side of the road. It passes through native rainforest with trees that are identified by wooden markers along the trailside.

Pua a kaa State Wayside Park: A well-marked auto stop on the Hana Highway, 5 miles southeast of Keanae. Beyond the swimming hole adjacent to the picnic area is a rough trail that heads up the stream to some additional swimming pools located in the small upper valley.

Waianapanapa Coastal Trail: 3.0 miles. The trail links Waiana-panapa State Park with Hana Bay. It follows a jagged lava coastline, with rugged headlands, blow holes, tidal pools, arches, and sea cliffs—an altogether extraordinary place. Begin at the Waiana-panapa campground, or in Hana near the old cemetery north of Hana Bay.

Other Maui Hiking Areas

To explore additional, less-known hiking areas, contact either the natural guide service "Hike Maui" (see Maui Nature Tours and Outdoor Excursions), the Maui Group of the Hawaii Chapter of the Sierra Club (P.O. Box 2000, Kahului, HI 96732), or the island's main community hiking club—Mauna Ala Hiking Club (P.O. Box 732, Puunene, Maui, HI 96784). Trail descriptions for 27 Maui hikes are in *Hiking Maui* by Robert Smith. *Hawaiian Hiking Trails* by Craig Chisholm describes 7 hiking routes.

MOLOKAI HIKING AREAS

The areas open to the public for hiking on Molokai are superior wilderness tracts. Molokai receives fewer tourists than the other islands, and its extensive natural areas provide an unparalleled tropical wilderness experience. The trail network is limited, though, by both geography and private landholdings. Much of the best hiking land is contained in The Nature Conservancy of Hawaii preserves or in state natural area reserves.

Natural Area Reserves

The two natural area reserves on Molakai are designed for plant and animal protection. Opportunities to explore these areas are therefore restricted. You must make advance arrangements with the reserve managers. The Pu Alii Natural Area Reserve contains 1340 acres of dense cloud forest above Waikolu and Pelekunu valleys. The Olokui Natural Area Reserve consists of 1635 acres of wet forest and bog above Wailau and Pelekunu valleys. Both of these

Mouth of Pelekunu Valley on Molokai

areas are pristine native cloud forest ecosystems. For information on hiking opportunities in these reserves, contact the Natural Areas Reserves System, 1151 Punchbowl Street, Honolulu, HI 96813. 808/548-7417.

The Nature Conservancy Preserves

The Nature Conservancy manages 2774 acres on the upper slopes of Makakupaia and Kawela mountains. You must arrange a visit to these areas through the preserve manager. A second Nature Conservancy preserve is at Moomomi—a dune ecosystem along the coast that contains 5 endangered plant species. It also provides habitat for the endangered Hawaiian green sea turtle and for numerous seabirds. To arrange a visit and obtain directions to these areas, contact: Preserve Manager, Kamakou Preserve, P.O. Box 40, Kualapuu, HI 96757. 808/567-6680. The preserve trails include:

Pelekunu Trail: 0.4 mile. Climbs to the rim of Pelekunu Valley, with magnificent views through the cloud forest of the valley and some of the north coast.

Pepeopae Trail: 0.6 mile. The trail goes to the Pepeopae Bog, where a wooden boardwalk has been constructed for hikers to avoid trampling the fragile bog ecosystem.

Puu Kolekole Trail: 2.0 miles. Begins near the Pepeopae trailhead, and ends at the 3951 foot summit of Puu Kolekole.

Other Molokai Hiking Areas

Halawa Valley Trail: 5 miles round trip. The trail is in the Halawa Valley, the only north shore valley accessible by car (take Hwy 450 to its east end). Near the back of the valley, the trail leads to Hipuapua Falls and Moaula Falls.

Kalaupapa Trail: 4 miles round trip. The trail begins at the end of Hwy 47, near the entrance to Palaau State Park. It switchbacks down 1600 feet of cliffs to the Kalaupapa Settlement—historical home for patients of Hansen's Disease. Permission to visit Kalaupapa must be obtained first from the Kalaupapa Settlement Administrator of the State Health Department. It is most convenient to arrange a tour through Damien Tours (808/567-6171).

Wailau Trail: This valley trail begins at the coast, which is accessible only by boat in calm weather. It is possible to traverse the mountains and enter Wailau Valley from above, but this route is extremely difficult and it crosses private property. Either way, the route requires the assistance and accompaniment of someone familiar with the trail and the permit procedures.

LANAI HIKING AREAS

There are few remaining undisturbed natural areas on Lanai, due to forest clearing and extensive cattle grazing. The current owners of most of Lanai (Castle and Cooke) have introduced reforestation programs in some areas, particularly in the upland central plateau. They have also recently designated the Kanepuu area on the northwest end of the central plateau a nature preserve. These areas contain some of the most nearly intact ecosystems on the island, and they have some of the best hiking land on Lanai. Additional areas along

Hawaii has the dubious distinction of harboring 30% of the total number of endangered species in the U.S.

Lanai's coasts provide good "beachcomber" hiking. But generally, the island appears to be heading toward resort development. Much of the island's natural areas will very likely become a playground for visitors spending their nights in expensive hotel rooms and their days on "wilderness safaris." Check first with the Koele Company (P.O. Box L, Lanai City, HI 96763) before heading out on any of the trails.

The established hiking routes include Kaiholena Gulch Trail (4 miles), Munro Trail (8 miles), North Hauola Trail (2 miles), and Polihua Beach Trail (2 miles). Trail descriptions and access information can be obtained from the Koele Company. Descriptions of Lanai trails are found in *Hawaiian Hiking Trails*.

Natural Foods and Farms

During the past decade Maui has become inundated with transplants from the hip centers of the mainland West Coast and from other areas that share an organic connection with good food, good times, and good vibrations. The crystal clarity of the New Age idyll fortunately includes an emphasis on things natural. As a result, Maui hosts a number of very good natural grocers.

Down To Earth Natural Foods: Offer a wide selection of bulk foods and locally grown organic produce. 1910 Vineyard St. in Wailuku. 808/242-6821.

Haleakala Herbs: Offer Maui's finest selection of naturally grown herbs and vegetables. They also provide permaculture design consultations that feature edible landscapes. In Haiku off Hana Hwy at 110 Pololei Street. 808/572-2758.

Makanali Farm: They produce and sell organically-grown fruits and vegetables in Hana along Hwy 31. Contact: P.O. Box 627, Hana, HI 96713. 808/248-7311.

Mana Foods: This is one of the best-stocked natural foods stores in Maui, run by a group of friendly hippies in Paia. It has just about everything you look for in a natural-foods store, making it a good place to stock up before heading off to Haleakala Crater or the Hana

Ruins of old fort on Lahaina's waterfront

Hawaiian Visitors Bureau

region. Located at 49 Baldwin Ave in downtown Paia. 808/579-8078.

Maui Natural Foods: Your run-of-the-mill natural-foods grocery. In the Maui Mall Shopping Center in Kahului. 808/877-3018.

Mountain Fresh Market: If you miss the Mana Foods market in Paia, you might try this place in Makawao. It's not quite as well-stocked as the Paia store, but it will do in a pinch if you're headed for the crater. In downtown Makawao at 3673 Baldwin Ave. 808/572-1488.

Paradise Fruit Maui: Formerly a small fruit stand, they have widened their inventory to include a variety of fresh produce and bulk natural foods. In Kihei across from McDonalds. 808/879-1723.

Upcountry Fishery and Dickie's Healthy Foods: Fresh seafood, organic produce and bulk natural grains are available at this funky little store on the corner of Bowen and Makawao Avenue in Makawao. 808/572-8484.

Westside Natural Foods: If you're in the Lahaina area, this place is conveniently located at 136 Dickenson St., off Front Street. 808/667-2855.

Tedeschi Winery: They grow grapes here, the only place in Hawaii and perhaps the entire tropical Pacific to do so. On that basis alone, it is worth a visit. But the best thing about the place is the drive to it. Kula Highway (Hwy 37) to the Tedischi vineyards winds through rolling upland pasture, past sheep farms that share outstanding views of the Maui isthmus, the West Maui mountains and the blue Pacific. The winery was established in 1974 by Emil Tedeschi and Pardee Erdman to make pineapple wine. In recent years they've produced a blush wine from locally grown grapes. Purchase a bottle at the visitor center for the sunset moments at your campsite or lodge. Contact: P.O. Box 953, Ulupalakua, HI 96793. 808/878-6058.

Molokai Natural Foods

The island of Molokai has one natural foods grocer: Outpost Natural Foods, in downtown Kaunakakai on Highway 460, around the bend from the Union 76 station.

Nature Tours and Outdoors Excursions

Maui is the second largest island of the Hawaiian Archipelago, containing a wide range of environments—from coast to cloud forest to volcanic caldera. The diversity of natural areas can be explored on your own or with the assistance of commercial tour operators.

Numerous operators on Maui cater to people with a desire to enter wild Maui.

BICYCLING

The coastal highway (Hwy 30) between Kihei and Lahaina is a busy route and is not recommended for cyclists, but other Maui roads offer excellent biking opportunities. Mountain bikers in particular will find a wide range of options on the remote, gravel outer roads that traverse the coasts between Hana and Wailea, and between Wailuku and Kaanapali. The premier bicycle journey for many cyclists, however, is the descent of Mt. Haleakala, from the summit to the seashore. For bikers traveling alone, there are limited sales and service outlets. Contact the bicycle-tour agencies listed below for current information. People without bikes, or those who want to travel as part of a chartered group, have several tour agencies to choose from.

Cruiser Bob's: During certain morning and afternoon periods, Haleakala Crater Road (Hwy 378) on the western flank of Haleakala sees groups of goggled bikers in yellow raingear. They most likely are members of a Cruiser Bob's bike tour. This is the first company to offer the exhilarating 38-mile coast down the world's largest dormant volcano. The ride descends 10,000 feet in 3 hours, downhill all the way. The tour company provides the gear (including bikes with "megabrakes") and the transportation (shuttle service to the summit). Contact: 505 Front Street, Lahaina, HI 96761. 808/667-7717.

New outfits offering the same volcano ride seem to appear each year. Shop around if you like.

Maui Downhill: They offer a sunrise tour, a full day tour, and an afternoon tour. Contact: 808/871-2155.

Maui Mountain Cruises: More of the same. Contact: 808/871-6014. From the mainland, call toll-free: 800/232-6284.

HORSEBACK RIDING

There are plenty of companies to help you explore Maui by horseback. The island's geographic diversity ensures a full range to the excursions offered—for example, Haleakala, coastal lava flows, or high-steppe ranch country. Choose your tour outfit with location in mind; the outfits differ most in their destinations.

Adventures on Horseback: "This is not a trail ride; this is an adventure," say the folks that lead you by horse to the craggy coasts, the tree-fern forests, and the waterfalls of the Haiku area on Maui's wet

northeast coast. The all-day affair includes a swim at Haiku Falls.
Price: $120/person. Contact: P.O. Box 1771, Makawao, HI 96768.
808/242-7445.

Aloha Nui Loa Tours: They combine a van tour of the Hana road
with a horseback ride along a secluded stretch of Hana's coast. This
makes it convenient if you wish to leave your car at the hotel.
Passenger pickup serves the Kaanapali and Kihei areas. Price:
$125/person (Hana tour, horseback ride, breakfast, lunch). Contact:
P.O. Box 10582, Lahaina, HI 96761. 808/669-0000.

Kaanapali Kau Kio: Their riding tours are conducted in the
ranchlands above Kaanapali, providing excellent views of the West
Maui mountains, and Molokai and Lanai. Three- and five-hour
excursions $46 and $69, respectively. Located near the Kaanapali
resort area, but the stables are accessible only by private 4-wheel-
drive roads (they arrange hotel pickups). Contact: P.O. Box 10656,
Kaanapali, HI 96761. 808/667-7896.

Kaupo Store: Charles Aki, owner of the funky little general store in
Kaupo (west of Kipahulu on Hwy 31) manages horseback tours into
the Haleakala crater. His tours include overnight stays in the crater
(park cabins if available, otherwise you camp; he provides the gear).
Price: $150/person for 4–6 persons; $200/person for groups of 2–3.
Contact: Kaupo Store, Kaupo, HI 96713. 808/248-8209.

Makena Stables: La Perouse Bay, the west slopes of Haleakala,
Ulupalakua ranchlands, coastal lava flows, and inland kiawe
woodlands are all part of the horseback tour available at Makena
Stables. The sunsets from these open rolling hills are exquisite, an
attractive part of the package. Contact: 7299-A S. Makena Road,
Makena, HI 96753. 808/879-0244.

Pony Express Tours: They specialize in Haleakala crater rides,
offering half-day and full-day tours. The rides are limited to small
groups and led by guides knowledgeable in local natural history and
folklore. They also offer shorter rides into the Haleakala ranchlands
on the volcano's grassy outer slopes. Price: $90/person for half-day
rides; $120/person for full day; $40/person for the shorter
ranchlands tours. Contact: P.O. Box 535, Kula, HI 96790.
808/667-2200.

Rainbow Ranch: The West Maui mountains and the north shore are
the twin locations for the tours offered by Rainbow Ranch. They
offer pineapple plantation rides, picnic rides, sunset rides, mountain
rides, and coastal rides of varying lengths and degrees of difficulty.
Prices vary from $25 to $70. Contact: P.O. Box 10066, Lahaina, HI
96761. 808/669-4991.

Landing a kayak on Molokai's north shore

Thompson Ranch: Canter along the grassy slopes of Thompson Ranchlands, located at 3700 feet elevation on Haleakala. Or slowly explore the crater on a half-day, a full-day or an overnight excursion. This outfit arranges it. The stables near the junction of Hwy 37 and 377 in Kula, on the way to Tedeschi Winery. 808/878-1910.

KAYAK TOURS

As it has elsewhere in the Hawaiian Islands, coastal kayaking has become popular on Maui. The island lacks the spectacular wilderness coasts of Kauai, Molokai, and the Island of Hawaii, so kayak tours here are less adventurous, but they still provide a wonderful opportunity to explore otherwise inaccessible areas. Two agencies lead kayak tours along Maui's coasts.

Maui Kayaks: They offer half-day and full-day guided tours of the gentle waters off Kihei for snorkeling or whale-watching in season. Contact: 50 J. Waiohuli Street, Kihei, HI 96753. 808/874-3536.

Maui Sea Kayaking: Group tours and personalized kayak adventures are arranged for various parts of Maui. Contact: 202 Kawehi Place, Kula, HI 96790. 808/572-6299.

NATURALIST GUIDE SERVICES

Several outfits on Maui arrange and lead wilderness tours for hikers. The main advantage they offer is guidance into places that would otherwise likely be missed. They also can deal with logistics, including equipment and permits.

Aumakua Adventures: This is a personalized guide service that includes hiking adventures in natural and scenic areas. They charge $150/day for 2 persons; $80/half-day for 2 persons (*kamaaina* rates are available). Contact: P.O. Box 1839, Makawao, HI 96768. 808/572-6212.

Hana Ranch: The owners of Hana Ranch now use their 4500-acre private preserve in east Maui for nature tours: hiking trips, horseback riding, hunting, and shoreline fishing. These guided activities capture the range of natural opportunities on the ranch. The ranch has been a driving force behind the community of Hana since 1946, and the new ranch activities present opportunities for tourists to explore areas formerly inaccessible. They probably won't appeal to die-hard hikers since the activities are organized and they generally cater to a more sedentary crowd. But if you're interested in an organized nature tour, with minimal strain, then it might be just the thing. They are located 1.5 miles south of Hana on Piilani Highway (Hwy 31). Contact: Hana Ranch, P.O. Box 278, Hana, HI 96713. 808/248-7238.

Hike Maui: Naturalist Ken Schmitt has formed a backcountry tour company that gets high ratings on Maui. He knows the island intimately, and he has the reputation of enthusiastically sharing his knowledge of natural areas with his clients. Private and group excursions can be arranged for dayhikes or week-long journeys into the most remote areas. Prices vary according to personal itineraries ($300/day for 2 persons for backpacking trips; $1000/person for week-long excursions). Contact: Hike Maui, P.O. Box 330969, Kahului, HI 96733. 808/879-5270.

Hunting Adventures of Maui, Inc.: Wild boar (puaa) and Spanish goat (kao) range the upper elevations of Haleakala's outer slopes. This guide service can lead you into the remote hunting regions. Contact: 645B Kaupakalua Road, Haiku, HI 96708. 808/572-8214.

Outer Island Adventures: This nature guide service based in the upcountry town of Makawao offers a variety of tours, hikes and explorations. Contact them at: P.O. Box 996, Makawao, HI 96768. 808/672-6396.

OCEAN TOURS

Maui is renowned for the excellent skin and scuba diving in its clear offshore waters, particularly around the tiny volcanic islet of Molokini. Maui's natural environment obviously includes marine as well as land areas, so it would seem appropriate to include some of the marine adventure options in this rundown of tour possibilities.

Hawaiian Visitors Bureau

Pineapple field in Maui's isthmus

However, there are so many outfits offering snorkeling and cruise excursions that the task is simply beyond this book.

The Pacific Whale Foundation (see Environmental Groups) operates charter excursions for snorkeling on Molokini. Given their excellent reputation for science and education excursions, and the fact that their snorkeling adventures combine fun with natural history education, you may want to check them out. The vessel *Machias* is reputed to offer some of the finest excursions on Maui— trips to Molokini and Molokai under the guidance of oceanographer Captain Bill Austin. His boat is an 80-foot sailing schooner, and his trips combine snorkeling with hiking in remote coastal locations. Make arrangements through the Ocean Activities Center (808/879-4485) or visit his representative at Maalaea Activities Center (808/242-6982); at the Maalaea boat harbor between Kihei and Lahaina.

You otherwise will encounter dozens of outfits offering snorkeling excursions to Molokini, the tiny tuff cone between Maui and Kahoolawe whose nearby waters provide some of the finest diving in Hawaii. Be aware that on any given day there are likely to be hundreds of other people in the water with you.

SNUBA of Maui provides personalized snorkeling and scuba adventures with an approach that combines ocean exploration with conservation education. Contact them at P.O. Box 2077, Kihei, HI 96753. 808/874-1001. If you remain at a loss as to how to arrange your marine adventure, you can contract Barefoot's Cashback

Tours, a commercial outfit in Lahaina that contracts with all the tour outfits on the island. Contact: 626 Front St. in Lahaina (P.O. Box 1775, Lahaina, HI 96767. 808/661-8889).

MOLOKAI NATURE TOURS AND OUTDOOR EXCURSIONS

There are no commercial nature tours on Molokai. However, a few of the agencies based on other islands frequently lead excursions to Molokai. Rusty Banana Oceanic Adventures organizes and leads 4–5 day kayak expeditions along the remote north coast. The trips demand stamina and a yen for adventure; they reward participants with solitude and excitement amid the splendid wilderness of the world's highest sea cliffs and Hawaii's most remote valleys. The 4-day excursions cost $395, 5-day $445, for everything—food, kayaks, air fare from Honolulu to Molokai, pre-departure orientations. Contact: 740 Kapahulu Ave., Honolulu, HI 96826. 808/737-9514.

Bicycling on Molokai is probably the best found anywhere in the Hawaiian Islands. The roads, offering magnificent vistas and rolling grades, are quiet. No services are available for bikers on Molokai. Inquiries into group bicycle tours can be made at Island Bicycle Adventures, 569 Kapahulu Avenue, Honolulu, HI 96815. 808/734-0700; 800/233-2226.

Snorkeling and Surfing

SNORKELING

Maui's beaches and clear water are renowned, and many leeward coastal areas offer good-to-outstanding snorkeling. The windward coast is generally treacherous, but for the expert diver it holds possibilities. Molokai and Lanai each offer limited snorkeling.

Kihei-Makena: A dozen beach parks are on the protected coast between Kihei and Makena. They are accessible from S. Kihei Road or Wailea Alanui Road. Snorkeling is good at many of them. Try a few. Between "Big" and "Little" beaches at Makena is a stretch of rocky shoal beneath Puu Olai (the 360-foot cinder cone between the beaches) that offers very good snorkeling when the seas are calm.

Honolua Bay: Designated a marine life conservation district, the bay is accessible from Hwy 30, 2 miles north of Napili Bay on Maui's west end. Summer snorkeling is fine for beginners through experienced.

Olowalu-Lahaina: Honoapiilani Highway (Hwy 30) skirts the ocean for several miles south of Lahaina, and passes many fine snorkeling areas. Try one that looks promising. The waters are protected by a fringing reef and so are generally quite calm.

Molokini Island: This submerged volcano is a marine life conservation district that attracts daily hundreds of snorkelers and divers. You can easily arrange a tour to the diving areas on one of the many tourist boats that advertise in Kihei and Lahaina.

For information on snorkeling or for guided tours, contact: Maui Dive Guide, P.O. Box 1461, Kahului, HI 96732. 808/879-5172.

Snorkeling on Molokai is generally mediocre. The best spots are at the west-end beaches near the Sheraton Molokai and Papohaku beach, and along stretches of the south shore accessible from Hwy 450. These places are not marked and require some exploring. Ask around on the island.

SURFING

Hookipa Park: Winter swells can be huge and are for experts only. This spot is most famous for world-class board sailing. Accessible from Hana Highway (Hwy 360), 2 miles east of Paia.

Lahaina: The breakwall is a popular spot, as is nearby "Hot Sands". Beginners can contact: Hawaiian Surfing Schools, P.O. Box 11713, Lahaina, HI 96761. 808/667-5834.

Honolua Bay: This summer-snorkeling spot is a favorite winter surfing spot among locals. Accessible from Hwy 30, 2 miles north of Napili Bay.

Maalaea: Small but fast waves reward surfers in the summer months. Popular with locals. Accessible from Hwy 30 northwest of Kihei.

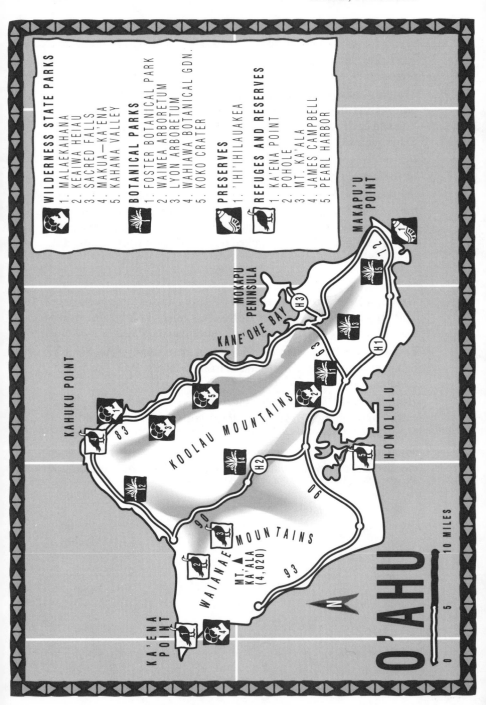

WILDERNESS STATE PARKS
1. MALAEKAHANA
2. KEAIWA HEIAU
3. SACRED FALLS
4. MAKUA–KA'ENA
5. KAHANA VALLEY

BOTANICAL PARKS
1. FOSTER BOTANICAL PARK
2. WAIMEA ARBORETUM
3. LYON ARBORETUM
4. WAHIAWA BOTANICAL GDN.
5. KOKO CRATER

PRESERVES
1. 'IHI'IHILAUAKEA

REFUGES AND RESERVES
1. KA'ENA POINT
2. POHOLE
3. MT. KA'ALA
4. JAMES CAMPBELL
5. PEARL HARBOR

MAKAPU'U
POINT

MOKAPU
PENINSULA

KANE'OHE BAY

KAHUKU POINT

KOOLAU MOUNTAINS

HONOLULU

WAIANAE MOUNTAINS

MT. KA'ALA
(4,020)

KA'ENA
POINT

O'AHU

N

0   5   10 MILES

Chapter Six

Oahu

Background

Visitors arriving at Honolulu International Airport are greeted immediately with outstanding views of the physical geography of Oahu. The low-lying mountains that appear to the northwest of the airport are the Waianae Range, aproximately 3 million years old. To the northeast is the younger Koolau Range, 2.5 million years old. Both of these mountain ranges are spiny remnants of former volcanic shields that once stood over 6000 feet in elevation. Between the two ranges is the Schofield Plateau, created where lava from the Koolau volcano flowed against the Waianae shield. The high points of the island are contained in the two ranges—Mt. Kaala (4020 feet) in the Waianaes, and Konahuanui (3150 feet) in the Koolaus.

But most visitors will probably first recognize the small, distinct volcanic landmarks that lie east of the airport, along the south coastline. Dominating the eastern skyline from the airport is Diamond Head, made famous in numerous movies and television series. This well-known geological feature is a tuff cone that is only 150,000 years old, an infant by Hawaii's geological standards. It was formed in a single violent eruption when ash, cinders, chunks of basalt, and limestone torn from the surrounding reefs were thrown into the sky. Settling amid the tuff debris were calcite crystals. Early sailors mistook these for diamonds, and hence the volcanic cone was misnamed Diamond Head.

Along the windward coast, the Koolau Range takes on its most spectacular form. There the range's flank has been eroded into a ragged face of 2000-foot fluted cliffs, known as the pali. The pali traces the long axis of a former shield volcano that extended west beyond the pali and east into the sea. The drive along the windward coast on Kahekili Highway (Hwy 83) provides an excellent opportunity to view the dramatic cliffs. The stark pinnacle of Olomana near Kaneohe and the magnificent buttress walls nearby show where the southwest edge of the old Koolau caldera was located. Everything to the east has been removed by erosion, subsidence and catastrophic wasting. If you visit the Byodo-In Valley of the Temples north of Kaneohe, you will see close up the full rise of the pali.

After rounding the windy north shore of the island, past the former sugar lands of Kahuku, Kamehameha Highway (Hwy 83) skirts Waimea Bay and then enters the coastal surfing village of Haleiwa. One mile south of Haleiwa, Hwy 83 intersects with Hwy 90, which heads south to Wahiawa, where it links up with H2. Near Wahiawa, the route passes through extensive fields of pineapple planted in the rich volcanic soils of the Schofield Plateau. This broad, elevated platform is bounded by the Koolaus to the east and the Waianaes to the west. Much of the land is owned by the Dole and Del Monte companies, and most of the plateau residents work in the sugar or pineapple industry. As H2 descends to Honolulu, clear views are obtained of infamous Pearl Harbor—a giant estuary

---

Early sailors mistook these for diamonds, and hence the volcanic cone was misnamed Diamond Head.

---

system that was formed as the island slowly subsided. West of downtown Honolulu, H1 traverses the Ewa Plain, formed from an elevated coral reef by changes in sea level. From Barbers Point on the Ewa Plain, Farrington Highway (Hwy 93) heads northwest along the leeward coast, west of the Waianae Range. The road skirts the broad Makaha and Waianae valleys before ending at Yokohama Bay, a couple of miles south of Kaena Point. The huge valleys of the leeward side of the Waianae Range are eroded from the west slope of the Waianae shield. Lava that had spilled over the western rim of the Waianae crater created the gradual slope observed at the valleys' upper ends. Weather conditions are dry along this coast because the Koolau Range and the windward side of the Waianae catch most of the rain brought by the northeast trades.

There are several vantage points from which the island's terrain can be viewed. Punchbowl and Roundtop Drive in Honolulu are good places to view the west slopes of the Koolaus, much of the Waianae Range, and the most recent Honolulu volcanic series, which includes Diamond Head, Koko Head, Punchbowl, and Hanauma Bay. Nuuanu Pali State Park off the Pali Highway (Hwy 61) provides an overlook for viewing the windward pali of the Koolaus and the caldera remnants near Kaneohe. The hikes described in this chapter provide opportunities to explore Oahu's varied volcanic terrain.

The volcanic surfaces on Oahu are now covered by a variety of things: urban development, recreational areas, agricultural fields, military establishments, planted gardens, and in some places natural vegetation. The once flourishing native coastal forests have been largely erased. Lowland dryland forests of lama (*Diospyros ferrea*) and wiliwili (*Erythrina sandvicensis*) still occur in remote pockets of the Waianae Range, among the outer foothills and talus slopes of the northwestern Koolaus, and in Koko Crater.

Some shoreline plants such as naupaka (*Scaevola sericea*) still flourish, but the flowering ilima (*Sida fallax*) that once grew profusely on the Ewa plain is now fairly scarce. Near the bustling urban centers it is still possible to discover small communities of native plants—for example, the coastal naio (*Myoporum sandwicense*) growing in Hawaii Kai. But other once-common beach species now are found only at more remote sites farther inland, or not at all. Oahu's wetlands have experienced some of the most severe rates of disturbance. One need go no farther than a Waikiki hotel lanai to imagine the massive transformations that led to the loss of the south shore marshes, first to taro cultivated by the early Polynesians, then to rice planted by Asian immigrants in the 19th century, and finally, irretrievably, to the coastline construction boom that began in earnest with Western development in the early 20th century.

The wet upland forests of Oahu have witnessed similar destruction and transformation. Sandlewood (*Santalum*) forests were cut for the China trade. Koa (*Acacia koa*) provided heavy, beautifully grained wood for ships, houses, and furniture. Huge tracts of ohia lehua (*Metrosideros polymorpha*) were cleared for agriculture. The specially adapted Hawaiian plants were displaced by cash crops

---

The presence of Honolulu and other large towns on Oahu means that environmental degradation is greater on this island, but to an alarming extent all the islands of Hawaii are sharing a similar fate.

(mainly sugar cane and pineapple), cattle grazing fields, or the numerous introduced trees such as the ironwoods (*Casuarina*), kiawe (*Prosopis pallida*), and banyans (*Ficus*).

To be sure, the transformation of Oahu's natural communities has a long history. But it was radically speeded up with the landscape manipulations and the plant and animal introductions of the ancient Polynesians. Next came Western cattlemen, farmers, and traders, who made even more dramatic alterations in the land. The impact of human activity in recent decades has caused even more

profound changes in Oahu's natural world. The presence of
Honolulu and other large towns on Oahu means that environmental
degradation is greater on this island, but to an alarming extent all the
islands of Hawaii are sharing a similar fate.

As you travel in Oahu, imagine what was here before, and how
significantly it has all changed. Explore some of the remaining
places where you will find part of the island's natural history intact,
in the island's natural-area reserves, wildlife refuges, nature
preserves, and parks. The nature-tour and outdoor-excursion groups
mentioned in this chapter can lead you into such areas for thought
and exploration. Several books also can help. *Anatomy of an
Island: A Geological History of Oahu* by Macdonald and Kyselka is
a complete discussion of Oahu geology. *Oahu Environments* by
Morgan and Street provides a description of Oahu's natural and cultural landscapes. *Islands in a Far Sea* by John Culliney and
Hawaii: A Natural History by Sherwin Carlquist contain extensive
sections on Oahu.

Alternative Lodging

Oahu has fewer alternative lodging opportunities than the outer
islands, even though it receives the bulk of island visitors. About
80% of incoming tourists never leave Oahu, and a majority of *them*
never leave Waikiki. The Waikiki Strip has an overwhelming
capacity to accommodate visitors. In 1988 there were 89 hotels in
Waikiki, with 26,911 rooms. The sheer density of tourists along this
sunny southern shore has made it one of the world's most famous
travel destinations.

Not so long ago, less than 80 years, most of the high-rise area
was swamp and taro fields. It now is densely packed with hotels and
condominiums, but new construction continues and is filling the
remaining empty spaces from Diamond Head to the airport. A
"second Waikiki" is currently being developed along the southwest
shore of Oahu, in an area of former scrub wildlands. This new
development, called West Beach, is located on the Ewa Plain south
of Waianae. But there exist a few alternative places to stay on Oahu,
scattered around the city or located in the rural windward and north-
shore areas.

BED AND BREAKFAST INNS

Most of the Oahu bed & breakfast establishments participate in
island-wide directories that link visitors with private homes. See the
directories to find the establishment that best meets your needs.

A 5 Star Bed and Breakfast—BRJ's: They advertise themselves as
a directory offering a "Special Experience in Hawaiian Living."
Find out for yourself. 808/235-8235.

Aloha Bed and Breakfast: Private homes and condos are listed by this group. They are at 1750 Kalakaua Ave., Suite 1002, Honolulu. 808/949-1881.

Bed and Breakfast: Studios and rooms in private homes are arranged by this directory service for tourists and residents. 808/595-7533.

Bed and Breakfast Hawaii: They do statewide bookings and are based on Kauai in Kapaa. Contact: P.O. Box 449, Kapaa, HI 96746; or call on Oahu 808/536-8421.

In addition to the B&Bs in the directories listed above, there are only a few unaffiliated bed & breakfast places on Oahu: Check with them directly for rates and amenities.

Akamai Bed and Breakfast: 808/263-0227.

Breakfast in Bed: 808/735-2626.

Manoa Valley Inn: 808/947-6019.

CABINS

Only a few cabins exist for visitors on Oahu; most of them are located at backcountry sites in the state forest reserves. These are normally used by hunters, but backcountry hikers with the proper permits are welcome to stay at them. The cabins are located in the Koolau Range, along some of the remote hiking trails. For information on cabin locations and permits, contact the Division of Forestry and Wildlife in Honolulu. 808/548-8850.

The Division of State Parks maintains a housekeeping cabin at Malaekahana State Recreation Area, north of Laie on Oahu's windward coast. Cost $5/person/night ($10 for a single person to use the entire cabin). Contact: Division of State Parks in Honolulu. 808/293-1736.

HOSTELS

These places are for low-budget travelers who do not mind trading privacy for cost savings. Many active young travelers, bicyclists, and international students end up at Oahu hostels, which have the transient and disheveled ambiance of a European-style youth hostel.

Hale Aloha AYH-Hostel: You need to be a member of the American Youth Hostel Association or the International Youth Hostel Association to stay here, and you must have your membership before coming to Hawaii—they don't sell the cards here. Dormitory bunks go for $10/night and private rooms cost $22/night. Book as far in advance as possible. Located in the Waikiki district. Contact: 2417 Prince Edward, Honolulu, HI 96815. 808/926-8313.

Honolulu International AYH-Hostel: No membership is needed here. Dorm bunks are $8/night for AYH members and $11/night for nonmembers. No private rooms. Located in the University district. Contact: 2323-A Sea View Ave., Honolulu, HI 96822. 808/946-0591.

Waikiki Prince Hotel: Not a hostel but it's located next to the Hale Aloha AYH, and it receives a lot of hostelers when the AYH is full. The resulting ambiance is youth-budget with an international feel. Prices are cheap for Waikiki—$29–$37/night. Contact: 2431 Prince Edward, Honolulu, Hawaii 96815. 808/922-1544.

Botanical Gardens and Parks

Foster Botanic Garden: Set amid the concrete and glass apartment towers of downtown Honolulu, this luxurious oasis of plant life is one of Oahu's premier botanical sites. The garden's founder, Dr. William Hillebrand, began importing flora from throughout the tropics in 1855. On five and one-half acres of land that he purchased from the Hawaiian royal family, he planted both native Hawaiian and introduced species. He added the magnificent bo Tree (*Ficus religiousa*), Chinese banyan tree (*Ficus microcarpa*), and baobab tree (*Adansonia digitata*) that now tower in the center of the garden. In 1867, he sold the property to Captain and Mrs. Thomas Foster, who continued to develop the garden until 1930, when they bequeathed it to the City of Honolulu. Since then the garden has been expanded to its current 20 acres, and it now contains several thousand plant species, including 24 of Oahu's "exceptional trees"—protected species of rare age, size, and endemic status.

Foster garden receives tens of thousands of visitors each year, and it functions as both an aesthetic park and an educational center. Self-guiding tours take visitors through the various settings: the prehistoric glen containing a variety of Paleozoic and Mesozoic plants, including numerous ferns (*Cyathea, Cibotium, Angiopteris, Blechnum* and *Adiantum*) and mosses (*Selaginella* and *Lycopodium*); the bromeliad collection (including examples of the best known family member, the pineapple); the Lyon orchid garden, with both New World and Old World species of *cattleya, epidendrum, dendrobium, vanda,* and many others; the economic garden, with plants that serve a variety of fiber, food, building, and medicinal purposes; the palm collection, with nearly 600 species of this important group of tropical plants; and the brilliant, flowering tropical plants found on the middle terraces of the garden—bird of paradise, yellow and white gingers, and heliconias.

Hibiscus

The garden is maintained by the Friends of Foster Garden, a community group responsible for a variety of horticulture outreach programs. They sponsor educational programs in the garden, give lectures and tours, conduct special events such as moonlight walks in the garden, and provide interpretive maps and booklets. To visit Foster Botanic Garden, take the Vineyard Blvd. exit off H1 in downtown Honolulu. The garden is between Liliiha street and Nuuanu Avenue on the mauka side of Vineyard Blvd. It is open daily 9–4 with a $1 admission charge. Their address is 50 N. Vineyard Blvd., Honolulu, HI 96817. 808/522-7066.

Hoomaluhia Park: This 400-acre natural park nestles beneath the impressive fluted cliffs of the Pali, on the windward side of Oahu, in Kaneohe. It is both a botanic garden and a nature preserve, with facilities for picnicking, hiking, camping, craftswork, and environmental study. Park personnel regularly offer tours for the public. These include bird walks, Hawaiian ethnobotany plant walks, moon walks, and other special events. The park is thematically divided into geographic regions of the tropics, each planted in native communities of rare and endangered species. But it emphasizes the preservation of endemic Hawaiian flora. Guided nature hikes are offered each Saturday (10–12) and Sunday (12:30–2:30). With its emphasis on ecology and ethnobotany, the park promotes visitor education. The interpretive center should be visited by everyone entering the park. Hoomaluhia is open daily 9–3. There is no charge, but many of the programmed activities require prior registration. The park is located at the end of Luluku Rd. off Likelike Hwy, approximately one mile mauka of Kamehameha Hwy near the Windward City Shopping Center in Kaneohe. 808/235-6636.

Koko Crater Botanic Gardens: The crater of the tuff cone that rises 1200 feet above the surrounding terrain in East Honolulu District contains Honolulu's newest botanic garden. The drought conditions that prevail here due to the rainshadow effect of the Koolau mountain range ensure a dry-forest plant assemblage. Numerous succulents and drought-tolerant trees have been planted on the caldera floor. The arid-lands garden is currently under construction, and many displays are not yet complete, but the walking trails and bridal paths that wander through the crater are well worth following. The quiet of the crater contrasts sharply with the noise of the city outside. The park is open daily 24 hours. It is reached by entering Queens Gate subdivision across Hwy 72 from Sandy Beach County Park. Proceed through the subdivision on Kealahou Street to the Koko Crater Stables. Park at the gate entrance; the crater and garden are directly ahead of you.

Lyon Arboretum: The Harold L. Lyon Arboretum is a botanical and horticultural research arm of the University of Hawaii, and one of Oahu's premier public gardens. The arboretum comprises 124 acres in lush upper Manoa Valley, including greenhouse and lab facilities for plant research and propagation work. The grounds contain over 4000 species and cultivars of palms, figs, taros, gingers, ti, orchids, and others. It contains extensive collections of native Hawaiian plants, including the Beatrice H. Krauss Hawaiian Ethnobotanical Garden, developed for the study of plants used by the ancient Hawaiians for food, medicine, clothing, and construction. Other areas are devoted to particular plant communities and habitats. From the high point on the botanical trail, "inspiration point," the view sweeps across the upper Manoa Valley's rugged topography of fluted cliffs and steep stream valleys. Bird songs and the sound of waterfalls fill the arboretum, while only minutes away is the nonstop buzz of Honolulu. Guided tours of the arboretum are conducted for both individuals and groups, or you can leisurely visit on your own. The park is open Mon.–Fri. 9–3. Contact: 3860 Manoa Road, Honolulu, HI 96822. 808/988-3177.

Senator Fong's Plantation and Garden: In 1976 Senator Hiram Fong resigned from the U.S. Senate and his influential position as the ranking minority member of the Appropriations Committee. He returned to Hawaii, where he established a plantation garden below the majestic Pali on Oahu's windward coast. The 725-acre estate is now open to the public. If you visit, don't let the commercial aspects of the place (tram tours, snack bar, gift shops) spoil the lovely gardens and the panoramic views. The estate is at 47-285 Pulama Road, Kaneohe, HI 96744. 808/239-6775. To reach there, head mauka on Pulama Road, off Kamehameha Highway (Hwy 83) in Kahaluu.

Wahiawa Botanic Garden: The Hawaii Sugar Planters' Association set up a nursery and a forestry experiment station during the 1920s in the hills above Wahiawa in central Oahu. In 1950 the land was turned over to the City and County of Honolulu for the purpose of developing a community botanic garden. The 27-acre wooded site remains only partly developed, but it contains rare spice trees, fruit trees, native Hawaiian flowering plants, a fern walkway and pleasantly cool surroundings. The garden is at 1396 California Ave., Wahiawa, north of the town center. To reach it, follow H2 north from Honolulu to its terminus in downtown Wahiawa.

Waimea Arboretum: The glitzy commercial atmosphere of Waimea Falls Park, one of Oahu's premier tourist attractions, disguises the fact that the Park contains one of the finest botanical gardens in the state. Tucked amid the concessions, restaurants, hula shows, and passing tour groups, is the semi-autonomous Waimea Arboretum and Botanic Garden. It contains 36 major plant collections, arranged by genus, family, and geographical region. The garden's emphasis is on "conservation through cultivation," and its scientific research staff collects and propagates threatened species from throughout the tropics. Of the approximate 3000 species of threatened plants native to the U.S., over one fourth are endemic to Hawaii. Waimea's collection includes a significant number of these endangered Hawaiian plants. Waimea's work receives cooperation from the International Union for the Conservation of Nature, the World Wildlife Fund, the U.S. Fish and Wildlife Service, and the Hawaii State Department of Forestry and Wildlife. To visit the garden, you must pay the Park entrance fee of $8.50. The Park is adjacent to Waimea Bay at 59-864 Kamehameha Hwy (Hwy 83), Haleiwa, HI 96712. 808/638-8511.

Camping Areas

Oahu's large urban population places a heavy demand on the island's campgrounds particularly on weekends. A problem with many of the campgrounds is their proximity to the city or to busy roads, and unless you are with a large group of people, some of the designated campgrounds simply are not safe places to spend the night. Since the parks that are safe and peaceful places to camp are popular and heavily used, reservations for camping permits must be made well in advance: for the state parks, 2 months is recommended for weekend dates; for the county parks allow at least 5 weeks.

There is little opportunity for camping on Oahu outside of the designated camping parks. Private campgrounds are closed to the general public, and there are no vast tracts of wilderness. On a few of the hiking routes into the Koolau Mountains, camping is permissable and pleasant (see Hiking). For the most part, though, camping on Oahu is restricted to the state parks and to the City and County of Honolulu beach parks.

The established campgrounds described below are the best on the island; others exist which you can inquire about from the Department of Parks and Recreation, City and County of Honolulu, 650 S. King Street, Honolulu, HI 96813. 808/523-4527. Camping is allowed in some forest-reserve areas. For information on regulations for them, contact the Division of Forestry and Wildlife in Honolulu.

Hiking in Keaiwa Heiau State Recreation Area

STATE PARKS

Permits are needed to camp at Oahu's state parks. Contact: Division of State Parks in Honolulu.

Kaiaka State Recreation Area: This 52-acre park has space for 7 tents. The park is located in a quiet coastal location at Kaiaka Point, on the south side of Haleiwa Village. The Kaiaka camping area is one of the best along Oahu's northeast coast. To reach the park from Honolulu, take H2 north to Wahiawa, and from Wahiawa, go north on Hwy 90 to Waialua Beach Road in Haleiwa; take this road south to Kaiaka Point. The state park is well-marked with a signboard.

Keaiwa Heiau State Recreation Area: This forest park is located on 385 acres of recreational land in the Koolau Range. It is situated at 880 feet elevation, and the weather can be windy, cool, and wet, particularly during the winter months. The park has 4 tent-campgrounds that combined can accommodate up to 100 persons. In addition to the campsites, it has picnic areas, a 4.8-mile loop trail, heiau remains, and lovely views of both the forests and the city. To reach the park from Waikiki, follow H1 west to Moanalua Highway (Hwy 72). Take the Aiea cutoff to Aiea Heights Drive and follow it for about 3 miles to the park at the roadend.

Malaekahana State Recreation Park: This camping park is arguably the premier beach campsite on Oahu. Its location on the far north shore isolates it from the urban problems encountered at many of the other beach parks. Unfortunately, even here problems of minor theft have occurred in recent years. But the incidents remain relatively infrequent, and Malaekahana is probably the nicest place on Oahu to beach camp. The adjacent beach is usually empty, and the swim-walk out to Moku Auia (Goat Island) offshore is a lovely way to spend some time. To reach the Park, go north from Kaneohe on Kamehameha Highway (Hwy 83) to Laie. The Park is one-half mile north of Laie on the makai side of Hwy 83.

Sand Island State Recreation Area: The finest points that this park has to offer as a campsite are the sunsets and the nighttime views of downtown Honolulu. It is a 140-acre urban camping area. The park experiences relatively few problems of theft or violence, probably because it is well-secured at night. To reach the park from Waikiki, take the Nimitz Highway (Hwy 92) west to the Sand Island Access Road, and follow this to the roadend.

Waimanalo Bay State Recreation Area: The beach at Waimanalo may well be one of the world's finest. The colors here are extraordinary, the fine-grained sand is the texture of talcum, and a

A wahine in Malaekahana State Park

fringing reef protects the bay, making for excellent swimming. This place rivals Malaekahana as one of Oahu's finest beach campgrounds. Its main drawback is the often-crowded conditions. In addition to the campsites, the 75-acre park contains picnic areas, an inland playfield, and popular body-surfing spots. To reach the park from Honolulu, follow Kalanianaole Highway (Hwy 72) east past Hanauma Bay, around Makapuu Point, and north along the windward shore to Waimanalo town. The park is about one mile north of town.

CITY AND COUNTY BEACH PARKS

The alternatives to the state park campsites are the many Honolulu City and County beach parks that allow camping. To spend the night in some of these is inadvisable; many of them are extended outdoor homes for local residents where transient campers are not particularly welcome. Thirteen city and county parks allow camping; I recommend it at only the 5 described below. One of these, Kualoa Park, is secured at night, but campers still occasionally report problems of theft and disturbance. The others are fairly remote and peaceful places. Permits are required but are free; make reservations in advance from the Department of Parks and Recreation in Honolulu. Or you can obtain permits from the satellite city halls; call the Department office for information on locations.

Bellows Field Beach Park: A windward coast park, adjacent to Waimanalo Bay. Camping in shady ironwood groves. Located off Kalanianaole Highway (Hwy 72) 2 miles north of Waimanalo.

Kahana Bay Beach Park: A lovely location amid a coconut grove at Kahana Bay. The ocean here is not very good for swimming due to the sediments that enter the bay from Kahana Stream, but the campsite itself is very picturesque. On Kamehameha Highway (Hwy 83), about midway up the windward coast, between Kaaawa and Punaluu.

Kualoa County Regional Park: The park is famous for the island offshore—Mokolii Island (Chinaman's Hat). Equally fine are the views of the windward coast, and the sunrises. The park is located on Kamehameha Highway (Hwy 83) about 10 miles north of Kaneohe.

Makapuu Beach Park: There is not much privacy at this campsite, but the coast is beautiful, the surf is excellent for body surfing, and the sunrise over Manana Island (Rabbit Island) is exquisite. Makapuu is on Kamehameha Highway (Hwy 72), across from Sea Life Park.

Mokuleia Beach Park: This park is located on one of the most remote stretches of beach on Oahu. Its isolated location recommends the Park as a place to camp. To reach the Park from Honolulu, head north on H2 to Wahiawa. Turn onto Hwy 99 and follow it west to Hwy 803, which leads to Waialua. In Waialua (at Thompson Circle) turn west onto Farrington Highway (Hwy 930) and follow it for 5 miles to the Park. The Park is well-marked with a signboard.

Ecomuseums

Oahu has two museums, both in Honolulu, that will fascinate and inform those with an interest in the natural or cultural history of Hawaii. They both sponsor frequent hikes, outings and other natural programs (see Hawaiian Islands Environmental Education).

Bishop Museum: This is the main museum in the Pacific region. Beneath its lofty gabled roof, the museum's impressive galleries and stately libraries document and chronicle the Polynesians and the land of Hawaii. The museum is a leading scientific research institution, with natural history collections of several million items. Scientists from throughout the world come to the Bishop Museum for purposes of scholarly research on diverse Pacific topics. The museum houses an archival library of maps, photographs, manuscripts, journals, and books. These collections are open to the public, but some require prior arrangement to visit. Bishop Museum regularly sponsors lecture programs by leading naturalists visiting from throughout the world, it provides environmental education materials, and it conducts natural history programs on Oahu. The main galleries are open Mon.–Sat. and the first Sunday of each month from 9–5. Admission is $4.95/adult; $2.50/children. It is located at 1525 Bernice Street, P.O. Box 19000-A, Honolulu, HI 96817. 808/847-3511. 808/848-4129 (recording). To reach the

---

Scientists from throughout the world come to the Bishop Museum for purposes of scholarly research on diverse Pacific topics.

---

museum, take the Houghtailing exit off H1 in downtown Honolulu. Follow the signs.

Waikiki Aquarium: In a small, unassuming building at the Diamond Head end of Waikiki is a splendid marine museum that houses artistically arranged and scientifically accurate exhibits of tropical Pacific marine life. It's only a 10-minute walk from Waikiki, but it shares with the glitzy tourist district only the name. As the third-oldest aquarium in the U.S. (founded in 1904) the Waikiki Aquarium has a long-standing tradition of community events—including their famous nighttime reef walks. The aquarium exhibits are arranged by ecological zone (intertidal, splash, surge, subtidal, sandy shore, coral reef, deep water). For each zone the associated marine life species are displayed with interpretive materials. The aquarium is affiliated with the University of Hawaii, and is a major research facility as well as a public museum. The aquarium is open daily 9–5. Admission is $2.50 donation/adult; children are free. It is at 2777 Kalakaua Avenue, Honolulu, HI 96815. 808/923-9741.

Environmental Organizations

Several environmental groups are located on Oahu. Their agendas include issues that have statewide significance, so while they appear here under the Oahu chapter, their work may be relevant for the outer islands as well. The groups are organized here according to their primary concerns: government, political action, preservation, research, or service. These categories often overlap, and the work of many of the groups will actually fall into more than one category. These groups complement the organizations that are described in the Hawaiian Islands chapter, under environmental education.

Government

Department of Land and Natural Resources: This is the state government agency that has the Division of Aquatic Resources,

Division of Conservation and Resources Enforcement, Division of Forestry and Wildlife, Division of Land Management, Division of State Parks and Recreation, and Division of Water and Land Development.

Political Action

Conservation Council for Hawaii: This is a nonprofit citizen's organization promoting the wise use and management of Hawaii's natural resources. Organized in 1950, it has since 1972 been the Hawaii state affiliate of the National Wildlife Federation. Active chapters exist on the outer islands, as well as a number of affiliated organizations. They publish a quarterly newsletter to inform members of current island environmental issues, they conduct workshops and education programs, and they prepare legislative materials and provide expert testimony for public hearings on current conservation issues. Contact: P.O. Box 2923, Honolulu, HI 96802.

The Hawaii Green Movement: This political action group based in Honolulu watchdogs environmental legislation in the state. Their environmental perspective links them with other state groups, including the Kaala Farm, the Opelu Project, and the Environmental Legislative Network. The group also publishes a newsletter, and it serves as a clearinghouse for environmental literature statewide. Contact: Hawaii Green Movement, P.O. Box 61508, Honolulu, HI 96839. 808/293-5891.

Life of the Land: This Honolulu citizen's group founded in 1970 is concerned with pollution, pesticides, and energy consumption. Contact: 19 Niolopa Place, Honolulu, HI 96817.

Natural Resources Defense Council: The Honolulu-based Hawaii office of the Natural Resources Defense Council is active on a number of environmental fronts. It is doing especially important work in the areas of biodiversity and Hawaii species extinction. Contact: 212 Merchant Street, Honolulu, HI 96813. 808/533-1075.

Sierra Club: The Honolulu-based Hawaii chapter of the Sierra Club, along with its outer island affiliates, is an important arm of the national environmental organization. Its work includes political lobbying, organizing community outreach programs, and conducting a variety of membership activities. The Club's newsletter, *Malama i ka Honua,* keeps members informed of club activities and Hawaii environmental issues. It regularly sponsors service trips to the outer islands, organizes trail clean-ups on Oahu, conducts dayhikes on Oahu with local naturalists, and sponsors special lectures and workshops. Contact: 212 Merchant Street, Suite 201, Honolulu, HI 96813. 808/538-6616.

Sierra Club Legal Defense Fund (SCLDF): This group provides legal representation for individuals and conservation groups when reason or persuasion (or existing laws) fail to protect natural resources. The Hawaii office, one of five regional affiliates of the San Fransisco-based SCLDF, opened in 1987. Since then, the office has been involved in issues relating to Hawaii endangered species, habitat protection, water resources, waste disposal, and construction development. Contact: Sierra Club Legal Defense Fund, Arcade Building, 212 Merchant Street, Suite 202, Honolulu, HI 96813. 808/599-2436.

Preservation

The Nature Conservancy of Hawaii: This group (TNC-H) is part of a national organization that is quietly buying up land throughout the U.S. for purposes of environmental preservation. A top priority for the national organization is the management of Hawaii's unique but threatened natural areas (680 Hawaiian plant species are on the federal register of endangered or threatened species, about one fourth of the nation's total). Currently, TNC-H protects over 17,000 acres on five islands and is supported by a membership of 3,500 persons. The Conservancy's preserves include Kaluahonu Preserve on Kauai (213 acres); Ihiihilauakea Preserve on Oahu (30 acres); Pelekunu Preserve (5759 acres), Moomomi Dunes (920 acres), and Kamakou Preserve (2774 acres) on Molokai; the Waikamoi Preserve (5230 acres) and Kipahulu Valley Preserve (500 acres adjacent to Haleakala National Park Kipahulu Extension Area) on Maui; and the Hakalau National Wildlife Refuge (15,053 acres now managed by the U.S. Fish and Wildlife Service) on the Island of Hawaii. TNC-H organizes interpretive hiking tours for the public in a few of its preserves (see island chapters under Hiking and Camping), and its regular newsletter sent to members keeps them informed of TNC-H activities throughout the islands. The Honolulu office is preparing a computerized data base of Hawaii's endangered natural areas, and it has recently embarked on a new "Islands of Life" campaign aimed at generating increased awareness of Hawaii's unique natural heritage. Contact: The Nature Conservancy of Hawaii, 1116 Smith Street, Suite 201, Honolulu, HI 96817. 808/537-4508.

Research

Environmental Center: Established in 1970 at the Water Resource Research Center at the University of Hawaii, it coordinates research and extension work at the university on environmental quality issues

Urban sprawl on Oahu

throughout the state. Contact: 2550 Campus Road, Honolulu, HI 96822. 808/948-7361.

Service

Clean Air Team: This group has been advocating clean air in Hawaii since 1975. A variety of fund-raising activities and lobbying efforts are organized each year. They sponsor the Diamond Head Summit Trail Cleanup and Anti-Litter Campaign, and they regularly offer environmental lectures and walking tours on Oahu. Every Saturday and Sunday, beginning at 9, they lead a "Look and Learn Excursion," which takes hikers from the Honolulu Zoo to the summit of Diamond Head—a 3-mile walk that has become popular for people of all ages. Contact: P.O. Box 4349, Honolulu, HI 96812. 808/944-0804.

Hawaii Audubon Society: The Hawaii chapter of the Audubon Society, established in 1939, is involved in a variety of activities that support community appreciation and understanding of Hawaii's natural heritage. The society's monthly journal, *Elepaio,* informs members about wildlife and wilderness in Hawaii. The organization also conducts guided field trips for members and the general public to various natural areas. Oahu hikes are scheduled once a month, usually on Sundays, and lengthier outer-island tours are often planned for birders. Contact: Hawaii Audubon Society, 212 Merchant St., #320, Honolulu, HI 96813. 808/528-1432.

Hoaaina O Makaha: "The land, the sea, the plants, the animals and people are one; we are all part of the same genealogical line to the Hawaiian way of thinking." This is the creed of Hoaaina o Makaha—a community group that sponsors sustainable forms of alternative development among the culturally rich but economically poor people who live on Oahu's leeward coast. The group organizes a variety of environmental outreach programs: education projects, family gardens, and a 3-acre demonstration farm where vegetables and herbs are grown. Hoaaina O Makaha is a part of a consortium of nonprofit groups coordinated through the Waianae Coast Community Alternative Development Corporation—a grassroots organization that seeks to re-connect Hawaiian society and people with their history and their land. Contact: 84-766 Lahaina Street, Waianae, HI 96792. 808/695-9730.

Kaala Farm: At the back of Waianae Valley, on Oahu's leeward coast, is this experimental taro farm that doubles as a youth education center. The farm organizers have reclaimed ancient farm terraces along the sloping valley wall, and they have dug new fields for subsistence crops of taro—the tuber that is the staple carbohydrate in the south Pacific. Much of the work is done by youths recruited from social-service programs on Oahu. The farm is open to the public but visits require prior arrangement. It recently has become involved in an alternative tourism program that brings visitors to the farm to study Hawaiian culture and land issues. The farm is operated in affiliation with the Waianae Coast Community Alternative Development Corporation. Contact: P.O. Box 630, Waianae, HI 96792. 808/696-7241.

The Outdoor Circle: The purpose of this 'soft' community group is to work toward the beautification of Hawaii. Many of their projects have to do with maintaining the 'sightliness' of Oahu's landscape. They do not get deeply involved in hard-hitting environmental tactics. Contact: 200 N. Vineyard Blvd. #506, Honolulu, HI 96817.

Upelo Project: This is a community group in leeward Oahu that works on the sustainable use and development of marine resources, the reef ecosystem, and water for subsistence agriculture. A big interest is to teach youth to deal responsibly with fishing issues and coastal resources. It's a nonprofit outfit associated with the Waianae Coast Community Alternative Development Corporation. Contact them at: P.O. Box 630, Waianae, HI 96792. 808/696-7241.

Heiaus

A large number of heiaus on Oahu have been destroyed in the past decades during the course of construction, especially in the Honolulu area. Many islanders believe that the mana of these places remains strong, however, thus accounting for the numerous reports of ghosts and odd occurrences at former temple sites. Despite the urban buildup and loss of natural areas on the island, numerous heiaus on Oahu remain fairly intact at both coastal and mountain sites. These are easily accessible by car (a few by bus) plus a little walking, and well worth the visit.

Kamaile Heiau: Four hundred feet up the Kamaileunu ridge, between Waianae town and Makaha Valley on the leeward coast, is a *luakini* temple heiau. It was used for human sacrifices and as a place of refuge by warriors between battles. The remnants include a platform terrace of coral pavement partitioned by rock walls. Its location near a former spring in the otherwise dry terrain and its prominence on the ridge gave it an advantageous position for battle and defense purposes. To visit the site, follow H1 to the Waianae coast and proceed past Waianae town to the far side of Waianae Regional Park. The heiau is on the ridge behind the residential district on the *mauka* side of the road. You must first secure permission from the Makaha Sheraton Hotel (808/695-9511), since the heiau is on hotel property.

Keaiwa Heiau: Above Aiea Heights in north central Honolulu, on a ridge between Kalauao and North Halawa streams, is Keaiwa Heiau State Recreation Area. The mountain heiau here is generally thought to have been a sacred healing place. A park has been developed around the site, with excellent picnicking and hiking possibilities in the surrounding Koolau forest (see Hiking and Camping at State Parks). From Waikiki, take H1 west to Moanalua Highway (Hwy 72), exiting at the Aiea cutoff. Follow Aiea Heights Drive mauka about 3 miles to the park at the roadend.

Pahua Heiau: This agricultural heiau is located at the end of a forested ridge where it drops down to the fast-growing residential district of Hawaii Kai in east Honolulu district. It overlooks Kuapa Pond and is reached by turning off Kalanianaole Hwy onto Lunalilo Home Road in Hawaii Kai. Take this to a cul-de-sac called Makahuena Street. The heiau is on the ridge at the end of the road. It is now difficult to envision the wetlands and extensive taro fields that once existed on the valley floor below the ridge, but the heiau reminds us of a time when this little corner of suburbia was a productive natural and agricultural area.

Puu o Mahuka Heiau: A broad plateau on the bluffs above Waimea Bay provides a spectacular natural platform for this large sacrificial heiau. It commands impressive views of Oahu's north shore from Pupukea to Kaena Point. Tradition attributes its construction to the Menehunes—mythological dwarfs of Hawaii's dim past. But according to historical records, it was built by early Hawaiian mortals to be used as a place of human sacrifice. It was recently restored and is now maintained as a historical monument by the City and County of Honolulu. Drive north past Waimea Bay on Hwy 83 and turn right onto Pupukea Road, which heads up the bluff next to the Foodland Supermarket. Follow the road as it winds up to the well-marked heiau turnoff. As you approach the heiau, notice the offerings of flower leis, ti leaves and rocks placed on the enclosure walls, altar, and platforms, indicating that it is still an active place of worship. Walk to the lower end of the structure and follow the trail to the end of the ridge. On your left look for a large sitting rock that juts out above Waimea Bay—it's a spectacular place to watch the huge winter surf at Waimea or a sunset any time of year.

Ulupo Heiau: Near the head of Kawainui Swamp in Kailua on the windward coast is an ancient heiau structure also credited to the Menehunes. It is a large (180' by 140') elevated platform (30' above the ground) that occupies a prominent position adjacent to the marshland that once was a fishpond. From Honolulu, take the Pali Highway to Kailua Road and go *makai* a little past Kalanianaole Highway to the YMCA building. Park behind the YMCA and walk through the gate to the heiau grounds.

Hiking Areas

Despite the intrusions of urban development into Oahu's natural areas, many places of wild beauty remain, and numerous trails provide the hiker with plenty of outdoor possibilities. Oahu's mountains, remote coasts, and forests are beautiful places. Do not let the bustle of Honolulu discourage you from exploring the island's natural assets. The island's hiking areas described below are organized into mountain environments and coastal environments, since these provide quite different experiences.

Mountain Hiking Areas

The Koolau Range and the Waianae Range are the two large mountain systems on the island, separated by a broad lava plateau, the Schofield Plateau. The Waianae Range, on the leeward side of the island, extends roughly from Kaena Point to Kahe Point. It contains the island's highest peak, Mt. Kaala (4020 feet). Except for the Mt. Kaala region, the summit of which is a bog (Mt. Kaala Natural Area Reserve), the Waianae Range is dry. In contrast, the Koolau Range, extending from the northern tip of the island south to Makapuu Point, receives a great deal of rainfall from the trade winds. The windward side of these mountains is very wet, and higher elevations on the leeward side also receive a good deal of precipita-

On the Makiki valley loop trail

tion. Partly as a result of these rainfall differences, the Waianae Range and the Koolau Range present very different conditions for the hiker. Wet upland forests and steep trails along eroded cliffs or deeply incised valleys predominate in the Koolaus; dry scrub vegetation, broad valleys and more gradual trails mark the Waianae Range. The major exception to this is Mt. Kaala in the Waianae Range; the summit trail to Mt. Kaala is one of the most difficult hikes on the islands and the summit itself is one of the wettest places in Hawaii. A handy nature guidebook to accompany you on your hikes into Oahu's upland forests is *Hawaiian Forest Plants* by Mark Merlin.

Waianae Range Hikes

Much of the land in the Waianae Range is privately owned, and the trails that traverse these areas require that hikers secure proper permits and waivers. The trail to Mt. Kaala Summit (the Dupont Trail—4 miles) requires a hiking permit from the Division of Forestry and Wildlife in Honolulu, and from the Waialua Sugar Company (808/637-3521). Trails that lead into the Mokuleia Forest Reserve (access from Farrington Highway at Yokohama Bay) also require a permit from the Division of Forestry and Wildlife. Trails that cross Mokuleia Ranch and Land Company require access permits from the Mokuleia Ranch and Land Co. (808/637-4241). Due to the complex land ownership and access rights, it is advisable for those planning a Waianae Range hike to link up with persons who are familiar with the routes.

The Oahu hiking clubs (Trail and Mountain Club, Sierra Club, Audubon Society, Friends of Foster Garden, The Nature Conservancy) regularly schedule pleasure hikes and service trips into the Waianae Range (see Nature Tours and Outdoor Excursions—Guided Hikes). They arrange transportation, secure all necessary permits, and provide an interpretive guide. So why not take advantage of them and join one of their outings? Trail descriptions for Waianae Range hikes are in *Hiking Oahu* by Robert Smith.

Koolau Range Hikes

Most of the mountain hikes on Oahu are in the Koolau mountains. The most popular trails are in the Makiki/Tantalus/Manoa trail complex. This system includes the following trails: The Kanealole Trail (0.7 mile) goes up the Makiki Valley; the Maunalaha Trail (0.7 mile) climbs the east ridge of Makiki Valley; the Nahuina Trail (0.8 mile) traverses the west side of Makiki Valley above Tantalus Drive; the Makiki Valley Trail (1.1 miles) contours up the back of Makiki Valley; the Ualakaa Trail (0.5 mile) goes past Ualakaa State Park; the Moleka Trail (0.75 mile) traverses along a bamboo grove above Round Top Drive; the Manoa Cliff Trail (3 miles) contours around the Manoa Valley; the Puu Ohia Trail (2 miles) goes to the Nuuanu Reservoir overlook; the Nuuanu Trail (0.8 mile) traverses upper Pauoa Valley and Pauoa Flats; the Aihualama Trail (1.3 miles) traverses the west side of Manoa Valley from Lyon Arboretum; the Manoa Falls Trail (0.8 mile) goes from Paradise Park to a small waterfall in the back of Manoa Valley; the Kolowalu Trail (1 mile) traverses the east side of Manoa Valley above Woodlawn; and the Waahila Trail (2.4 miles) follows the ridge between Manoa and Pololo valleys. Many of these trails intersect and form loops. The best entry point for the system is at the Hawaii Nature Center at 2131 Makiki Heights Drive, Honolulu, HI 96822 (808/973-0100). They can provide trail guides, maps, and expert information about trail conditions, access roads, and connecting loops.

Another trail system in the Koolau Range is the Hauula trail system, located along the northern stretches of the windward Koolaus. Three intersecting trails compose the system: The Hauula Loop Trail (2.5 miles) crosses the Waipilopilo Gulch to Kaipapau overlook; the Maakua Gulch Trail (3 miles) goes straight up the narrow canyon of Maakua Gulch along a streambed; and the Maakua Ridge Trail (2.5 miles) heads across dry, open country with good views of the northern windward coast. Trail permits and maps for these routes can be obtained from the Division of Forestry and Wildlife.

One of the most popular Koolau hikes is to Sacred Falls (2.2 miles). It begins at the Sacred Falls State Park trailhead on Kamehameha Highway (Hwy 83), 1 mile south of Hauula (the park is marked with a signboard). The trail leads through a narrow gorge to a 90-foot waterfall. No permits are required for this hike, and the trail is well marked.

Coastal Trails

Hiking along Oahu's coastline provides opportunities to beachcomb, to explore tidal pools, and to examine unique coastal strand vegetation. A handy guidebook to beach vegetation is *Hawaiian Coastal Plants* by Mark Merlin.

Kaena Point: The best shoreline hike on Oahu is to the Kaena Point Natural Area Reserve. This is located at the western tip of the island, where talus slopes from the towering cliffs of the Waianae Range de-

---

The reserve is a refuge also for seabirds such as the wedge-tailed shearwater, the red-footed booby, and the Laysan albatross.

---

scend to an isolated stretch of sand dunes and rocky coastline. The natural area reserve was established in 1983 to protect the endangered native plants that inhabit the area. The reserve is a refuge also for seabirds such as the wedge-tailed shearwater, the red-footed booby, and the Laysan albatross. During the winter months, humpback whales are commonly observed offshore.

The hike into the reserve is hot and dry on most days; bring a hat and sunscreen. If you can spare the time, stay for a sunset—magic and color descend onto the reserve with the setting sun. The reserve can be reached from two directions. From Haleiwa, head west on Highway 930 past Mokuleia to the roadend, and begin walking along the coast trail. From the Waianae coast, go north to the end of Farrington Highway (Hwy 930), park at the turnout near Yokohama Bay and begin walking along the coastal trail. From either direction, the walking trail is about 2.5 miles long. For information about the Hawaii Natural Area Reserve System, contact the NARS Office in Honolulu (808/548-7417). *A Nature Walk to Kaena Point* by Edward Arrigoni provides detailed comments on the natural and cultural history of the area.

Makapuu Peninsula Hike: An undeveloped hiking trail traverses the coastline between Queen's Beach, northeast of Sandy Beach County Park, and Mokapuu Point, trailing along the sea cliffs below Mokapuu Point. The trail is rocky and unmarked, but not too difficult. It passes deep tidal pools and interesting coastal lava forms as it leads to a lava platform below Makapuu Lighthouse. The area has a wild and free feel about it, even though it is easily accessible from Kalanianaole Highway (Hwy 72). To reach the trailhead, park along the highway near the Coast Guard road that heads up to Makapuu Point (The road is marked by a gate that is generally closed.) Follow the dirt track on foot through the kiawe scrub terrain to the coast, where you will intersect the north-heading trail.

Natural Foods and Farms

Oahu has several natural food stores (not to mention the hundreds of Asian groceries that supply bulk grains, spices, and produce). The stores listed below can provide you with a healthy selection of foods for backcountry trips or for daily consumption. Naturally, most of these stores attempt to use locally produced goods, and they tend also to support the small-scale growers on the island. There is no main supplier on Oahu of freeze-dried backpacking food, so the natural food grocers are your best bet for backcountry staples.

Celestial Natural Foods: If you're on the north shore or driving around the island, look for this store on the circum-island road (Hwy 83). Located at 66-443 Kam Hwy in downtown Haleiwa. 808/637-6729.

Down To Earth Natural Foods: This is a popular natural-foods store in the University district of Honolulu. They have a well-stocked bulk food department where you can buy trail food. At 2525 S. King Street in Moilili district. 808/947-7678.

Huckleberry Farms Natural Foods Ranch Market: If you're a meat-eater but you want your beef and poultry chemical-free, this is the place. They also stock produce and dry goods. Located in Nuuanu Valley at 1613 Nuuanu Ave. 808/524-7960.

India Bazaar Madras Cafe: This new place specializes in South Asian foods. They stock an assortment of grains, lentils, breads and spices. They also have a small deli where you can get a quick and tasty South Indian meal for a cheap price. Located in a small shopping center near the University district in Honolulu at 2320 S. King St.—Unit B4. 808/949-4840.

Kokua Co-op: This is the largest food co-op in the state. It has an excellent selection of natural groceries and produce, including chemical-free meats. Located in the University district of Honolulu at 2357 Beretania, near the corner of Isenberg St. 808/941-1922.

Nature Tours and Outdoor Excursions

Several Honolulu-based groups conduct outdoor excursions to natural areas on Oahu and to outer islands. You will find further references to some of them in the other island chapters under the sections on Nature Tours and Outdoor Excursions. The outfits listed below provide the most extensive opportunities for Oahu-bound people.

BICYCLING

Touring Oahu by bicycle is not a particularly good idea. The traffic on the island is heavy, the road shoulders are narrow or nonexistent, opportunities for roadside camping are limited, and the urban bias of the island presents many of the potential problems of urban society anywhere—mainly theft and vandalism for bikers. Many people nonetheless tour the island by bike, out of choice or because they have no real choice. If you plan a cycle tour of Hawaii, Oahu is where you can initially contact bike service centers. In addition to sales and service, the bike shops are a source of information about cycling conditions and routes on the outer islands.

Bike Shops

Island Triathlon and Bike: This is one of the best bike shops in Hawaii. The service department provides fast, expert repairs at reasonable rates. They also organize outer-island bicycle tours (see Island Bicycle Adventures below). At 569 Kapahulu Ave. in Honolulu, near the Diamond Head area, 808/732-7227. Open Mon.–Fri. 10–7; Sat. 9–5; Sun. 11–4.

McCully Bicycle: This is the oldest bike shop on the Islands (ca. 1923). They carry a full line of bikes and accessories, and they provide full repair service. Two locations—in Honolulu at 2124 S. King St (near the intersection of King and McCully), 808/955-6329; and in Waipahu at 94-320 Depot Road, 808/671-4091. Both locations are open Mon.–Fri. 9–8 and Sat./Sun. 9–5.

The Bike Shop: Four locations each provide a full range of sales and service. In Honolulu at 1149 S. King St., 808/531-7071; in Hawaii Kai at the Hawaii Kai Shopping Center, 808/396-6342; in Aiea at 98-019 Kam Hwy, 808/487-3615; and on the windward coast in Kaneohe at the Windward City Shopping Center, 808/235-8722. The S. King St. location is also Hawaii's main center for back-packing and camping equipment (see Outdoor Equipment and Supplies).

Island Bicycle Adventures

The people at Island Triathlon and Bike also organize and lead cycling trips in Hawaii. They can help with an Oahu itinerary, but their organized cycling journeys are on the outer islands (6- and 12-day excursions to the Island of Hawaii, Kauai, and Maui are offered). Contact: Island Bicycle Adventures, 569 Kapahulu Ave., Honolulu, HI 96815. 808/734-0700 or toll-free 800/233-2226.

GUIDED HIKES

Several Oahu community organizations conduct outings that enlist the services of island naturalists to lead hikers into Oahu's wildlands. These guided hikes serve several purposes: they provide access to natural areas that otherwise might be off-limits to individuals, they provide the interpretive services of experts on Hawaii's natural history, and they bring together people of similar interests in groups kept small to maximize enjoyment and minimize impact.

Friends of Foster Garden: The people that work to maintain the Foster Gardens Botanic Park also organize hikes on Oahu and on the outer islands. Many of the outer-island trips are overnight journeys, and some combine hotel stays with camping. On Oahu, their hikes take you to little-visited places. Contact: 50 N. Vineyard Blvd., Honolulu, HI 96817. 808/537-1708.

Hawaiian Trail and Mountain Club: This voluntary association of hikers and campers regularly heads into Oahu's wilderness for day and weekend journeys. They hike on more than 80 trails on Oahu, many of which they maintain. The hikes are open to club members and to the general public for a modest fee; visiting hikers are particu-larly welcome. The club was organized in 1910, and most of the club's members have extensive experience in and knowledge about Oahu's natural areas. Contact: P.O. Box 2238, Honolulu, HI 96804.

Whale mural in Honolulu

Hawaii Nature Center: These folks do an excellent job educating youngsters about nature, and do an equally fine job organizing day hikes into Oahu's wilderness areas (see also Environmental Education in Ch. 1). Their hikes are open to all interested persons. Contact: 2131 Makiki Heights Drive, Honolulu, HI 96822, 808/973-0100.

Sierra Club: The Hawaii chapter of the Sierra Club organizes a number of different types of environmental outings (see also Environmental Groups in Ch.1). It regularly conducts pleasure backpacking tours on both Oahu and the outer islands. The Oahu hikes are generally dayhikes, scheduled for each Sunday ($1 fee). A variety of hikes are offered on Oahu—from easy strolls in the valleys and along the coasts to strenuous mountain climbs. On Oahu, the Sierra Club also organizes weekend service trips to the island's natural areas reserves—Mt. Kaala and Kaena Point. These trips are geared primarily for people who live in Honolulu and want to escape the city for a day or more. An advantage of the Sierra Club-sponsored hikes is that they provide access to otherwise restricted natural areas (national wildlife refuges and The Nature Conservancy preserves).

The Club also organizes service trips, during which part of your time is devoted to working on various projects: trail maintenance, shelter construction, constructing fences around nature preserves, weed eradication, and so forth. The service component of the Sierra Club effort is a popular local program. The trips generally take place over a weekend, although some service trips to the Big Island and to Molokai last a week. The cost is minimal (usually $25/person, all inclusive). Once the work is contracted to the Sierra Club by a state or federal agency (for example, a national park), the Club gathers a work group of volunteers no larger that 6–12 persons and handles the logistics of transportation, food, equipment, work-sharing, and so forth.

The trips generally involve manual labor, and require youthful vigor, with days off between work periods on the longer trips. Many of the trips fill up quickly, so if you're interested, contact them for upcoming trips and make your commitment well in advance. Service trips in the past have taken people to Kamakao Nature Preserve and Kalaupapa peninsula on Molokai; Kilauea and Hakalau nature preserves, and Waimanu Valley on the Island of Hawaii; Haleakala National Park on Maui, and the Alakai Swamp Wilderness Preserve and Kilauea National Wildlife Refuge on Kauai.

Miscellaneous

Numerous other community groups regularly offer hiking tours on Oahu. These groups include the Hawaii Audubon Society (808/528-1432), the Hawaii Geographical Society (808/538-3952), the Moanalua Gardens Foundation (808/839-5334), and The Nature Conservancy (808/537-4508). Call them for information.

HORSEBACK RIDING

A few stables on Oahu offer trail rides into the island's backcountry.

Koko Crater Stables: Located adjacent to the Koko Crater Botanical Park off Kalanianaole Hwy near Hawaii Kai. They lead horseback rides into the crater. Contact: 808/395-2628.

Kualoa Ranch: This windward-shore ranch offers trail rides to vista viewpoints and across rolling hills. Located at 49-560 Kam Hwy, along the circum-island road (Hwy 83). Contact: 808/237-8515.

Sheraton's Makaha Lio Stables: The Sheraton Makaha resort on Oahu's leeward coast near Makaha offers trail rides into the surrounding valley. The landscape is dry savanna with scrub kiawe and towering valley walls—a fine place for a horseback ride, just like the wild west. Contact: 84-626 Makaha Valley Road. 808/695-9511.

OCEAN/LAND EXCURSIONS

Opportunities to explore Oahu's offshore ocean environment are virtually limitless. Most of the outfits that conduct ocean tours rely on a flotilla of engine-powered vessels. Nowhere is this more apparent than in the busy waters off Waikiki. Para-sailors, dinner

The stream in Maakua Gulch

cruises, waterjets, ski boats, and fishing launches scream and dream their way across the open waters, creating havoc for marine life in the wake of their fun. A few outfits are doing something a bit different.

Kayaking Adventures

Exploring Oahu's coastline by kayak has become popular in recent years and two outfits on Oahu now offer low-keyed, non-mechanized kayaking adventures along the island's coasts.

Adventure Kayaking International: They specialize in international expeditions to Fiji and Thailand, but they also offer a limited number of half-day trips along Oahu's windward coast. Contact: P.O. Box 61609, Honolulu, HI 96839.

Rusty Banana Oceanic Adventures: The owner of "Go Bananas" kayak supply store also operates a kayak expedition company that leads tours to the outer islands as well as to a variety of Oahu destinations. Their 4- and 5-day Molokai trips are classic adventures (see Molokai section on Kayaking). The Oahu excursions are tamer, but they nonetheless get you into areas that are otherwise inaccessible, and they show you the spectacular Oahu coastal mountains from the ocean—an outstanding perspective on the island. Rusty Banana's Oahu trips include journeys to Kahana Bay, Mokulua Island, Kaneohe Bay and Kepapa Island, and moonlight tours off Diamond Head. The Oahu trips average 3–4 hours, and they vary in cost from $30 to $50. Contact: 740 Kapahulu Avenue, Honolulu, HI 96816. 808/737-9514.

SNUBA of Oahu: This new company arranges marine excursions that include underwater training in the use of snuba gear—a hybrid of snorkeling and scuba—that gently orients the user to the ocean world. Their approach to marine exploration is gentle and slow, and their tours include education in ocean conservation. Contact: 2233 Kalakaua Avenue, B 205 A #1271, Honolulu, HI 96815, 808/922-7762.

TRAVEL AGENCIES

Two travel agents on Oahu specialize in island tours that include significant time in Hawaii's natural areas. For visitors from the mainland or from abroad, they can assist with all aspects of the trip, including itineraries for backcountry touring.

Kailua Travel: Contact Lee Miller-Kalama, a travel consultant who specializes in adventure travel. 404 Uluniu Street, Kailua, HI 96734. 808/261-8919.

The Haina Group: Contact Annette Kaohelaulii, an active member of the Sierra Club knowledgeable about Hawaii's natural areas. She arranges tours to fit most needs, but she specializes in trips for less hardy persons who nonetheless want to get out and see some of Hawaii's wildlands. 45-403 Koa Kahiko Street, Kaneohe, HI 96744. 808/235-5431.

MISCELLANEOUS

Youth Adventures Unlimited, Inc.: This new outfit caters exclusively to children, and they provide custom excursions for youth groups into the Oahu forests. Activities are adult-supervised and restricted to young people between the ages 6–17. The company prefers working with groups of about 20 persons, and they specialize in children of convention-goers. If that is you, and if you want to farm out your children to a group that will take their energies out of the hotel room and into the mountains, you might want to contact them: P.O. Box 462, Kaneohe, Oahu, HI 96744. 808/235-4206.

Outdoor Equipment and Supplies

BACKPACKING AND CAMPING

Oahu has few places that carry a complete line of backpacking and camping equipment. This is somewhat surprising, given the size of the city and the heavy use of the natural areas on Oahu and the outer islands. Many camping visitors to Hawaii bring their own gear, so the local places cater primarily to local residents.

The Bike Shop: The upstairs part of this combined bike/hike shop is devoted to backpacking equipment. They carry the most complete line of name-brand gear in Hawaii. Boots, backpacks, tents, foul weather gear, and all of the necessary knick-knacks can be obtained here. At 1149 S. King Street, Honolulu, HI 96814. 808/531-7071.

Omar the Tent Man: If you need to rent a tent, you can try this outfit. They don't carry high-tech camping equipment, but they do stock a large supply of basic family tents and camping equipment. Located at 650 A. Kakoi Street, Honolulu, HI. 808/836-8785.

MAPS

Maps and Miscellaneous: This store is run by a lively lady who loves her maps, and she generally keeps a good collection of USGS topos and island road maps in stock. At 404 Piiloi Street, Suite 216, in Honolulu, across from Ala Moana Center. 808/538-7429.

Pacific Map Center: This is your best bet for a full line of maps, including USGS topos, nautical charts, street maps, NOAA maps, and island trail maps. At 647 Auahi Street in Honolulu. 808/531-3800.

The Hawaii Geographical Society: They carry a full line of USGS topographic maps, the University of Hawaii Press island maps (good for general orientation and auto touring), and some trail maps. At 49 S. Hotel Street, Suite 218, in downtown Honolulu, or contact: P.O. Box 1698, Honolulu, HI 96806. 808/538-3952.

Snorkeling and Surfing

SNORKELING

The most famous beach in Hawaii, and perhaps the world, is Waikiki beach, but it offers little for snorkelers. The best snorkeling spots on Oahu are listed below.

Hanauma Bay: Ten miles east of Waikiki off Kalanianaole Highway (Hwy 72). This is a favorite of tourists, and the beach here gets quite jammed with glistening white-and-pink bodies by mid-morning on most days. The protected waters inside the reef are heavily used, and frequent collisions with other snorkelers occur. Fortunately, the outer reef receives few visitors and the waters there are the best for

snorkeling. The rich coral reef is protected by a deep bay and is now
an underwater park and marine conservation district. Best times are
very early mornings (around 6–7 a.m.), before the tour groups
arrive.

Kaluanui to Aukai: South of Hauula for 2 miles, the Kamehameha
Highway skirts the ocean between Kaluanui beach and Aukai Beach
County Park. The nearshore waters are protected by a fringing reef
and provide good snorkeling. This is a popular spot for local spear-
fishermen.

Malaekahana State Recreation Park: Offshore is Mokuania (Goat
Island), which provides a sheltered lee area for snorkelers. Accessible from Hwy 83, 2 miles north of Laie (see Camping).

Shark's Cove: Don't let the name frighten you. This is an excellent
summer snorkeling spot. Located next to Pupukea Beach County
Park on Hwy 83, one-half mile north of Waimea Bay. The summer
waters are crystal-clear, and the interesting underwater rock formations and colorful fish make for excellent snorkeling. In winter, the
cove is extremely treacherous—stay away.

Waimea Bay: The world's largest rideable surf occurs here in winter, but in summer the bay is calm and flat, with clear water for
snorkeling. The sandy bottom makes for rather uninteresting sights,
though.

Yokohama Bay: Accessible from Farrington Highway (Hwy 93), 8
miles northwest of Waianae on the leeward coast. The rocky coast
here provides interesting snorkeling during calm days in the summer.

SURFING

Waikiki: This is where surfing made its name and gained fame for
Hawaii. A multitude of surf breaks are here, with ample opportunities for beginners. Rentals and lessons are available. Ask around.

Diamond Head: Frequently large summer swells roll in off
Diamond Head, making this area a popular surf spot. Accessible
from Diamond Head Road; watch for surfer vehicles parked along
the roadside. The waves can be seen from numerous lookouts along
the road.

North Shore: Internationally famous surfing spots are located here,
including Sunset Beach, the Bonzai Pipeline, and Waimea Bay. The
huge waves here are for experts only. Accessible from Kamehameha
Highway (Hwy 83), north of Haleiwa.

Makaha: Some of Hawaii's best surfing occurs here during the winter. Several surfing spots are located between Yokohama Bay and Maili Beach County Park, south of Waianae. This area is a heavy local scene, and novice haole surfers should probably avoid it.

Riding the shorebreak at Sandy Beach

Thomas Winnett

Bibliography

Arrigoni, E., 1988. *Exploring Nature Safely.* Honolulu: Nature Safety Consultants.

Arrigoni, E., 1978. *Nature Walk to Ka'ena Point.* Honolulu: Topgallont Publishing Company, Ltd.

Atlas of Hawaii, 1983. Honolulu: Department of Geography, University of Hawaii.

Beckwith, M.W., 1970. *Hawaiian Mythology.* Honolulu: University of Hawaii Press.

Carlquist, S., 1980. *Hawaii: A Natural History.* Lawai, HI: Pacific Tropical Botanical Gardens.

Chisholm, C., 1989. *Hawaiian Hiking Trails.* Lake Oswego, OR: The Fernglen Press.

Cooper, G. and G. Daws, 1985. *Land and Power in Hawaii.* Honolulu: Benchmark Books, Inc.

Culliney, J., 1988. *Islands in a Far Sea.* San Fransisco: Sierra Club Books.

Daws, G., 1968. *Shoal of Time: A History of the Hawaiian Islands.* New York: Macmillan Co.

Daws, G., 1988. *Hawaii: The Islands of Life.* Honolulu: The Nature Conservancy of Hawaii.

Degener, O., 1945. *Plants of Hawaii National Park.* (privately published).

Fielding, Ann, 1985. *Hawaiian Reefs and Tidepools.* Honolulu: Oriental Publishing Company.

Hagmann, M., 1988. *Hawaii Parklands.* Helena and Billings, MT: Falcon Press Publishing Co., Ltd.

Hawaii's Birds, 1986. Honolulu: The Audubon Society.

Kamakau, S.M., 1976. *The Works of the People of Old.* Honolulu: Bishop Museum Press.

Kirch, P.V., 1985. *Feathered Gods and Fishhooks: An Introduction to Hawaiian Archaeology and Prehistory.* Honolulu: University of Hawaii Press.

Kuykendall, R.S. and A.G. Day, 1948. *Hawaii: A History.* New York: Prentice-Hall, Inc.

Lamoureux, C.H., 1976. *Trailside Plants of Hawaii's National Parks.* Hawaii Volcanoes National Park: Hawaii Natural History Association.

Liliuokalani, 1979. *Hawaii's Story by Hawaii's Queen*. Rutland, VT: Charles E. Tuttle Co.

MacDonald, G. and W. Kyselka, 1967. *Anatomy of an Island: A Geological History of Oahu*. Honolulu: Bishop Museum Press.

MacDonald, G., A. Abbot, and F. Peterson, 1986. *Volcanoes in the Sea*. Honolulu: University of Hawaii Press.

Malo, D., 1951. *Hawaiian Antiquities*. Honolulu: Bishop Museum Press.

Merlin, M., 1980. *Hawaiian Forest Plants*. Honolulu: Oriental Publishing Company.

Merlin, M., 1986. *Hawaiian Coastal Plants*. Honolulu: Oriental Publishing Company.

Morgan, J., 1983. *Hawaii: A Geography*. Boulder: Westview Press.

Morgan, J. and J. Street, 1979. *Oahu Environments*. Honolulu: Oriental Publishing Company.

Pukui, M.K. and S.H. Elbert, 1971. *Hawaiian Dictionary*. Honolulu: University of Hawaii Press.

Pukui, M.K., S.H. Elbert, and E.T. Mookini, 1975. *Pocket Hawaiian Dictionary*. Honolulu: University of Hawaii Press.

Pukui, M.K., S.H. Elbert, and E.T., Mookini, 1989. *Place Names of Hawaii*. Honolulu: University of Hawaii Press.

Riegert, R., 1987. *Hidden Hawaii*. Berkeley: Ulysses Press.

Sohmer, S.H. and R. Gustafson, 1987. *Plants and Flowers of Hawaii*. Honolulu: University of Hawaii Press.

Smith, R., 1989. *Hiking Hawaii*.

Smith, R., 1989. *Hiking Oahu*.

Smith, R., 1989. *Hiking Maui*.

Smith, R., 1989. *Hiking Kauai*. Long Beach, CA: Hawaiian Outdoors Adventures Publications.

The State of Hawaii Data Book, 1988. Honolulu: Department of Business and Economic Development.

Valier, K., 1988. *On the Na Pali Coast*. Honolulu: University of Hawaii Press.

Appendix

Island of Hawaii:
Hawaii Volcanoes National Park, HI 96718
808/967-7311

Division of State Parks
P.O. Box 936
Hilo, HI 96721
808/933-4200
street address: 75 Aupuni St., Hilo

Hawaii County Department of Parks
25 Aupuni St.
Hilo, HI 96720
808/961-8311

Kauai:
Division of State Parks
P.O. Box 1671
Lihue, HI 96766
808/241-3444
street address: 3060 Eiwa St., Lihue

Kauai County Division of Parks
4280 A Rice St., Bldg. B
Lihue, HI 96766
808/245-8821

Maui, Molokai, Lanai:
Haleakala National Park
P.O. Box 369
Makawao, HI 96768
808/572-9306

Division of State Parks
P.O. Box 1049
Wailuku, HI 96793
808/243-5354
street address: 54 High St., Wailuku

Maui County Department of Parks
War Memorial Center
Wailuku, HI 96793
808/244-9018

Oahu:
Division of State Parks
P.O. Box 621
Honolulu, HI 96809
808/548-7455
street address: 1151 Punchbowl St., Honolulu
Honolulu City and County Department of Parks
650 S. King Street
Honolulu, HI 96813
808/523-4525
Divsions of Forestry and Wildlife
1151 Punchbowl St.
Honolulu, HI 96813
808/548-8850
Department of Land and Natural Resources
P.O. Box 621
Honolulu, HI 96809
808/548-6550
DLNR Divisions:
  Division of Aquatic Resources—808/548-4002
  Division of Conservation and Resources—808/548-5919
  Division of Forestry and Wildlife—808/548-2861
  Division of Land Management—808/548-7517
  Division of Land and Water Development—808/548-7533

Index